117933

THE OLD TESTAMENT
AS THE BOOK OF CHRIST

THE OLD TESTAMENT AS THE BOOK OF CHRIST

An Appraisal of Bonhoeffer's Interpretation

By
MARTIN KUSKE

Translated by
S T KIMBROUGH, JR.

THE WESTMINSTER PRESS
Philadelphia

Translated from the German *Das Alte Testament als Buch von Christus, Dietrich Bonhoeffers Wertung und Auslegung des Alten Testaments* (Evangelische Verlagsanstalt, Berlin, 1970)

Published by The Westminster Press ®
Philadelphia, Pennsylvania

PRINTED IN THE UNITED STATES OF AMERICA

Grateful acknowledgment is made to the following for use of copyrighted material:

Macmillan Publishing Co., Inc., and SCM Press Ltd: Dietrich Bonhoeffer, *Creation and Fall*, © SCM Press Ltd 1959; Dietrich Bonhoeffer, *Letters and Papers from Prison*, Revised, Enlarged Edition, copyright © 1953, 1967, 1971 SCM Press Ltd.

Library of Congress Cataloging in Publication Data

Kuske, Martin.
   The Old Testament as the Book of Christ.

   Translation of Das Alte Testament als Buch von Christus.
   "List of D. Bonhoeffer sources": p.
   Bibliography: p.
   1. Bible. O.T.—Criticism, interpretation, etc.—History—20th century. 2. Bible. N.T.—Relation to the Old Testament. 3. Bonhoeffer, Dietrich, 1906–1945. I. Title.
BS1160.K8713   225.6   76–25495
ISBN 0–664–20772–3

For Ruth

CONTENTS

II. Bonhoeffer's Appraisal of the Bible

III. The Old Testament as the Book of Christ

ABBREVIATIONS

WORKS BY DIETRICH BONHOEFFER

AS   *Akt und Sein. Tranzendentalphilosophie und Ontologie in der systematischen Theologie,* 1931; Munich, 1956. *Act and Being,* Collins, London, and Harper, New York, 1962.

SC   *Sanctorum Communio. Eine dogmatische Untersuchung zur Soziologie der Kirche,* 1930; 3d expanded edition, Munich, 1960. *The Communion of Saints,* Collins, London, and Harper, New York, 1963.

SF   *Schöpfung und Fall. Theologische Auslegung von Genesis 1 bis 3,* 1934; Munich, 1958.[4] *Creation and Fall,* SCM Press, London, and Macmillan, New York, 1959.

N   *Nachfolge,* 1937; Berlin, 1954. *The Cost of Discipleship,* SCM Press, London, and Macmillan, New York, 1959.

GL   *Gemeinsames Leben,* 1939; Munich, 1961[10]. *Life Together,* Harper, New York, 1954.

E   § *Ethik,* ed. by E. Bethge, 1949; Munich, 1963[3]. *Ethics,* Collins, Fontana, London, and Macmillan, New York, 1964.

WE   § *Widerstand und Ergebung. Briefe und Aufzeichnungen aus der Haft,* ed. by E. Bethge, 1951; Berlin, 1961[2], Munich, 1955[7]. *Letters and Papers from Prison,* The

Enlarged Edition, SCM Press, London, and Macmillan, 1971.

GS I–IV *Gesammelte Schriften,* ed. by E. Bethge. Vol. I: *Ökumene. Briefe, Aufsätze, Dokumente 1928–1942,* Munich, 1958. Vol. II: *Kirchenkampf und Finkenwalde. Resolutionen, Aufsätze, Rundbriefe 1933–1943,* Munich, 1959. Vol. III: *Theologie—Gemeinde. Vorlesungen, Briefe, Gespräche 1927–1944,* Munich, 1960. Vol. IV: *Auslegungen—Predigten 1933–1944,* Munich, 1961.

§References to *E* and *WE* have two sets of pages cited always as follows: *E*, 6th edition/1st-5th edition; *WE*, Berlin, 1961²/München, 1955⁷.

OTHER WORKS

AELKZ	*Allgemeine evangelisch-lutherische Kirchenzeitung*
BEvTh	*Beiträge zur Evangelischen Theologie*
BK	*Biblischer Kommentar,* ed. by M. Noth
CAT	*Das Christuszeugnis des Alten Testaments,* Vol. I: *Das Gesetz,* 1934, 1946⁷; Vol. II: *Die frühen Propheten,* 1942, W. Vischer
DB	*Dietrich Bonhoeffer,* E. Bethge
EKG	*Evangelisches Kirchengesangbuch*
EvTh	*Evangelische Theologie*
JK	*Junge Kirche*
KAT	*Kommentar zum Alten Testament*
KD	*Kirchliche Dogmatik,* K. Barth
MPTh	*Monatsschrift für Pastoral Theologie*
MW I–IV	*Die Mündige Welt* Vol. I: *Dem Andenken Dietrich Bonhoeffers. Vorträge und Briefe,* Munich, 1955, 1959³. Vol. II: *1. Weissensee—2. Verschiedenes,* Munich, 1956. Vol. III: *Weissensee 1959,* Munich, 1960. Vol. IV: *1. Weissensee 1961—2. Verschiedenes,* Munich, 1963

PAH	*Probleme alttestamentlicher Hermeneutik,* ed. by C. Westermann
PhB	*Philosophische Bibliothek,* ed. by G. Lasson
RGG	*Religion in Geschichte und Gegenwart*
ThBl	*Theologische Blätter*
ThEx	*Theologische Existenz heute*
ThEx NF	*Theologische Existenz heute* (new series)
ThLZ	*Theologische Literaturzeitung*
ThR NF	*Theologische Rundschau* (new series)
ThSt(B)	*Theologische Studien,* ed. by K. Barth
ThZ	*Theologische Zeitschrift*
WA	*Weimarer Ausgabe,* M. Luther
WADB	*Weimarer Ausgabe, Die Deutsche Bibel*
ZZ	*Zwischen den Zeiten*

INTRODUCTION
TO THE ENGLISH EDITION

Das Alte Testament als Buch von Christus was written by Martin Kuske, who is now Director of Studies for the Predigerseminar of the Evangelical Church in Gnadau, East Germany. Following its publication in East Germany by the Evangelische Verlagsanstalt in Berlin (1970), it was published by Vandenhoeck & Ruprecht in Göttingen, West Germany. It now appears in an English edition not only because it contains new interpretations of Bonhoeffer, in whom there is continued interest, but also because of its merits as a book. Eberhard Bethge says of Kuske's work: "It is not a popular treatise. It is a careful study which throws light on Bonhoeffer's development and his handling of the Old Testament. It illuminates as well Bonhoeffer's shift from Barthian theology to the theology of his prison letters. Any scholar working on Bonhoeffer's relation to the Bible should not neglect this study, with its subtle differentiations and observations. The book will remain on the very short list of the most serious books about Bonhoeffer."

Throughout the works of Bonhoeffer there are traces of his interest in and dependence upon the Old Testament for the development of his theology. These references are more than incidental. They indicate the author's conscious participation in the new theological emphasis on the Old Testament in the first half of the twentieth century. There are occasions, moreover, such as in *Letters and Papers from Prison,* where his Old

xv

Testament hermeneutic is developed with clarity and perception.

Bonhoeffer is not known per se as an Old Testament specialist, and certainly it is the more revolutionary aspects of his theology that have captivated his readers. Nevertheless, Martin Kuske, having immersed himself in Bonhoeffer's work, has found the Old Testament to be a guiding force for Bonhoeffer. Therefore he has been motivated to produce this volume. Although Bonhoeffer's Old Testament interpretation has often been viewed as comparable to the Christological interpretation of Wilhelm Vischer, Kuske shows that Bonhoeffer's concept of the Old Testament as "the book of Christ" is quite the opposite. Kuske places Bonhoeffer's Old Testament perspective in the context of his total writings as well as the scholarship of his period.

The author has drawn from Bonhoeffer's sermons, sermon outlines, Bible studies, devotions, devotional aids, occasional speeches, meditations, exegeses, letters, poems, a series of lectures, a confirmation teaching plan, an address, an "Introduction to the Psalms," and a confession. There are references to almost all his major works. These materials are carefully scrutinized to form a kernel view of Bonhoeffer's Old Testament interpretation. Kuske is extremely sensitive that each of these various sources has a different *Sitz im Leben* and he attempts to deal with them within their context. He does so by a wise use of footnotes.

Before treating Bonhoeffer's basic position on the Scripture, Kuske devotes Chapter One to a résumé of the confrontation of Bonhoeffer with certain Continental theologians (Adolf von Harnack, Reinhold Seeberg, Ernst Sellin, Friedrich Baumgärtel, Karl Barth, and Wilhelm Vischer), who were influential in molding his Biblical position. Such a background is the *raison d'être* for Chapter Two, which discusses Bonhoeffer's essential appraisal of the Bible. As in Chapter One, Bonhoeffer's views are set within their particular period of development. This is no scissors-and-paste exercise, for quotations are related to the man, his time and theology, as well as to the historical and theological milieu within which he functioned.

The larger framework of Bonhoeffer's view of Scripture is sketched so that his view of the Old Testament may be seen within it. In Chapter Two it becomes apparent that for Bonhoeffer the message of the cross becomes the matrix of his interpretative perspective for the Bible as a whole. The Bible is the book of the church (the church under the cross), witnessing to one God, who in Jesus Christ loves the world.

Chapter Three is the core chapter. Here Kuske develops the theme of the book: the Old Testament as the book of Christ. His method procedurally overlaps a chronological and objective approach. Following Bethge, Kuske shares the opinion that Bonhoeffer addressed particular themes at certain periods of his life, and within these themes one finds a development of his views on the Old Testament. He saw it constantly as the book of Christ, but Kuske illustrates in this chapter how he said it in different ways. He uses numerous quotes which allow Bonhoeffer to say what he had to say without a strained effort to be systematic. Yet Kuske's arrangement keeps the quotations from standing alone, unrelated to one another. His skillful footnoting provides a running commentary of the theological climate as well as a contemporary evaluation of Bonhoeffer's thought. The footnotes enhance the work as a whole and prove helpful to the reader.

The first half of Chapter Three discusses Bonhoeffer's own "Christological" interpretation of the Old Testament, which moves in two directions—from Christ to the Old Testament and from the Old Testament to the New Testament. Here he shares in what Hans Walter Wolff, Walther Zimmerli, Alfred Jepsen, and Gerhard von Rad have also asserted on Old Testament interpretation. Not only is there a double-direction hermeneutical principle, but Bonhoeffer's use of the phrase "Christ in the Old Testament" is explained.

This chapter also includes selections from Bonhoeffer that deal directly with Old Testament passages—for example, Gen. 1:1 (in which all the interpretative elements mentioned above appear to be present); II Sam., chs. 11 to 19; and the Song of Songs. Bonhoeffer claimed that the Old Testament must be read from this side of the incarnation, crucifixion, and resurrection; that is, from the perspective of the revelation which has taken place. Otherwise, one remains within the Jewish or heathen understanding of the Old Testament. Kuske states this position tersely and clearly, helping one to see how Bonhoeffer read the Old Testament from such a perspective.

Bonhoeffer's phrase "Christ in the Old Testament" is subsequently explored. Claus Westermann, W. Rupprecht, and H. Pfeiffer have said that Bonhoeffer interpreted the Old Testament directly and strictly from a Christological standpoint. Kuske finds such criticism much too narrow. He supports this view as he develops Bonhoeffer's position from a lecture entitled "Christ in the Psalms," a Bible study on the restoration of Jerusalem according to Ezra and Nehemiah, and a sermon on Psalm 58. He also discusses such important concepts in Bonhoeffer as the "real presence" and the "personal presence." Comments of many theologians, as well as Kuske's own, are appropriately used to sharpen and clarify Bonhoeffer's position.

In the phrase "Christ was in David," Bonhoeffer had certainly moved beyond the general concept of the real presence of Christ in the Old Testament. The question of whether he thereby surrendered the Old Testament comes to the surface. If one means the Old Testament as object of historical-critical research per se, perhaps Yes. To the contrary, however, Kuske replies No. There occurs the conquering of the Old Testament for the church. It is discovered as the book of the wandering people of God, through which worship and justice are under way in the world, and through which the voice of the living God may be heard and received.

The phrase "Christ in the Old Testament" in the light of the sermon on Psalm 58 suggests that Bonhoeffer had moved another step beyond the personal presence. Understanding the Old Testament from the standpoint of Christ leads to the knowledge that it is from Christ, for us. He makes it valid. It belongs to him. Nothing stands outside this, for in Christ the entire Old Testament is fulfilled.

The last half of the chapter is devoted to the New Testament from the perspective of the Old Testament. Here some key words and phrases from Bonhoeffer—such as, "How do we speak of God in a worldly sense?" and the "actuality" of the Old Testament—enter the discussion as Kuske follows the development of the influence of the Old Testament on Bonhoeffer's theology. On the basis of his letters and works it becomes clear that Bonhoeffer's world view was largely shaped by the Old Testament. He saw man living within reality as the Old Testament presented it.

Kuske has succeeded in letting Bonhoeffer speak from his works. Thus he enters into conversation with Baumgärtel, Brunner, Barth, and others, so that his view of the New Testament from the perspective of the Old is lively.

By no means does Bonhoeffer view the Old Testament as the mere counterpart of the New. Rather, the presupposition of the New brings a relevant interpretation of the Old Testament message. The Old Testament has a growing importance for Bonhoeffer which is reflected in his New Testament interpretation as well. Kuske has included examples in this chapter.

Finally, Kuske addresses the contribution the Old Testament makes to understanding Bonhoeffer's statement "the world come of age." In this concluding chapter he moves into the arena of what in Bonhoeffer's Old Testament interpretation is valid for men today. He has drawn the lines clearly so that Bonhoeffer can be placed neither in the camp of Friedrich Baumgärtel, Rudolf Bultmann, and F. Hesse, who tend to devalue the Old Testament, nor in that of Arnold Albert van Ruler, who tends to overvalue it. Rather, for Bonhoeffer (as with G. von Rad, H. W. Wolff, and W. Zimmerli) both Testaments are of practically the same value, since both witness to Christ. From this basic position, Kuske approaches the question, Can the Old Testament lead to a better understanding of Bonhoeffer's last theological thoughts? His answer is, Yes; and through further analysis of Bonhoeffer's materials, supports this position effectively. The pros and cons of Bonhoeffer's views are thoroughly considered.

Kuske's goal in this chapter is to understand Bonhoeffer's phrase "the world come of age" in correspondence to the Old Testament message of justice. The writer suggests that Bonhoeffer is much more influenced by the Old Testament prophets than is often recognized. Although Kuske might have developed this assertion more thoroughly, it is clear that Bonhoeffer himself in a few places recognized that his thoughts on "nonreligious interpretation" were rooted in the Old Testament.

Kuske has elucidated the "tension" hermeneutic which exists in Bonhoeffer's interpretation of the Scripture—the "reciprocal" movement between the Old Testament and the New. He has shown that it is *actually* a reciprocal movement. Furthermore, it is here that his Christological interpretation is profitable for, rather than a hindrance to, an understanding of the Old Testament.

There are valuable implications in this work for the life of the contemporary church, since Kuske has set Bonhoeffer's thought in the context of its development. Most suggestive are Bonhoeffer's interpretative comments on social justice. Implications may be drawn on the importance of the Old Testament for the church as it faces particular social issues in the present, since Bonhoeffer found the Old Testament such a great resource at this point.

Kuske's work is significant especially since it is the first study to treat extensively Bonhoeffer's Old Testament interpretation. In the long line of material reflecting the sustained interest in and the importance of Dietrich Bonhoeffer it will be an invaluable resource.

TRANSLATION NOTES

1. Abbreviations: Kuske's abbreviations for the German titles of Bonhoeffer's original works have been maintained. A key to these abbreviations is included and corresponding En-

glish translations have been listed.

2. Book titles: The first time each of Bonhoeffer's works is cited the complete German title is given with an English translation in parentheses. German titles by other authors cited by Kuske have been retained as they appear in the German edition, generally without translation.

3. Quotations: Whenever an existing English translation of a work of Bonhoeffer has been used, the original German citation is followed by the full title and page number of the English translation. If a translation is cited more than once, succeeding references include only the original German reference and the notation "Eng. tr." ("English translation") plus the page number.

ACKNOWLEDGMENTS

When the translator first picked up Kuske's volume in a Leipzig bookstore at the suggestion of a fellow traveler, Ralph Zorn, pastor of the Tempelhof Evangelical Church in West Berlin, he was struck by the need for an English translation. But the project could not have reached completion without the sustained assistance of Dr. Darrell Guder and Professor Hans Klimkeit, who generously read the translation to ensure that it would do justice to the original German text. In addition, Eberhard Bethge and the author, Martin Kuske, graciously supplied helpful information when consulted. To all of these who have contributed time, help, and advice toward the completion of this translation a deep sense of gratitude is joyfully expressed.

S T KIMBROUGH, JR.

Bonn, Germany

FOREWORD

The first thing to be said here is a word of gratitude in memory of Professor Heinrich Benckert. He was the doctoral adviser for this work, which was submitted to the Theological Faculty at Rostock University in 1967 under the same title and which now appears in somewhat altered form. Professor Benckert's availability to his students during the final months of his life, when he already knew of his impending death, will not be forgotten.

A word of gratitude is also extended to Rector Eberhard Bethge, D.D., who during the entire period of the preparation of this work lent assistance through correspondence and even made available the proofs of his then forthcoming biography of Dietrich Bonhoeffer.

With this volume the author wishes to present more than a mere contribution to the discussion about Bonhoeffer's theology and its analysis. That is certainly a high expectation, especially since in this work a personal point of view is very reserved. However, through occupation with Bonhoeffer's work the Old Testament has been opened up to the author, and the work of God surprisingly disclosed anew. The publication will have achieved its purpose if someone gains new courage, perhaps stronger than before, to draw both life and proclamation from the Old Testament, because from it as an essential part of the Bible we can both see and learn anew of the reality of God and our own reality.

MARTIN KUSKE

INTRODUCTION

1. *The Task*

Dietrich Bonhoeffer loved the Old Testament. When engaged with his work, we encounter the traces of this love again and again, and when we pursue these traces we will find ourselves well rewarded. In so doing, we can recognize that Bonhoeffer has a share in the new theological consideration of the Old Testament before and during the church struggle, when the Confessing Church discovered the Old Testament; that he is, moreover, a partner in the discussion which, since the end of the Second World War, has been directed to the Old Testament;[1] and that finally some of the controversial thoughts from *Nachfolge (The Cost of Discipleship)* are based upon and conditioned by his interpretation of the Old Testament.

1. It is not without reason that C. Westermann, editor of *PAH*, in his overview of "Weitere Literatur zur Hermeneutik des Alten Testaments" cited *WE*. In H. W. Wolff's article "Zur Hermeneutik des Alten Testaments" (*PAH* 140–180), Bonhoeffer is directly and indirectly quoted (see below, pp. 128 and 136). In looking at Bonhoeffer as a whole, H. Ott says that his thought "is not dated but extends directly into our present time and lays a binding claim on us" and that he stands next to us "as our theological contemporary." These claims are also valid for Bonhoeffer's conversation with the Old Testament (H. Ott, *Wirklichkeit und Glaube*, Vol. I: *Zum theologischen Erbe Dietrich Bonhoeffers*, 1966, 61). For the subsequent consequences for an interpretation of the Old Testament, see the comments in fnn. 28 and 150.

These realizations have in part already been indicated in the literature. Although Bonhoeffer as an interpreter of the Old Testament caused much less of a stir than the monklike, orthodox, political, and liberal Bonhoeffer,[2] nevertheless some direct and indirect discussions of our theme have already appeared.[3] They have dealt with or referred to separate or chronologically related Old Testament interpretations by Bonhoeffer.[4] This has led to conflicting judgments that on the one hand Bonhoeffer's interpretation of the Old Testament must be likened to that of Wilhelm Vischer,[5] and on the other hand that, unlike Vischer, Bonhoeffer did not interpret the Old Testament as the proclamation of Christ.[6] As a matter of fact, Bonhoeffer appears to have interpreted the Old Testament in contradictory fashions. In 1937 he allows the picture of the bloody Savior to emerge in the midst of the Psalm of Vengeance (Ps. 58, *GS* IV, 421), while in 1944 he finds that probably the "best 'Christological' interpretation" of the Song of Songs is the one that regards the book

2. E. Bethge, "Dietrich Bonhoeffer. Person und Werk," *MW* I, 18 f.; "Dietrich Bonhoeffer. Der Mensch und sein Zeugnis," *MW* II, 102. The Bible studies "König David" ("King David") and "Der Wiederaufbau Jerusalems nach Esra und Nehemia" ("The Reconstruction of Jerusalem According to Ezra and Nehemiah") (1935/36) constitute an exception to which F. Imholz (see *GS* II, 292) and F. Baumgärtel (*Die Kirche ist Eine—die alttestamentlich-jüdische und die Kirche Jesu Christi?* 1936) strongly react.

3. In Bibliography I, the writings of H. Hellbardt, F. Baumgärtel, J. Fichtner, R. Grunow, and H. Schulte belong to the direct contributions. To the indirect ones, on the one hand, belong the works on the other problems of Bonhoeffer's theology in which longer or shorter statements on the Old Testament are to be found: Bibliography I, J. D. Godsey, K. H. Nebe, H. Pfeifer, E. Bethge, B.-E. Benktson, and also W.-D. Zimmermann; and, on the other hand, other theological works of Bonhoeffer which have to do with the Old Testament: Bibliography I, G. von Rad, K. Barth, H. W. Wolff, K. H. Miskotte, C. Westermann, W. Rupprecht, H.-G. Fritzsche, W. Kreck, C. Nicolaisen.

4. In addition to the contributions of R. Grunow, C. Westermann, E. Bethge, and B.-E. Benktson, all the works cited in Bibliography I belong here as well.

5. Baumgärtel, *Die Kirche ist Eine,* Foreword; W. Rupprecht, *Die Predigt über alttestamentliche Texte in den lutherischen Kirchen Deutschlands,* dissertation, Nürnberg, 1962, 372.

6. K. H. Nebe, *Religionslose Interpretation bei D. Bonhoeffer und ihre Bedeutung für die Aufgabe der Verkündigung,* dissertation, Hamburg, 1961, 205.

2

as an "ordinary love song" (*WE* 172/173). "The problem of caesura" in Bonhoeffer's theological development[7] is also to be considered in this work, the purpose of which is to draw together all important and available Old Testament interpretations and statements by Bonhoeffer on the Old Testament in their context.

2. *The Sources*

A wide variety of sources serve as the basis for this work: sermons,[8] sermon outlines,[9] Bible studies,[10] devotions and devotional aids,[11] pastoral addresses,[12] meditations and exegeses,[13] letters,[14] poems,[15] a series of lectures,[16] a curriculum for confirmation instruction,[17] an address,[18] an "Introduction to the Psalms,"[19] and a confession.[20] In addition, there are many passages from the other works of Bonhoeffer, with the exception of *Akt und Sein (Act and Being),* in which he uses or interprets individual verses or larger sections from the Old Testament.[21]

These sources are very different in their *Sitze im Leben* (for the podium and for the pulpit, for the many and for the individual); and the manner in which they have been passed on to us is just as varied. They were printed[22] in part during Bon-

7. See the summary report in *DB* 964 f.
8. List of D. Bonhoeffer Sources: numbers 1, 2, 4, 6, 7, 9, 10, 11, 25.
9. Numbers 12, 15, 16, 17, 22, 23.
10. Numbers 14, 20, 24.
11. Numbers 3, 33, 35.
12. Numbers 18, 26, 27, 32.
13. Numbers 29, 31, 36.
14. Numbers 19, 34.
15. Number 37.
16. Number 5.
17. Number 21.
18. Number 13.
19. Number 30, also 28.
20. Number 8; Bonhoeffer only coeditor.
21. See the indexes of *SC, N, E, GS* I-III.
22. *SF,* 1934; address on Ps. 90 at the memorial ceremony for Mrs. J. Bonhoeffer, a special family publication; Bible study "King David," *JK* 4

3

hoeffer's lifetime, and in part published posthumously by Bethge.[23] A few of these sources have been preserved in the original handwriting or typewriting, while others had to be reconstructed from notes.[24] The different types of material, *Sitze im Leben,* and the manner in which we have received them must be considered along with the interpretation.

3. The Method

The types of material reveal the way in which Bonhoeffer customarily approached the Old Testament texts, not as an Old Testament specialist, but as a dogmatician and preacher.[25] But before one supposes for that reason that Bonhoeffer's Old Testament interpretations can be laid aside as considerations of a dilettante, one should ask himself whether approaching a Biblical text as preacher is not the most relevant way to deal with the Bible and whether here the dogmatician as dilettante cannot at the same time be the leader.[26]

This fact among others is the reason why, before turning to individual interpretations of Bonhoeffer, we say something in Chapter Two about Bonhoeffer's fundamental position on the Bible. In Chapter One a brief overview of the appraisal of the Old Testament in Bonhoeffer's setting is given in order to place his own appraisal and interpretation in its time context. In Chapter Four we shall attempt to summarize the contribu-

---

(1936), 64–69, 157–161, 197–203; Bible study "The Reconstruction of Jerusalem . . . ," *JK* 4 (1936), 653–661 (statement in *GS* IV, 632 f.); *Das Gebetbuch der Bibel (The Prayerbook of the Bible),* 1940.

23. *E,* 1949; *WE,* 1953; *Versuchung (Temptation),* 1953; *GS* I-IV, 1958–1961.
24. See the evidence in *GS* I, 528; III, 550–553; IV, 630 ff.
25. W. Rott, in *Begegnungen mit Dietrich Bonhoeffer,* 1966², 106.
26. Compare K. H. Miskotte, "Der moderne Dogmatiker als Dilettant und Dirigent," *EvTh* 20 (1960), 245–262. According to K. Schwarzwäller ("Das Alte Testament in Christus," *ThSt*[B] 84 [1966], 6) in order to be able to solve the prescribed task of the relationship of the Old and New Testaments, Old and New Testament exegetes are led back in increasing degree to a grasp of systematic principles "in order to achieve fundamental unity."

tion of the Old Testament to an understanding of Bonhoeffer's statements on "the world come of age."

The main part, Chapter Three, treats the development of the theme of this work: the Old Testament as the book of Christ. In regard to method, generally speaking chronology and content overlap. That is rooted in the sources and the subject. In an overall look at Bonhoeffer's works, Bethge determined that he had definite addressees[27] for a specific theme at a specific time. His conclusion is valid in modified form here as well. From the volume *Schöpfung und Fall (Creation and Fall)* onward, Bonhoeffer certainly always says the same thing with

27. The "knowledge about the preciousness of the word of Jesus Christ" is "the theme that runs throughout Bonhoeffer's life." "In the 1920's Bonhoeffer said to the theologians: Your theme is the *church!* In the 1930's Bonhoeffer said to the *church:* Your theme is the *world!* In the 1940's Bonhoeffer said to the world: Your theme, the abandonment, is God's *theme* itself." (Bethge, *MW* I, 8, see also 24.)

28. Time and again a systematized oversimplification has been warned against, for instance by H. Müller ("Zur Problematik der Rezeption und Interpretation Dietrich Bonhoeffers," *MW* IV, 53), Chr. Hinz ("Christliche Verkündigung angesichts atheistischer Anfechtung," *MPTh* 51 [1962], 32), and H. Ott (*op. cit.,* 58). For Müller a legitimate acceptance of Bonhoeffer entails the following: "taking up his development, his way, the tendency and the inclination of his work and at the same time not systematizing the living movement in him" *(loc. cit.).* So far as an interpretation of Bonhoeffer is concerned, we agree with this claim, but we differ from Müller in that we can find no way of speaking about a "qualitative break" in Bonhoeffer's theological development (H. Müller, *Von der Kirche zur Welt,* 1966², 355). That may lie in the fact that the object of our investigation was almost completely ignored by Müller. He also lacks a discussion of *SF.* The "qualitative break" need not necessarily be reflected in Bonhoeffer's Old Testament interpretation. On the other hand, a few interpreters have succeeded in developing a contrasting view of the question of Bonhoeffer's relationship to Vischer, because they review either his interpretations from 1935/36 or *WE* (see above, Introduction, sec. 1, and fnn. 5 f.). A difference does appear to exist here. What Ott says about Bonhoeffer's work in general is appropriate and valid for his intercourse with the Old Testament as well. He says that "with all the exterior imbalance" he still possesses "an unusual inner uniformity, a clear inner 'direction' " *(op. cit.).* In a chapter entitled "Das Erbe D. Bonhoeffers und die Methode seiner Entfaltung" *(ibid.,* 57–84), Ott provides some evidence for a Bonhoeffer interpretation. For further reference to this evidence, see fnn. 141, 147, and 150.

regard to the Old Testament—it is the book of Christ—but he says it in different ways. The chronological arrangement points sometimes simultaneously to an objective arrangement. In order to prevent a systematizing structure, the interpretation of individual texts stands in the foreground. These texts do not stand next to one another unrelated or in opposition, but move toward the already mentioned uniformity; one notices the chronological place of the texts, a movement in a definite direction: the Old Testament gains a greater and greater significance for Bonhoeffer.[28]

I

THE EVALUATION
OF THE OLD TESTAMENT
IN BONHOEFFER'S SETTING

In order not to represent Bonhoeffer's evaluation and interpretation of the Old Testament in a vacuum, but to let them
come alive in the historical milieu of the time, it is necessary
to cite some voices addressed to the Old Testament that were
heard in Germany after the First World War. They are certainly manifold and very different;[29] but three basically distinct
positions are easy to recognize: that of the *rejection* of the Old
Testament because it is not a witness to the Christian religion;
that of its *retention* because it is a witness to the pre-stage of
Christianity; and that of its *acknowledgment* because it is the
Word of God along with the New Testament. Bonhoeffer came
into contact with each of them.

1. *The Rejection of the Old Testament*

a) *Anti-Semitic–Nationalistic Movement*

At the infamous Sport Palace demonstration of the Berlin
German Christians on November 13, 1933, the district chair-
man, Dr. R. Krause, and others demanded "the liberation

29. For a closer orientation, see the dissertation of C. Nicolaisen,
Die Auseinandersetzungen um das Alte Testament im Kirchenkampf 1933–1945, Hamburg, 1966, who differentiates much more strongly in the position presented
by us above under sec. 1.a. Compare Chapters I.2.c to III.B.3 and III.D.2 to
III.E.3.a.

from the Old Testament with its Jewish money morality, from these stories of livestock handlers and pimps," because true Christianity and clinging to the Old Testament would be self-exclusive.[30] This demand is taken over almost word for word from A. Rosenberg's *Mythus des 20. Jahrhunderts*.[31] That which was already prepared was now put into words in public: the fight against the Old Testament. Aside from the theological struggle of Adolf von Harnack, it was fed from three sources: the racial anti-Semitism of Gobineau and Chamberlain, the rejection of the Bible on the basis of the scientific criticism of Friedrich Delitzsch or Th. Fritsch, and the culture-critical conclusion of the end of Christianity, as it was represented by F. Nietzsche and A. Bonus.[32] The German Christians in part made the arguments of these opponents of the Old Testament their own,[33] even if after the Sport Palace demonstration such

30. J. Gauger, *Chronik der Kirchenwirren*, 1935, 109.

31. 1930; 17th-20th edition, 1934, 603 and 614. But National Socialism not only issued a verdict on the Old Testament, which though implied was clearly included under number 24 of the German National Socialist Workers Party (National Sozialistische Deutsche Arbeiter Partei, or NSDAP) platform (see, in addition, Nicolaisen, *op. cit.*, 61 f.), but on the New Testament and Christianity as a whole. In this context Nicolaisen cites the following statement of Hitler from H. Rausching, *Gespräche mit Hitler*, 1940, 50: "Fascism may make its peace with the church. I will do the same. Why not? That will not deter me from exterminating Christianity in Germany down to its last roots and fibers. . . . What's the difference, Old Testament or New, . . . it is all the same Jewish swindle. It is all one and the same and cannot make us free. One is either a Christian or a German."

32. Compare R. Abramowski, "Vom Streit um das Alte Testament," *ThR*, NF 3 (1937), 68 ff.; Gobineau, *Essai sur l'inégalité de races humaines*, 1884; Chamberlain, *Die Grundlagen des 19. Jahrhunderts*, 1889; F. Delitzsch, *Die grosse Täuschung*, 1920; Th. Fritsch, *Der falsche Gott. Beweismaterial gegen Jahwe*, 1912; and three works by A. Bonus, *Deutscher Glaube*, 1897; *Von Stöcker zu Naumann. Ein Wort zur Germanisierung des Christentums*, 1896; *Religion als Schöpfung*, 1902.

33. Rather than the theological uncertainty about the value and authority of the Old Testament, which rested on the uncertain relationship of Old Testament science over against the Old Testament itself, Nicolaisen sees the self-assuredness of the German Christians as the foundation of their polemic against the Old Testament. "One thing that was certain to the German Christians was the experience of the 'hour of the Germans,' the certainty that God reveals himself in the historical moment, in the people and the blood. Everything which was disturbing through its uncertainty or strangeness had to be sacrificed to this certainty. . . . The one-sided and stubborn adherence to the

radical voices as that of Dr. Krause are not to be heard from their ranks as often.[34] However, the fight against the Old Testament continued.[35] Bonhoeffer himself became conscious of it. His Bible study "King David," from October, 1935, provoked the indignation of a certain F. Imholz, who calls it "obnoxious, vulgar nonsense about King David, whose method of treatment, by the way, offends the morality and ethic of the German race "[36]

b) *Adolf von Harnack*

These opponents of the Old Testament just mentioned also thought they could find support for themselves in the conclusions of Adolf von Harnack.[37] In his book on Marcion is the oft-quoted sentence, "To reject the Old Testament in the second century was a mistake which the universal church rightly had rejected; to retain it in the sixteenth century was a fate from which the Reformation was not able to disentangle itself; but to conserve it since the nineteenth century as a canonical document in Protestantism is the result of a religious and church paralysis."[38] The Old Testament certainly is not to be rejected simply because the Christian element cannot be perceived in it; but it should be conceded a place no higher than at the head of the list of those books "which are good and useful to read," but Harnack would only let that apply to selective portions of the Old Testament. To give honor to

---

regulations of the people, state, and history, allegedly based on creation itself, kept them from seeing the revelation of God in the word of the Scripture" (Nicolaisen, *op. cit.*, 97, see also 116 f.).

34. See "Die Richtlinien der Kirchenbewegung Deutsche Christen in Thüringen vom 11.12.1933," or the so-called "Pommersche Bekenntnis Deutscher Christen Weihnachten 1933," in K. D. Schmidt, *Die Bekenntnisse und grundsätzlichen Äusserungen zur Kirchenfrage des Jahres 1933*, 1934, 102 f.

35. Compare, in addition, Nicolaisen, *op. cit.*, 134–148: "Der Kampf um das Alte Testament mit Staat und Partei."

36. F. Imholz, "Durchbruch," Stuttgart, March 26, 1936, in *GS* II, 292.

37. Compare Nicolaisen, *op. cit.*, 12–15: "Die Kritik des theologischen Liberalismus: Adolf von Harnack."

38. Adolf von Harnack, *Marcion. Das Evangelium vom fremden Gott*, 1921, 248 f.

truth and no longer maintain the Old Testament as holy and infallible Scripture, "that is the great deed which today—although almost too late—is demanded of Protestantism."[39] This opinion of Harnack is a "total rejection of the Old Testament as a Christian book,"[40] even if on completely other grounds than those which the anti-Semitic motive asserted.

Adolf von Harnack strongly influenced the student Bonhoeffer. Bonhoeffer wrote to him in 1929: "That you were our teacher for many hours is passed, that we may call ourselves your students remains." Bonhoeffer accepted his legacy proudly.[41] But in Old Testament matters he did not accept quite all of it!

2. The Retention of the Old Testament as Witness of the Pre-Stage of Christianity

Many other theologians of that period expressed a more middle-of-the-road position on the Old Testament and did not, as did Harnack, demand a rejection of the Old Testament as a Christian book. To the contrary, they polemicized against him and his untheological partisans, but also they were not ready to decide with Karl Barth and Wilhelm Vischer on an equal status for both the Old and the New Testament. To these theologians belong R. Seeberg, Bonhoeffer's doctoral supervisor; E. Sellin, with whom Bonhoeffer studied the Old Testament "rather late" in Berlin;[42] and F. Baumgärtel, who vehemently disputed Bonhoeffer's interpretation of the Old Testament in 1936.[43]

a) Reinhold Seeberg

If Harnack could write that the Old Testament must be rejected because "the largest number of objections which peo-

39. *Ibid.*, 254 f.
40. Nicolaisen, *op. cit.*, 15.
41. *GS* III, 59; see also *DB* 95 ff., 175 f.
42. *DB* 101, see also 115.
43. See fn. 2.

ple raise against Christianity and the truthfulness of the church stem from the authority which the church still gives to the Old Testament,"[44] Reinhold Seeberg could see in the Old Testament a protection against a "gross nationalism," which supposes that immoral thoughts could penetrate Christianity through the Old Testament.[45] But this defense of the Old Testament, on the other hand, had its depreciation close at hand, because the difference between Old and New Testament religion is the "characteristic difference between two stages of religion in which one should overcome the other." The difference exists not only in the "difference between the religious feelings and the moral purpose" but also in the "limitation of the pure spirituality of the religious relationship as it results from the maintenance of natural and mythological conceptions."[46] Old Testament religion is a "pre-stage of Christianity." The Old Testament is certainly important for the understanding of the New Testament, but the New Testament alone is "to be considered as the source of the dogmatic knowledge,"[47] the source which is "for all times in Christianity both creative and decisive authority."[48] That means, however, no fundamental disqualifying of the Old Testament. Through the Holy Spirit the Old Testament can also "become effective as God's Word,"[49] for it likewise has authority for Christian doctrine, but only because "it stands in relationship to the New Testament as one of the pathmaking and preparatory developmental stages."[50]

44. Harnack, *op. cit.*, 254.
45. R. Seeberg, *Christliche Dogmatik* II, 1925, 424.
46. *Ibid.*, 240.
47. *Ibid.*, 241.
48. *Ibid.*, 412. In the table of contents, number 41 reads, "Das Wort Gottes im Neuen Testament" (XII) ("The Word of God in the New Testament"), while on p. 408 it reads only, "Das Wort Gottes" ("The Word of God"). Seeberg's opinion is better rendered by the first heading, since the Word of God is limited to the New Testament.
49. *Ibid.*, 424.
50. *Ibid.*, 240.

b) *Ernst Sellin*

Ernst Sellin's position on the Old Testament is similar. On the one hand, he could oppose the well-known Harnack thesis in *Marcion* as follows: "To do away with the Old Testament as canonical record in the twentieth century would directly contradict the witness of Jesus and the apostles, who found divine will and purpose in the Old Testament; it would have fatal religious results, and, above all, simply be an anachronism and the greatest blunder the evangelical church could commit."[51] On the other hand, he could call[52] a "sickness" the "practical equation of the Old Testament and the New Testament in spite of theoretical distinctions, the dying out of the knowledge that the divine revelation . . . has had its historically bound stages and limits," and he remembers that he has always "stressed energetically" that "an equation of the Old Testament and the New Testament can no longer be mentioned."[53]

c) *Friedrich Baumgärtel*

Like Seeberg and Sellin, Friedrich Baumgärtel also rejected Harnack's radical thesis.[54] Many an attack was aimed at Friedrich Delitzsch.[55] In spite of that, he comes very near Harnack when he says, for example, that the Old Testament "lacks specific Christian ideas," that it conveys "many sub-Christian and anti-Christian ideas."[56] Yahweh, the God of the Old Testament, may not be equated directly with the God of Jesus Christ,[57] since Jesus takes up only the god concepts of the prophets and high priests of the Old

51. E. Sellin, *Das Alte Testament und die evangelische Kirche der Gegenwart,* 1921, 93.
52. *Ibid.,* 96; see also E. Sellin, *Abschaffung des Alten Testaments?* 1932, 37.
53. Sellin, *Das Alte Testament und die evangelische Kirche der Gegenwart,* 84.
54. F. Baumgärtel, *Die Bedeutung des Alten Testaments für den Christen,* 1925, 15.
55. *Ibid.,* 9, 11, 15.
56. *Ibid.,* 19; compare Harnack, *op. cit.,* 254.
57. Baumgärtel, *Die Beudeutung des Alten Testaments,* 14, 19.

12

Testament.[58] But the Old Testament is of value because it "trains us for a correct and intensive kind of piety,"[59] because "we as Christians stand in the midst of the Old Testament and, as the Old Testament and with the Old Testament, strive toward the New Testament."[60]

We will meet Baumgärtel twice more in the course of this work, once in his attack on Bonhoeffer in 1936 and another time in the context of Bonhoeffer's own ideas on the Old Testament in *Letters and Papers from Prison,* which appear very similar to the statements of Baumgärtel on our movement from the Old into the New Testament.[61]

The position of R. Seeberg, E. Sellin, and F. Baumgärtel on the Old Testament can be labeled with the word "retention." They resist a rejection of the Old Testament, because they do not want to renounce certain parts of it.[62] However, thereby they set an impossible alternative in opposition to the rejected position. According to G. Gloege, the church in that period did not have to decide between "retention" and "rejection" of the Old Testament, rather between "conquest" and "surren-

58. *Ibid.,* 34, and F. Baumgärtel, "Das Alte Testament," in Künneth/ Schreiner, *Die Nation vor Gott,* 1934[3], 102.
59. Baumgärtel, *Die Bedeutung des Alten Testaments,* 25, 31 f.
60. Sellin, *Das Alte Testament und die evangelische Kirche der Gegenwart,* 106 f.
61. See below, Chapter II.D.3 and III.E.2.a,b. (*WE* 92/112 f.)
62. Compare the presentation of Sellin and Baumgärtel in Nicolaisen, *op. cit.,* 50–55, and his summary opinion about both (and J. Hempel), 55: "The Old Testament always has only a conditional authority for everyone: . . . Sellin sees only in the 'ethical prophetical' line a connection with the New Testament with respect to salvation history. For Baumgärtel the validity of the Old Testament is limited to those witnesses who have analogous counterparts in the New Testament with respect to religious history. In this way the representative Old Testament specialists in the 1920's applied critical measures to the Old Testament from many different viewpoints and everything that did not comply with these critical measures was disposed of as nonobligatory for Christian belief." However, it must be pointed out that during the years after 1930, the "representative Old Testament specialists" were those who attempted to work out the continuity between the Testaments in a positive manner. Among them were W. Eichrodt, *Theologie des Alten Testaments,* Vol. I, 1933, especially 1–8; and G. von Rad, see below, the beginning of Chapter III.

der." The church as a whole since the eighteenth century had not possessed the Old Testament at all and stood in 1934 before the possibility of gaining it again. Up until then only a few had recognized this task.[63]

3. *The Acknowledgment of the Old Testament as the Word of God*

Wilhelm Vischer and Karl Barth furnished the weapons that were necessary for the church in its conquest of the Old Testament. This had a decisive effect on Bonhoeffer's theological development, but Bonhoeffer encountered the former only when he himself had already acknowledged the Old Testament as the Word of God.

a) *Karl Barth*

After the First World War, Karl Barth pointed toward the only power "from which all theology could experience a new consciousness: *the Word of God.*"[64] And Barth indeed referred to the Word of God which he perceived from the New *and* the Old Testament; for in the sentence, "that *the Bible* . . . is qualitatively distinguished from all other possible authorities as *God's Word,*" "a *fundamental* difference" in relationship "between the Old and the New Testament *cannot* be acknowl-

---

63. G. Gloege, "Die Deutschkirche," in Künneth/Schreiner, *op. cit.,* 413. Gloege mentions Vischer, Brunner, Fendt, and Maurenbrecher. A few remarks on Brunner are necessary, because ideas from his article "Die Bedeutung des Alten Testaments für unseren Glauben," *ZZ* 8(1930), 30–48 are also found in Bonhoeffer. See fnn. 305, 337, 361, and 379. Since chronologically these ideas appear later in Bonhoeffer, one must consider the possibility of whether Brunner, along with Barth and Vischer, has not also influenced Bonhoeffer here. In September, 1932, both became acquainted (*DB* 190, 218, 303). Bonhoeffer was grateful to Brunner for the afternoon that they were able to spend together, *GS* I 36 f. During those years Bonhoeffer was especially interested in Brunner's book *Das Gebot und die Ordnungen,* 1932; compare *GS* I, 31, 33; *DB* 1087 ff. After 1933, Bonhoeffer lost interest in discussing further Brunner's themes.

64. H. J. Kraus, *Geschichte der historisch-kritischen Erforschung des Alten Testaments,* 1956, 379; compare the entire number 86: "Religion, Wort Gottes und Theologie."

edged."[65] Although the witness of the Bible is varied,[66] very incomplete and imperfect in the Old and the New Testament,[67] we are to teach its "identity" in regard to that to which it witnesses. "Revelation, by virtue of the term itself, can mean only one thing: the revelation of God,"[68] who as the "God of Moses, Jeremiah, Job, of Psalms 39 and 139, is also the God of Capernaum and Nazareth, of Gethsemane and Golgotha." The prophets speak with the apostles "in the face of an indivisible, perfect revelation of the triune God," and they "proclaim God speaking in Christ."[69]

This passionate call to the central issue found its echo in the entire expanse of theological science in Germany,[70] and also with Bonhoeffer, who discovered Barth in the winter of 1924. According to Bethge that was a liberation and permitted a self-assured definiteness to take the place of a certain restless wandering.[71] To what extent Bonhoeffer was impressed by Barth with regard to the Old Testament at this time is not possible to establish; however, he must have examined rather soon the views of Barth also on this question.[72]

65. K. Barth, "Das Schriftprinzip der reformierten Kirche," *ZZ* 3(1925), 222, 217.

66. *Ibid.*, 223.

67. K. Barth, *Die Lehre vom Wort Gottes. Prolegomena zur christlichen Dogmatik*, 1927, 242.

68. *Ibid.*, 244.

69. *Ibid.*, 243; compare Nicolaisen, *op. cit.*, 55–59: "Die neue Konzeption der 'Dialektischen Theologie': Karl Barth."

70. H. J. Kraus, *op. cit.*, 382.

71. *DB* 102–107.

72. During the summer semester of 1925 in a seminar with Seeburg, Bonhoeffer wrote a paper entitled "Lässt sich eine historische und pneumatische Auslegung der Schrift unterscheiden, und wie stellt sich die Dogmatik dazu?" ("Can a Distinction Be Drawn Between a Historical and Pneumatical Interpretation of the Scriptures and What Is the Attitude to This of Dogmatic Theology?" *DB* 109; Eng. tr., E. Mosbacher, P. and B. Ross, F. Clarke, and W. Glen-Doepel, *Dietrich Bonhoeffer*, 1970, 59). So far as the question of the interpretation of Scripture is concerned in this paper Bonhoeffer stands fully on the standpoint of dialectical theology (*DB* 109 f.). This work was not accessible to us, so that the question regarding the Old Testament must remain open. In a work written for Sellin in his eighth semester, "Die verschiedenen Lösun-

b) *Wilhelm Vischer*

Necessitated by the new consciousness which Barth brought to Protestant theology, Wilhelm Vischer tried "to interpret the Bible again as Bible, and in its own strange sense quite foreign to us."[73] That means for the Old Testament that he sought to lift up its "witness of Christ," for "Jesus Christ is the cornerstone and keystone" of the Old Testament.[74] The Old and New Testaments testify to him like two choirs facing each other in a church and pointing to the same center, to the mediator between God and man.[75] Therefore, Vischer resisted all attempts to disqualify the Old Testament witness as opposed to the New Testament. A "church" which does that will no longer be a church, for the "Christian church stands and falls on the acknowledgment of the unity of both Testaments."[76]

Vischer's *Das Christuszeugnis des Alten Testaments (The Old Testament Witness to Christ)* struck "alarm throughout theological science." Not groping and precautious, but with daring abandon breaking through to the Reformation message, Vischer achieved the new orientation of Old Testament science.[77]

---

gen des Leidensproblems bei Hiob" ("The Various Solutions to the Problem of Suffering in Job"), winter semester 1926/27, he says, however, nothing about "theological exegesis." To the contrary, he uses the entire vocabulary of the discipline: "heightened ethical consciousness," "deeper Christian understanding," "overwhelming remonstrance" (*DB* 115). On Dec. 16, 1927, on the other hand, one day before the defense of his dissertation, he debated with Franz Hildebrandt, who took sides with Marcion, about the relationship of both Testaments. In numerous discussions afterward Hildebrandt defended Harnack and attacked Bonhoeffer for his defense of Hegel and Barth (*DB* 174).

73. *CAT*, Vol. I: *Das Gesetz*, 1934, 1946[7], 35.

74. *Ibid.*, 21; see also "Das Alte Testament als Gottes Wort," *ZZ* 5(1927), 380, where, however, only cornerstone is mentioned.

75. *CAT*, Vol. I, 29.

76. *Ibid.*, 32.

77. H. J. Kraus, *op. cit.*, 387; compare V. Herntrich, "Theologische Auslegung des Alten Testaments? Zum Gespräch mit W. Vischer," *MPTh* 32(1936), 178: concerning Vischer's work it can only be said "that he has called the church to consider the relevance of the Old Testament." This judgment carries a lot of weight, because Herntrich himself already saw clearly

Bonhoeffer first met Vischer at Bethel during the work on the Bethel Confession in August, 1933.[78] From this encounter Vischer reported that on the question of the Old Testament he was united with Bonhoeffer "in the crucial issues and in all particulars." He had spoken much with Bonhoeffer about these things during those days.[79] Bethge supposes that Bonhoeffer was not influenced by Vischer, but rather thought parallel to him, "because *Creation and Fall* appeared before Vischer's book. But Bonhoeffer felt himself a close ally"[80] of Vischer and Vischer as one of Bonhoeffer's.[81] Whether and to what extent Bonhoeffer might have had knowledge of or can have been influenced by Vischer's preliminary essays[82] for *Das Christuszeugnis des Alten Testaments* can no longer be determined. However, parallels exist.[83]

---

in 1933 that the fight against the Old Testament was a fight against the foundation of the church (V. Herntrich, *Völkische Religiosität und Altes Testament*, 1933, 11) and then in 1936 he acknowledged that Vischer's book could help the church to secure its foundation. Abramowski, *loc. cit.*, 91 (see fn. 32) and Nicolaisen, *op. cit.*, 173 ff., share a similar opinion.

78. *GS* II, 83.
79. Vischer's letter to this author, Oct. 14, 1965.
80. Bethge's letter to this author, March 12, 1966.
81. Compare fn. 79.
82. Vischer, "Das Alte Testament als Gottes Wort," *ZZ* 5(1927), 379–395; "Der Gott Abrahams und der Gott Isaaks und der Gott Jakobs," *ZZ* 9(1931), 282–297; "Das Alte Testament und die Verkündigung," *ThBl* 10(1931), 1–12; "Das Alte Testament und die Geschichte," *ZZ* 10(1932), 22–42. In addition, compare Nicolaisen, *op. cit.*, 150–152, with these articles.
83. See fn. 121.

II

BONHOEFFER'S
APPRAISAL OF THE BIBLE

The framework within which Bonhoeffer's appraisal and interpretation of the Old Testament operate is his fundamental
appraisal of the Bible, which includes a fundamental appraisal
of the Old Testament.[84]

1. *The Bible as the Place of God's Speech*

On April 8, 1936, Bonhoeffer writes a letter to his brother-
in-law, R. Schleicher, in which he wants to answer a question
that he read between the lines of Schleicher's statements on
Bonhoeffer's sermons: "How do I live a Christian life in the
world of reality and where are the final authorities of such a
life which in itself is worth living?" To begin with, Bonhoeffer
admits quite simply: "I believe that the Bible alone is the
answer to all our questions and that we need only to ask
persistently and somewhat humbly in order to receive the
answer from it." He then enlarges on why the Bible has this

84. Compare R. Grunow, who says in the first part of his article "Dietrich
Bonhoeffers Schriftauslegung" "something about Bonhoeffer's interpretation
of Scripture as a whole." (1) "The Holy Scripture is interpreted by Bonhoeffer
as the book of the church"; see Chapter II.4. (2) "The entire Holy Scripture
is interpreted from the standpoint of Jesus Christ, who is its center, its meaning, and its goal"; see Chapter II. 2 and 3. (3) "The Holy Scripture is to be
interpreted with all the tools of historical and literary research and with all aids
of scientific criticism"; see Chapter II.4. (4) "The Holy Scripture is to be
interpreted nonreligiously for a world come of age" (*MW* I, 64 ff.).

authority. "It has to do with the fact that God speaks to us in the Bible" (*GS* III, 26). A later passage in the letter says: "The whole Bible is the place where God intends for us to find him" (*GS* III, 28).[85] How does Bonhoeffer come to this admission? He speaks of a bold venture and a decision, which must be made in regard to the Bible. We must risk "getting involved with the Bible as though God, who loves us and does not want to leave us alone with our questions, were really speaking to us here. Only in this way will we rejoice in the Bible" (*GS* III, 27). A part of this bold venture requires that we do not "simply *read* the Bible as we do other books" (*GS* III, 26). If we read it in that way, it does not open itself to us in its own essence. As an example of the right intercourse with the Bible, Bonhoeffer cites the way in which we deal with the word of a person whom we love: If we want to comprehend it, we may not "dissect" it, but must simply accept and ponder it. The pondering in the heart, as Mary did it, is the persistent questioning; the simple acceptance is the "somewhat humble" reading. Bonhoeffer expands these ideas.[86]

For him there are two ways in which God is to be found: "Either I determine the place where I want to find God, or I let God determine the place where he wants to be found" (*GS* III, 27).[87] Bonhoeffer admits that for him only the second

85. Compare from the "Finkenwalder Homiletik" (1935): "It has pleased God to speak to us through the word of the Bible" (*GS* IV, 253).

86. Compare the following sentence from the "Finkenwalder Homiletik" (1936–1939): "The knowledge of the Scripture should not serve fame and pride. Humble intellect is better than clever intellect. We study the Scripture vicariously for the community of Christ. We do that in order to be able to preach and pray from it more effectively. Hurried and hasty reading is disgraceful and inappropriate. Thorough and comprehensive Scripture knowledge is necessary" (*GS* IV, 256).

87. Bonhoeffer has suggested a similar "either-or" in the response to the question regarding the "re-presentation of the New Testament message." "Either one means by it that the Biblical message must be justified in the face of the present and hence the re-presentation must be proven valid, or one means that the present must be justified in the face of the Biblical message and hence the message must be contemporary" (*GS* III, 303, lecture: "Vergegenwärtigung neutestamentlicher Texte" ["Re-presentation of New Testament Texts"]).

comes into question. Whoever goes the first way always finds a god "who somehow conforms to me, is pleasing, who belongs to my being" (*GS* III, 27). Bonhoeffer knows that he would only encounter a "divine double" in this fashion. He is afraid of this (*GS* III, 29).[88] He wants to let God determine the place where he intends to be found. The place determined by God "does not conform at all" to the being of men and is "not at all pleasing. . . . This place is the cross of Christ. And whoever wants to find God there must take up this cross, as the Sermon on the Mount demands" (*GS* III, 28).[89] This is the message of both Testaments (*GS* III, 28).

Bonhoeffer attempted to read the Bible from the assumption that God speaks to him there. In this way he learned that this occurs quite differently from what he had anticipated. Therefore, he reads the Bible "somewhat humbly," in that he prefers to admit that he "does not understand this or that passage, but in the assurance that they will also one day be revealed, rather than to presume: that is godly, that is human" (*GS* III, 29).[90] He confesses that he "can no longer really live"

88. This "divine counterpart" is also God as "so-called eternal truth" (*GS* III, 28). In the lecture cited in the previous footnote Bonhoeffer suggests as an example for the "either" the method of interpretation that relates "Scripture to the eternal truth which I already know—be it an intellectual truth, an ethical principle, or a myth" (*GS* III, 310).

89. In letters from Jan., 1935, and the beginning of 1936, Bonhoeffer declares what effect the Sermon on the Mount had had on him. "I believe I know that I actually would be inwardly clear and honest, if I would begin really to be sincere about the Sermon on the Mount. Herein lies the only source of strength, which can shatter all magic and apparition once and for all" (1935). From that perspective Jesus Christ has been made an advantage for Bonhoeffer, and the Sermon on the Mount has freed him from the negligence of prayer (1936), *DB* 249. One of the central ideas in the lectures on the Sermon on the Mount delivered in 1935/36, which appeared as *N* in 1937, is that this sermon calls to discipleship under the cross. The closeness to Luther's Heidelberg debate is apparent. The "either-or" of both ways along which God is to be found is readily to be recognized as the "either-or" of *theologia gloriae* and *theologia crucis.* Compare R. Prenter, "Bonhoeffer und der junge Luther," *MW* IV, 33–51.

90. In the 1935 lecture cited in fn. 87, Bonhoeffer mentions the "false understanding of re-presentation," which relates the Scripture to eternal truths. "Thus the interpreter claims to be able to distinguish the Word of God

without reading the Bible in this manner and he is "glad" that "he has found this way back again from the wrong track of some theology to these primitive matters" (*GS* III, 29 f.).

Those are the most important thoughts from Bonhoeffer's letter to his brother-in-law which allow us to take a look not only at his personal relationship to the Bible but also at what is fundamental for his whole theology. Bonhoeffer read the Bible with the expectation[91] that God speaks to us there.

---

and the word of man in Holy Scripture. He himself knows where God's Word and where man's word are" (*GS* III, 310).

91. In the letter (April, 1936) Bonhoeffer writes that it is not so long ago that he learned to read the Bible in this way (*GS* III, 29). According to Bethge, in 1931/32 Bonhoeffer had finished "The Theologian Becomes a Christian" (*DB* 146–150). A part of becoming a Christian is that "for the first time Bonhoeffer came to the Bible" (letter of Bonhoeffer from the beginning of 1936 [see above, fn. 89] considered by Bethge as a glance back to the time before 1933), which he learned to read not for himself but over against himself. Compare the sentence about "a great concern" that weighed heavily on him during the Youth Conference in Gland from Aug. 25 to 31, 1932. "Has it not become terrifyingly clear again and again, in everything that we have said here to one another, that we are no longer obedient to the Bible? We are more fond of our own thoughts than of the thoughts of the Bible. We no longer read the Bible seriously, we no longer read it against ourselves, but for ourselves. If the whole of our conference here is to have any great significance, it may be perhaps that of showing us that we must read the Bible in quite a different way, until we find ourselves again" (*GS* I, 166; Eng. tr., J. Bowden with E. Bethge, *No Rusty Swords*, 1970, 181). How has Bonhoeffer come to his "humble" encounter with the Bible? According to R. Grunow, undoubtedly Karl Barth exerted "the decisive influence on him in the ecclesiastical interpretation of the Holy Scripture," but also Adolf Schlatter must be recalled (*MW* I, 64), for it was he who was of primary interest to Bonhoeffer in 1923 at Tübingen (*DB* 80 f.). According to J. Glenthoj, ecumenical work "made a Biblical interpreter" out of Bonhoeffer ("Bonhoeffer und die Ökumene," *MW* II, 145, 130). Franz Hildebrandt was Bonhoeffer's first close friend, and according to Bethge his turning to a stronger Biblicism greatly influenced Bonhoeffer (*DB* 174, 161).

Bonhoeffer also puts the Bible at the center of his work with those entrusted to him. In a report compiled by a participant in Bonhoeffer's ecumenical circle of students at the Technical University at Charlottenburg in Berlin, where Bonhoeffer served as a student minister beginning on Oct. 1, 1931, about the work in this group one reads: "At that time we divided the questions (which concerned the attitude of Christians toward the world, Glenthoj) according to specific subjects (body, law, etc.) and read the New Testament on that basis. Then in this context each one dealt with those points within his area of specialty. This took place without considering the pertinent literature. Then

Therefore he is able to say: The Bible alone is the final authority for a Christian life in the real world—and for a correct theology.[92] Bonhoeffer is bound to the text, and *the* message of the Bible is the message from the cross.

Bonhoeffer's decision regarding the Bible is not to be forgotten when his Old Testament interpretations are examined. The "humble acceptance" of the Biblical word, which results from the central theological insight that God lets himself be found by men at the strange place of the cross of Christ, is employed by Bonhoeffer in his interpretation of the Old Testament, when, for example, he does not reject the Psalms of Vengeance as being opposed to the higher morality of the New Testament or understand them as an early religious stage, rather preaches on a psalm such as Psalm 58 so that we may learn to pray it.[93]

2. *The Whole Bible as Witness of the One God*

In the letter to Schleicher, Bonhoeffer writes that not only the New Testament but also the Old Testament (Isa., ch. 53) proclaims that the cross of Christ is the place where God

---

we determined from the direct readings the point of view that applied to the concrete questions such as law, nature, etc., in the New Testament" (reported by J. Glenthoj, *loc. cit.,* 129 f.).

In a circular letter dated Oct., 1935, the brothers of the Finkenwalde Preaching Seminar wrote, "The Bible stands at the center of our work." The letter continues: "It has once again become for us the starting point and the center of our theological work and of all our Christian action. We have learnt here to read the Bible once again prayerfully. That is the significance of our morning and evening devotions in which we hear the word of the Bible continuously (*GS* II, 454; Eng. tr., E. H. Robertson and J. Bowden, *The Way to Freedom,* 1966, 35). . . . In the daily meditation period we consider a short biblical text which is selected for an entire week" (*ibid.*). In the circular letters the former candidates were called on time and again for text meditations (*GS* II, 463, 475, 495, 507, 515; see also the "Introduction to Daily Meditation," *GS* II, 478–482).

92. Second Catechism attempt (Oct., 1936): "For whom is the Holy Scripture written? It is written for everyone (at this point "for the theologians" is crossed through), who wants to say something about God and Jesus Christ, that he may measure every truth by the Scripture" (*GS* III, 337).

93. *GS* IV, 413–422; see Chapter III. D.4.

intends for himself to be found. In the letter he continually speaks of "the Bible." But after the sentence in which he mentions the Old Testament, one reads: "In any case Jesus and Paul looked at it that way: with the cross of Jesus the Scripture—that is, the Old Testament—is fulfilled. The whole Bible is the place where God intends for us to find him" (*GS* III, 28). The *whole* Bible—for Bonhoeffer there is no problem of an authorization of the Old Testament in distinction from a fully established and unproblematical authority of the New Testament. The distance of Bonhoeffer from his mentors, Harnack and Seeberg, as well as his nearness to Barth, Vischer, and Luther is clear in this one sentence.[94]

Bonhoeffer perceives God's Word in the New and Old Testaments, because it is the *One* God who speaks in both Testaments. We encounter this principle again and again in Bonhoeffer.

Together with other writers of the first draft of the Bethel Confession (among others Vischer) in August, 1933, under point I, "Of the Holy Scripture," Bonhoeffer says: "The Old Testament is God's Word, because it is the *One* God who calls Israel to be the church, who is rejected by Israel, and who founds the church of the New Covenant" (*GS* II, 92).[95] In 1933 when Bonhoeffer writes[96] the introduction for *Creation and Fall,* the publication of his lectures "Creation and Sin" from the winter semester of 1932/33, he ends with the sentence:

94. "The conviction of the . . . unity of Scripture . . . is plainly the foundation of Luther's entire exegetical work." This conviction is based on the assumption that "the God of the entire Scripture is the Father of Jesus Christ" (H. Bornkamm, *Luther und das Alte Testament,* 1947, 165).

95. On the significance of the Bethel Confession regarding the question of the Old Testament, Nicolaisen says (*op. cit.,* 103): "For the first time during the development of the Confessing Church an encompassing *damnatio* has been uttered, which has in view Stapel's doctrine of the law of the people, as well as the original-revelation doctrine of Althaus, and which deals with both the rejection and the curtailment of the Old Testament by the German Church. Furthermore, it sets the witness of the unity of salvation history in both Testaments in opposition to the religious-scientific significance of the Old Testament."

96. *DB* 261.

"The church and theological science stand and fall on the faith that God is the *One* God in the whole of Holy Scripture" (*SF*, 1958[4], 8). In the "Finkenwalde Homiletic" in answer to the question as to which text is concrete are found the following statements: "Fundamentally each text. It is one and the same God who speaks in each word of the Scripture" (*GS* IV, 253). In the discussion about his Bible study "King David" (October, 1953), Bonhoeffer notes: "The God of the Old Testament is the Father of Jesus Christ. The God who appears in Jesus Christ is the God of the Old Testament. He is a triune God" (*GS* IV, 320). And as his reason for the fact that he does not want to designate the very human stories of the Old Testament as an early religious stage, he states in a letter of December, 1943: "He is indeed one and the same God" (*WE* 93/113).

The initial decision with which Bonhoeffer approaches the interpretation of the Bible is that God is the *One* God in the whole Bible. This decision is not the result of exegesis; it is a faith event (*SF* 8).[97] If we consider what was said under the first point about his fundamental appraisal of the Bible, it should be clear that Bonhoeffer does no violence to the text with this decision.

3. *The Bible as Witness of the Love of God in Jesus Christ*

Bonhoeffer sees the whole Bible as the place where the *One* God speaks to us. Beyond this statement in his letter to Schleicher about the cross of Christ being the place where God meets us, he mentions only in a subordinate clause who he thinks God is. In the Bible "the God who loves" speaks to us

97. In like manner, Bornkamm expresses his opinion about Luther's conviction that the Father of Jesus Christ is the God of the entire Scripture. "The exegetical proof does not confirm this conviction, but presupposes it and makes it . . . intelligible for every interpreter with linguistic and logical arguments." While this is Luther's approach as well, it is not that of the Jews (Bornkamm, *op. cit.*, 169).

(*GS* III, 27). Here we have a key term, which is especially important for Bonhoeffer in his *Ethik (Ethics):* the love of God.[98]

The Bible proclaims to us: God is love (I John 4:16). For the sake of clarity this sentence must be read by stressing the word "God." For "only he who knows God knows what love is; however, the reverse is not true: one does not know first—that is, by nature—what love is and on the basis of that what God is" (*E* 55/155).[99] In order to know God, he must reveal himself to us.

Since Jesus Christ is *the* revelation of God,[100] he is "the only definition of love" in that "which he does and suffers" (*E* 55 f./156). According to the Scripture the content of the love of God exists "in the reconciliation of man with God in Jesus Christ" (*E* 57/157, 217/68). Bonhoeffer defines this content of the love of God more closely in another passage of the *Ethics,* when he speaks of Christ as the incarnate, crucified, and

98. In the following excerpts from Bonhoeffer's *Ethics* he speaks about the love of God: (1) "Love," 1939/40, *E* 53–58/154–158; (2) "The Despiser of Men," "The Successful Man," "The Idolization of Death," "Conformation," Nov., 1940, to Feb., 1941, *E* 74–91/16–28; (3) a few pages from the section "Christ, Reality and Good," Aug., 1940 or summer 1941, *E* 217 ff./68 ff.; (4) a few pages from the section "The Structure of Responsible Life," Aug., 1941, to April, 1942, *E* 235/172, 244–247/178–181; (5) one page from the article "On the Possibility of the Word of the Church to the World," during the time at Tegel prison(?), *E* 379/279.

99. Just as in the letter to R. Schleicher, Bonhoeffer speaks here also of the Bible, which proclaims to us the God of love. *E* 217/68 relates this message to the New Testament: "That God loved the world in Christ and reconciled it to himself is the central proclamation of the New Testament." Such a sentence may not lead astray to the assumption that only the God of the New Testament is a God of love for Bonhoeffer. Indeed, there are no explicit statements in the Scripture that the God of the Bible is the God of love other than those two quoted above; indeed, in *E* 55/155 f. Bonhoeffer cites only passages from the New Testament (I John), but since he can say at another point emphatically that God is *one* in the entire Bible, it stands to reason that the God of the Old Testament is the God of love. On this question, see below, Chapter III. C.4.

100. "The extent of the intensity to which Bonhoeffer's theological thinking was oriented to Jesus Christ needs no proof" (G. Ebeling, "Die 'nicht-religiöse Interpretation biblischer Begriffe,' " *MW* II, 19).

resurrected Lord.[101] The incarnate God is the "unfathomable mystery of God's love for the world" (*E* 75/16); the mystery of the judgment which God accomplishes in the cross "is the love of God for the world and for man" (*E* 79/19); in the risen One it becomes clear that "God's love for man was stronger than death" (*E* 83/22).[102] The perfect love of God for man confronts this death in Christ and overcomes it (*E* 74/16). "What befell Christ, befalls all men in him (*E* 80/19, 77/17, 84/23, 88/26).[103] Summarized, that means: God loves the world in the incarnate, crucified, and risen Lord, because he accepts it, judges it, and awakens it to new life, and thus mankind is reconciled.[104]

101. The section *"Ecce homo!"* begins with the sentences *"Ecce homo!*—Behold the man! In Him the world was reconciled with God" (*E* 74/15; Eng. tr., N. H. Smith, *Ethics*, 1970, 70). Then follow the sections "The Despiser of Men," "The Successful Man," and "The Idolization of Death." They begin with: *"Ecce homo!*—Behold the God who has become man." *"Ecce homo!*—Behold the man sentenced by God." *"Ecce homo!*—Behold the Risen One." (*E* 75/16, 79/19, 83/22).

102. In the following sentence from the section "Das Vorletzte" ("The Penultimate"), Bonhoeffer associates the love of God only with the incarnation. "In the incarnation we recognize the love of God for his creation; in the crucifixion we recognize the judgment of God upon all flesh; in the resurrection we recognize the will of God for a new world" (*E* 139/83). The following sentence, however, follows one page later: "Jesus Christ who rose again—this means that God out of His love and omnipotence sets an end to death and calls a new creation into life, imparts new life" (*E*, Eng. tr., 132).

103. Compare Hegel, *Die absolute Religion, PhB* 63 (1929), 159: The death of Christ "is atoning for us, because it represents the absolute history of the God idea, namely, that which has already come to pass and which eternally comes to pass." On the next pages, pp. 160 f.: The history of Christ "is not the history of one individual, rather it is God who fulfills it, i.e., from this point of view this history is the common, existing history in itself." Bonhoeffer scrutinized Hegel intensively. See the indexes to *SC* and *AS*. In the summer of 1933 he held a seminar on dogmatics, "Religionsphilosophie bei Hegel" ("Hegel's Philosophy of Religion," *DB* 266). On the relationship of Bonhoeffer and Hegel, see fnn. 120 and 389.

104. Compare R. Schulze, "Hauptlinien der Bonhoeffer-Interpretation," *EvTh* 25 (1965), 699 f.: the history of the world "is the movement of being accepted, judged and raised" by God.—"The man whom God has taken to Himself, sentenced and awakened to a new life, this is Jesus Christ. In Him it is all mankind. It is ourselves. Only the form of Jesus Christ confronts the world and defeats it. And it is from this form alone that there comes the formation of a new world, a world which is reconciled with God" (*E* 84/23;

The community of Christ must acknowledge and bear witness to the world of God's love for the world, which accomplishes the reconciliation of the world with God (*E* 218/69, 379/279).[105]

The love of God is recognizable in Jesus Christ, who is the incarnate, crucified, and risen Lord. This Christ stands at the center of Bonhoeffer's theology. That is verifiable in sources from 1930 to 1944.[106] Bonhoeffer's thought about the incar-

---

Eng. tr., 79). "Now there is no more reality, no more world, but it is reconciled with God and at peace" (*E* 75/16; Eng. tr., 71). Bonhoeffer did not describe everywhere in *E* the relationship of love and reconciliation and the occurrence of love in Jesus Christ as he did on pp. 55 ff./155 ff. and 74–84/16–23, so that it could be summarized in one sentence as attempted above. That sentence was not formed on the basis of passages from the sections "Christ, Reality and Good" and "The Structure of Responsible Life" cited in fn. 98. Now and then in both sections, as in "History and Good," Bonhoeffer speaks of the world "loved, judged and reconciled" in Christ (*E* 235/172, 244/178, 245/179, 247/181) or the world "born, received and reconciled" in Christ (208/61, 235/172). Also mention is made of the "incarnate, crucified and resurrected" Christ, or Christ come in the flesh, dead and risen (218/67 f., similarly 219/69). The result of the appearance of Christ, the content of the love of God, is always reconciliation.

105. On love as "Law and Gospel," see the discussion of K. H. Nebe in Chapter III.E.3.c of this work.

106. We agree with G. Ebeling's view that Bonhoeffer's theological thought involves a "basic Christological presupposition," but stress that the incarnate, crucified, and resurrected Jesus Christ is the basic presupposition or center of his theology. Compare J. D. Godsey, *The Theology of Dietrich Bonhoeffer*, 1960, 264: "Throughout the continuing development of his theology, as he faced the various situations of his life, it was the figure of the incarnate, crucified, and risen Lord that captivated his attention and evoked his faithful obedience." It can be said in favor of such a statement that through Bonhoeffer's involvement with Barth's theology his attention was drawn to this Christ. An account of Christ encountered as incarnate, crucified, and resurrected is available in Bonhoeffer's report on Barth's theology delivered in 1930/31 at Union Theological Seminary in New York under the title "The Theology of Crisis and Its Attitude Toward Philosophy and Science." "The fact of God's incarnation in Christ, the fact of Christ's suffering and the fact of his resurrection are the revelation of God" (*GS* III, 113, see also 112). On Hegel's influence, see fn. 103 and 389. This Christological concept was adopted and expanded by Bonhoeffer in his summer course on theology in 1933 at Berlin: Part IV, (1) The Incarnate One, (2) The Humbled and Exalted One (*GS* III, 231–242). In the lecture "Re-presentation of New Testament Texts" (1935), he says a few things about the "New Testament as witness . . . of the God-man Jesus Christ," who is "incarnate, crucified, and risen" (*GS* III, 314 f.). Bonhoeffer goes into

nate, crucified, and risen Lord will also contribute to his understanding of his Old Testament interpretation in a few passages.

4. The Bible as the Book of the Church

The framework within which Bonhoeffer's dialogue with the Old Testament moves would be described imperfectly if we should not consider the following: namely, the Bible is for him "the book of the church." Almost everything that has been said up to now about his appraisal of the Bible could be said about his personal opinion of the Bible. Bonhoeffer used the phrase "the book of the church" in the introduction to *Creation and Fall* in the "Theological Interpretation of Genesis 1–3" (subtitle). "Theological interpretation takes the Bible as the book of the church and interprets it as such" (*SF* 7). Theological interpretation is a controversial term. Since the end of the First World War, its pros and cons have been discussed in many scholarly contributions to the subject.[107]

---

more detail on this Christ in *Nachfolge* (1937) in the context of the incarnation of Christ in his community (*N*, Berlin, 1954, 280 ff.). In his *Ethics* these ideas are found in four sections: (1) "Ethics as Formation" (74–91/16–28); (2) "The Last Things and the Things Before the Last" (139 ff./83 ff.); (3) "Christ, Reality and Good" (217 ff./68 ff.); (4) "The 'Ethical' and the 'Christian' as a Theme" (313 ff./230 ff.). These sections originated between Sept., 1940, and the winter of 1942/43 (foreword to the 6th edition by Bethge). For the time prior to this the following writings of Bonhoeffer should be considered: "Theological Letters" for Christmas 1939, "Resurrection" Easter 1940, and the "Ascension of Jesus Christ" 1940 (*GS* III, 383–388, 405–415). This Christological concept endures to the time of *WE*. The letter from May 5, 1944 (*WE* 149/184), and the "Outline for a Book" (*WE* 209/259) should also be examined. The result of the examination of the sources is that we are left with the problem of how the knowledge of Jesus Christ as incarnate, crucified, and risen in Bonhoeffer relates to other knowledge that the cross of Christ is *the* location of the knowledge of God. The problem cannot be discussed here. Only one inference: contrary to the interpretation attempted by H. Müller (*op. cit.*, 355) that the Bonhoeffer of *WE* is "completely committed to the *theologia crucis*" (see, however, Müller's epilogue to the second edition of his book, 1966, 433), the thesis could be asserted that this is the Bonhoeffer of *N*.

107. Fundamental: K. Barth, Preface to *Der Römerbrief*, 1922, viii–xiii. See

With the sentence about theological interpretation, Bonhoeffer moves along the line of interpretation already laid down by Barth (1935) and K. H. Miskotte (1936). For them, as for Bonhoeffer, an essential aspect of theological interpretation is that the Bible and the church are viewed as belonging together.[108] In the introduction to *Creation and Fall*, Bonhoeffer discusses this intimate relationship. The church "lives, thinks, acts, and proclaims in the light of the end," that is, in the light of Jesus Christ, who is "the end of the Old . . . and therefore the New." The church lives in the light of the end, "because it is founded on the witness of the Holy Scripture." "There is no other 'church' " than the "church of the Holy Scripture." The church reads all of Holy Scripture "as the book . . . of Christ." Since the church is only the church when it is founded on the Holy Scripture, the sentence is also valid for Bonhoeffer when inverted: "Indeed the Bible is nothing but the book on which the church stands. This is its essential nature or it is nothing" (*SF* 6 f.).

The church lives from Christ, who testifies to it in the Bible. Consequently theological interpretation attempts to express the Biblical witness to Jesus Christ, which is the source of the life of the church.[109]

This goal and this task are to be reached through a method which Bonhoeffer describes with the words: "Its (that is, the theological interpretation) method is this presupposition (that is, the Bible as the book of the church); it incessantly refers

---

also the contributions of the following authors cited in Bibliography III: K. Girgensohn, R. Bultmann, J. Behm, H. Frick, A. Oepke, O. Weber, K. H. Miskotte, V. Herntrich, G. Eichholz, and A. Bea.

108. K. Barth: Theological exegesis is the "attempt to understand Holy Scripture within the sphere of the church" (*Credo*, 1935, 153). K. H. Miskotte writes, "I live and read and understand from the church outward, . . . I recognize in the canon of the Holy Scripture the holy church listening to God." That is the result of the "subjection of theological exegesis" to the "belief that Holy Scripture is God's Word" ("Das Problem der theologischen Exegese," in *Theologische Aufsätze, K. Barth zum 50. Geburtstag*, 1936, 58, 63).

109. What Bonhoeffer says in the "Finkenwalder Homiletik" about the relationship of text and sermon is an expansion and application of this fundamental idea. *GS* IV, 243, 246 ff., 267.

back from the text (which has to be ascertained with all means of philological and historical research) to this presupposition. That is the objectivity of theological interpretation." Just after these sentences Bonhoeffer offers an example of it. "When Genesis says 'Yahweh,' historically or psychologically it means nothing but Yahweh. Theologically, however—that is, from the church's viewpoint—it is speaking of God." This example signifies: If we interpret Genesis with the methods of historical-psychological research, whose goal and task it is to establish and understand past occurrence, thought, speech, and emotion, then we will never come to the conclusion that the "Yahweh" of Genesis is the God of Jesus Christ. Only a theological interpretation can determine that, because it moves outward from the presupposition that God is the one God in the whole Bible.

Bonhoeffer views textual inquiry according to "all rules of philological and historical research" as also belonging to theological interpretation. Bonhoeffer enclosed this requisite for theological interpretation in parentheses. Do these parentheses mean that such investigation is incidental or self-evident for him?[110] That problem will engage us further.[111]

Theological interpretation interprets the Bible as the book of the church. Many of the Old Testament sermons and interpretations that Bonhoeffer delivered during the church struggle move within this framework. In them he attempted to proclaim to "the church under the cross" (*GS* IV, 313) the witness of Christ, which it needed for life.

Since Bonhoeffer dares to confront the Bible with the expectation that God speaks in it, the Bible becomes for him—as a result of his intercourse with it—the book of the church with

110. Through his studies in Berlin, Bonhoeffer was well acquainted with the methods of historical-critical research (*DB* 105, 115, 119). However, already in the summer semester of 1925 he criticized this "art" in one of R. Seeberg's seminars. "Can a Distinction Be Drawn Between a Historical and a Pneumatical Interpretation of the Scriptures, and What Is the Attitude to This of Dogmatic Theology?" "Textual criticism leaves nothing behind but dust and ashes" (*DB* 109; Eng. tr., 59).

111. See below, Chapter III.D.2 and 3.

the witness to the One God who loves this world in Jesus Christ. With this appraisal of the Bible the fundamental decision about the Old Testament is formulated. Along with the New Testament, the Old Testament is the place where God speaks to us.[112]

112. According to K. Schwarzwäller (*ThSt*[B] 84 [1966], 10), one "can treat the question concerning the relationship of both Testaments profitably only ... if one is not bound to the duty of proving the validity of the Old Testament and is therefore free to develop one's Old Testament position subsequently along with the New Testament," i.e., if one does not attempt to argue on another basis for "the validity of the Old Testament as witness to the triune God in the community of the new covenant." Compare *ibid.*, 33 f. Bonhoeffer fulfills these conditions.

III

THE OLD TESTAMENT
AS THE BOOK OF CHRIST

The phrase "the Old Testament as the book of Christ" was never used by Bonhoeffer in the preserved sources. He formulates it only indirectly when he writes in the introduction to *Creation and Fall* in 1933 that "the church of the Holy Scripture" reads "all Holy Scripture as the book . . . of Christ" (*SF* 7). Bonhoeffer reads *all* Holy Scripture as the book of Christ, therefore the Old Testament as well. He attempted to solve the task which had been raised in that sentence. That is revealed in many passages where he interprets the Old Testament. Hence, with the phrase "the Old Testament as the book of Christ" we are able to summarize appropriately Bonhoeffer's appraisal and interpretation of the Old Testament.[113]

Before the beginning of the church struggle Bonhoeffer had recognized with regard to this task what the evangelical churches were not to learn until after 1933 from G. von Rad: On the question of the Old Testament there is only an either-

---

113. This opinion appears to be contrary to a comment of Bethge, who in the context of the excursus on "The New Theology" *(WE)* defends the following view: "There are also examples in Bonhoeffer's life of his taking on themes alongside a major work in order to relinquish them again soon to the experts in the field, as, for example, his christocentric interpretations of the Old Testament" *(DB* 968; Eng. tr., 766). This remark is somewhat inaccurate. Indeed, Bonhoeffer did develop a particular manner of interpreting the Old Testament ("Christ in the Old Testament") for a period of time, but from *SF* to *WE* he always interpreted the Old Testament fundamentally in relationship to Christ, and this relationship is not unimportant, for Christ is its center.

or. Either the Old Testament speaks "with the New of the Christ revelation of God . . . or we deny that; then in spite of its highly noteworthy particularities we must assign it to the remaining religions . . . but *tertium non datur.*"[114]

A. The Three Viewpoints of Old Testament Interpretation in Bonhoeffer

What is meant by the small word "of" in the phrase "the Old Testament as the book of Christ"? Its contents are supplied in a threefold manner. In Bonhoeffer's Old Testament interpretations a double movement and a resolution of this movement can be discerned. It is a movement from Christ to the Old Testament, but also from the Old Testament to the New Testament. On the one hand, Bonhoeffer says that the Old Testament "must be read in the light of the incarnation and crucifixion, that is, the revelation which has taken place for us" (*GS* IV, 320; Oct., 1935), while on the other hand, he states regretfully that "we read the New Testament much too little in the light of the Old Testament" (*WE* 148/182; April 30, 1944).[115]

114. G. von Rad, *Fragen der Schriftauslegung im Alten Testament,* 1938, 5. Compare V. Herntrich, *MPTh* 32 (1936), 119 ff.—In reflecting on *SF*, Bethge writes: "Bonhoeffer set vigorously about drawing conclusions from Barth's christocentric treatment of the Old Testament and the First Article, before Barth himself or others had yet got so far. . . . Nor can it be denied that he provided the defences with good armour and equipment to detect and resist the enemy of the day" (*DB* 261, 263; Eng. tr., 162, 163). In a certain sense H. Vogel had already arrived at this point. In "Kreuz und Hakenkreuz. Thesen des Protestes, der Frage und der Bitte an die 'Glaubensbewegung Deutscher Christen' " he explains: "18. Christ is the *entire* content of the Holy Scripture. 19. Christ is the content of the *entire* Holy Scripture. 20. Whoever rejects the Old Testament as the Word of God also rejects the New Testament as the Word of God" (*ZZ* 11 [1933], 202). Here one thinks once again of Brunner. See above, fn. 63.

115. B.-E. Benktson refers to this twofold movement. "Previously Bonhoeffer was clearly Barthian in his thought on the unity of the Scripture: the church must see creation from the standpoint of Christ ('from the standpoint of Christ . . . , and only from this viewpoint move forward toward him,' *SF* 7), hence in *WE* he tended to see the matter from the other side. Namely, 'God is in the midst of our life to come. . . . Hence, it is in accordance with the Old Testament, and in this sense we read the New Testament much too

In seeking to understand the Old Testament in the light of Christ and the New Testament in the light of the Old Testament, Bonhoeffer utilizes the double direction movement in his interpretation of the Bible and in so doing shares in the discussion of such Old Testament specialists as H. W. Wolff, W. Zimmerli, A. Jepsen, and G. von Rad in their contributions to Old Testament hermeneutics in recent years. They speak of the "double movement of a mutual understanding" (Von Rad), which is necessary in order to arrive at a relevant interpretation of both Testaments.[116]

However, there is another point of view in the Old Testament interpretation of Bonhoeffer, which has no equivalent in that which the theologians just mentioned require for an interpretation of the Bible. This point of view consists no longer in a movement between Christ, the Old Testament, and the New Testament, but in Christ being found in the Old Testament. "Christ in the Old Testament" is a phrase used by Bonhoeffer (*GS* IV, 294; Oct., 1935).

If we do not wish to present properly Bonhoeffer's interpretation of the Old Testament historically nor on the basis of different *Sitze im Leben*, then the three so-called viewpoints offer themselves as the organizing principle. In this way the historical points of view and those which result from the actual *Sitz im Leben* need not be neglected. Indeed they may not be. Since in one part of the interpretation of Gen. 1:1 f. in *Creation and Fall* all three viewpoints are mentioned one after another, this interpretation will be examined in section B, below. It forms an overture which includes all the themes which will be pursued subsequently.

---

little from the standpoint of the Old Testament' " (*Christus und die Religion*, 43).

116. H. W. Wolff, "Der grosse Jesreeltag (Hos. 2:1–3)," *EvTh* 12 (1952/53), 1021; "Hauptprobleme alttestamentlicher Prophetie," *EvTh* 15 (1955), 468; "Zur Hermeneutik des Alten Testaments," *EvTh* 16 (1956), 361; W. Zimmerli, "Verheissung und Erfüllung," *EvTh* 12 (1952/53), 54; A. Jepsen, "Wissenschaft vom Alten Testament," *PAH* 241 f.; G. von Rad, *Theologie des Alten Testaments*, Vol. II, 1960, 387 (quotation), 400.

B. Interpretation of Gen. 1:1 f. in "Creation and Fall"

It is appropriate to begin the investigation of Bonhoeffer's Old Testament interpretation with one of the excerpts from *Creation and Fall* for another reason. This book, which goes back to lectures delivered in 1932/33, stands between two periods in Bonhoeffer's life. *Creation and Fall* originated in the academic-scientific realm of theology just as did the previous works *Sanctorum Communio* and *Act and Being*. But it is different from each of these books, because it is exposition of the Bible to which Bonhoeffer was directing his attention in those years and which progressively was going to influence his theological work even more strongly. This intermediate period is even clearer if we consider which texts of the Old Testament Bonhoeffer interpreted: Gen., chs. 1 to 3, the classical text for the dogmatic teaching of creation, primeval state, and fall. It may be more justifiable to choose *Creation and Fall* as an example for an "eschatological teaching of creation"[117] than to attempt to explain with it how Bonhoeffer interprets the Old Testament.[118] But just as Gen., chs. 1 to 3, is not only the classical text for the dogmatic teaching of the creation but also the beginning of the Old Testament, even so Bonhoeffer's interpretation of this chapter is not only "eschatological teaching of creation" but also the beginning of his numerous interpretations in which he seeks to read the Old Testament as the book of Christ.[119]

117. *DB* 263.

118. Compare H. Hellbardt, "An essay such as the one presented belongs in essence more in the systematic than in the Old Testament discipline," *ThBl* 13(1934), 112. Bethge describes the impression evoked by *SF* in the following words: "Bonhoeffer had again fallen between two stools. The exegetes regarded the work as systematics, and the systematicians regarded it as exegesis" (*DB* 261; Eng. tr., 163).

119. In the interpretations before *SF*, that was decidedly not the case: Sermon on Ps. 63:4 for Erntedankfest (harvest celebration) 1931 (*GS* IV, 17–25); Confirmation sermon 1932, on Gen. 32:25–32; 33:10 (*GS* IV, 44–50);

(1) On Gen. 1:1 f. Bonhoeffer says:

The void between God's freedom and the creation is not
an attempt to explain what is; it is thus not the matter out
of which the world has then paradoxically come into being, the necessary point where what is comes through.
Nor is it a thing, not even a negative thing. It is the definition which alone can express the relation of God's freedom to his creation. . . . The world stands in the void. This
means that it stands in the beginning; and that means
nothing except that it is rooted in the freedom of God.
. . . But the God of the creation and of the real beginning
is, at the same time, the God of the resurrection. From the
beginning the world is placed under the sign of the resurrection of Christ from the dead. Indeed it is because we
know of the resurrection that we know of God's creation
in the beginning, of God's creation out of nothing. The
dead Jesus Christ of Good Friday and the resurrected
Kurios (Lord) of Easter Sunday: that is creation out of
nothing, creation from the beginning. The fact that Christ
was dead did not mean the possibility of the resurrection,
but its impossibility; it was void itself, *nihil negativum.* . . .
If it were possible to intensify the *nihil negativum* we would
have to say here of the resurrection that with the death of
Christ on the cross the *nihil negativum* was taken into God
himself. "O great affliction, God himself is dead"—but
he who is the beginning lived, destroyed the void and

fragment of a meditation from Dec. 1, 1932, on Dan. 10:1,2,8,9,15–19 (*GS* IV,
144–146); sermon from May 8, 1932, on II Chron. 20:12 (*GS* I, 133–139). If
at the time of his Bible study "King David," or of the interpretation of Gen.
12:1–3 in *N* (1954, 73 ff.), Bonhoeffer had preached on Gen. 32:25–32, it is
highly probable that he might have called the figure who wrestled with David
—Christ. Compare W. Vischer in *CAT,* Vol. I, 189. On March 13, 1932, that
figure is God for Bonhoeffer. Naturally Christ is mentioned not only in this
sermon but in other Old Testament sermons as well—e.g., in the one on II
Chron. 20:12. In one place Bonhoeffer cites the text ("We do not know what
we should do, but our eyes are fixed on Thee") and then continues, "on the
Lord, on the resurrected Lord" (*GS* I, 138). The reflection on the interpretation begins, however, first in *SF.*

created the new creation in his resurrection. By his resurrection we know of the creation—for if he were not resurrected the Creator would be lifeless and would not bear witness to himself" (*SF* 16–18; Eng. tr., J. C. Fletcher, *Creation and Fall* 1971, 19–20).[120]

In these sentences Bonhoeffer conveys what he presented in the introduction as the task: the creation story is "to be read in the church only in the light of Christ" (*SF* 7). Here he reads it from the standpoint of the risen and crucified Lord.[121] The statements he makes are radical. "O great affliction, God's Son lies dead," sings the church today.[122] Bonhoeffer, however, cites the original version of the hymn: "O great affliction, God himself is dead."[123] Patripassianism appears to have a voice here. These are not statements in the noetic realm, but in the last sentence a statement in the ontic realm is made. Therefore, it is not only important that we *know* of the creation of God, "because we *know* of the resurrection," but more. This noetic statement has an ontic basis: "for if he were not resurrected the Creator would be dead and would not bear witness to himself." In regard to the resurrection of Christ, according

120. Compare Hegel, *Die absolute Religion*, "God is dead, God is dead—this is the most terrible thought that everything eternal, everything true is not, the negation itself is in God; the greatest pain, the feeling of perfect hopelessness, the abandonment of everything lofty is bound up with that. —The process does not stop here, but there is a reversal; namely, God preserves himself in this process and this alone is the death of death. God rises once again to life and the process is reversed" (*PhB* 63, 167 f.). "This humanness in God, and indeed . . . the deepest degree of frailty, is, however, natural death. 'God himself is dead,' says a Lutheran hymn. In this way the idea is expressed that the human, the infinite, the frail, the weak, the negative are themselves aspects of God" (*ibid.*, 172 f.). Compare, in addition, fnn. 103 and 389.
121. Bonhoeffer's sentences are very close to those which Vischer wrote in 1927: "As absurd as it may appear to base the Easter faith on the interpretation of the book of Genesis, it is significantly and essentially necessary. The Christ message of creation is the presupposition of the Easter message" ("Das Alte Testament als Gottes Wort," *ZZ* 5 [1927], 388).
122. *EKG* 73, v.2.
123. Compare J. Kulp, *Die Lieder unserer Kirche. Eine Handreichung zum Evangelisches Kirchengesangbuch*, Berlin, 1958, 129. "The second strophe originally began: '*O grosse Not! Gott selbst is tot!*' ('O great need! God himself is dead!')"

to Bonhoeffer it is also a matter of the being and non-being of the Creator. The cross without the resurrection would only mean that the disillusioned hope of the two on the way to Emmaus must be the final word of Luke's Gospel; it would not only mean that Jesus Christ has been proven a failure forever, but it would mean also the death of the Creator. It was necessary for God to show himself in the resurrection of Christ as the Creator of the world. Only through the resurrection of Christ does God bear conclusive witness to himself as the Creator, and—we go back to the noetic level—only on the basis of the resurrection can we know the Creator. Thus Gen., ch. 1, can be the witness of God the Creator for us only through the resurrection of Christ. Reading the creation story in the light of the resurrected Lord has an ontic and a noetic basis and is necessary.

If Gen. 1:1 f. is seen in the first instance not as the proof text for a dogmatic doctrine but as representative for the whole of the Old Testament, then it is necessary to read the Old Testament in the light of Christ, because only through the raising of Christ did God, whose word and deed the Old Testament reports to us, conclusively prove himself to be the living God. Bonhoeffer does not say that, but it is appropriate to him.[124]

In the discussion concerning his Bible study "King David," Bonhoeffer himself notes: "The Old Testament must be read in the light of the incarnation and crucifixion" (*GS* IV, 320). It is striking that Bonhoeffer speaks only of the incarnation and crucifixion. The failure to mention the resurrection is due to the fact that this sentence is more of a marginal note. Yet Bonhoeffer does not mean that the incarnation and crucifixion comprehensively describe the revelation which has taken place, since only through the raising of Christ is it certain "that

124. Compare with our interpretation of the exposition of Gen. 1:1 f. by Bonhoeffer the exposition of Rom. 10:4 by Schwarzwäller: The occurrence of the Old Testament, "which lies before the *telos*, . . . preserves its inherent ontological dimension with its goal and end without which it would not be what it originally was, without which it could not exist" (*loc. cit.*, 40).

God has said 'yes' to his Son and his work" (*GS* III, 405). Moreover, in the Bible study the risen Lord himself is not lacking.[125] Through the resurrection the work of Jesus is declared valid for us.[126] Therefore, reading the Old Testament in the light of the incarnate, crucified, and risen Lord is necessary. Jesus Christ as *the* revelation of God stands between us and the Old Testament.

(2) Bonhoeffer continues in his interpretation of Gen. 1:1 f., separated only by a semicolon from the previous quotations from *Creation and Fall:* "but by his creation we know once more of the power of his resurrection, because he remains the Lord" (*SF* 18).

In the preceding sentence the sequence was from resurrection to creation—"by his resurrection we know of the creation"—now he goes from the creation to the resurrection. In this sentence Bonhoeffer only says that by the creation we know of the power of the resurrection and goes no further as to what comprises the knowledge. It is nevertheless clear that he understands the resurrection, a New Testament message, also in the light of the creation, an Old Testament message.[127]

(3) Just after the sentence discussed above come the following sentences:

> In the beginning, out of freedom, out of nothing, God created the heavens and the earth. That is the comfort with which the Bible addresses us who are in the middle, who are anxious before the false void, the beginning with-

125. See below, Chapter III.B.1.
126. R. Grunow comments on Bonhoeffer's view of the meaning of Christ for the Old Testament. "One can speculate that if Jesus had not withstood the temptation of the devil, and had not said 'Yes' to the cross, then the entire Old Testament would crumble like a house of cards! Then everything would be lies; everything would be like an invalid banknote. God would be the greatest bankrupter of world history! Only in Christ does the Old Testament have its existence and its reality" (*MW* I, 70). From Bonhoeffer's viewpoint, however, one may not stand still at the cross! The cross without the resurrection means that the Old Testament would crumble like a house of cards!
127. In *WE* he expands this sentence; see below, Chapter III. E.2.c.

out a beginning and the end without an end. It is the gospel, it is the resurrected Christ of whom one is speaking here. (*SF* 18; Eng. tr., 20)

Bonhoeffer speaks here of the "Christ in the Old Testament." The creation and the resurrection message discussed above in (1) and (2) are not only related to each other; they are identical. The resurrection of Christ is witnessed to in the creation message.

To think this thought of Bonhoeffer's along with him is difficult, and we shall see that the interpretations in which he speaks further of "Christ in the Old Testament" will give us even more difficulties. Perhaps one of Bonhoeffer's metaphors can make clear how he could arrive at that conclusion. It is the frequent metaphor of light, used in the context of clarifying the relationship of the Old and New Testaments. The light goes out from Christ and falls upon the Old Testament.[128] If one understands the Old Testament in the light of Christ, then this otherwise obscure book is illumined. The light that proceeds from Christ and falls upon the Old Testament, however, is then reflected by the Old Testament. Consequently it can be shed upon the New Testament, thus serving a better understanding of it as well, that is, to understand the New Testament in the light of the Old Testament. The main point at present, however, is that the light of Christ which is only reflected from the Old Testament can be considered as the Old Testament's own light. If I recognize that the creation story reflects the light of the resurrection, but say that it is the resurrected Lord himself of whom Gen. 1:1 f. speaks, then I speak unclearly as if I speak of moonlight, which is actually reflected sunshine from the moon. Or in order to take up again the metaphor of movement: if one is to speak of "Christ in the Old Testament," then a movement between Christ and the Old Testament is no

128. K. Galley, *Altes und neues Heilsgeschehen bei Paulus*, 1956, 59; O. Weber, *Grundlagen der Dogmatik*, Vol. I, 1959², 339; G. von Rad, *Theologie des Alten Testaments*, Vol. II, 343.

longer possible, because Christ as it were has passed over into the Old Testament.

In the exegesis of Gen. 1:1 f., Bonhoeffer already expressed the three points of view of his Old Testament interpretation, in part very strongly in order to expand them subsequently.

C. The Understanding of the Old Testament in the Light of Jesus Christ

How Bonhoeffer understood Old Testament texts as the book of Christ may be explained in three examples. The first is an excerpt from the Bible study "King David" (Oct. 8–11, 1935), the selected exposition of II Sam., chs. 11 to 19; the second is an excerpt from the letter of the Second Sunday in Advent, 1943; and the third is a short letter about the Song of Songs from June 2, 1944. With the first example it is easy to see that Bonhoeffer understood Old Testament texts in the light of Christ, but with the second and third it must be deductively concluded.

1. Interpretation of II Sam., chs. 11 to 19 (Oct. 8–11, 1935)

Bonhoeffer entitles his exposition of these chapters "David the Justified Sinner" (*GS* IV, 311–318). He understands David according to the New Testament witness, as the "prototype and shadow" of Christ (*GS* IV, 294–297).[129] At the conclusion of the exposition he asks how David, "who became a sinner," is "the prototype and shadow of Christ." His answer:

> David is not these "in his moral qualities, in his holiness." In such manner he never was. But he is both and remains the same through the election, the anointing, and God's grace which remains faithful to him. As the one whom

129. Bonhoeffer cites the following passages: Rom. 1:3; Matt. 1:1; John 7:42; II Tim. 2:8; Matt. 22:4 ff.; Acts 2:30 f.; Luke 1:32, 69; Mark 11:10; Heb. 2:12; 10:5; Luke 23:46; John 19:28; Matt. 27:46; Rev. 22:16.

God humbles, brings low, and punishes and who bears God's judgment as a sinner and takes upon himself the punishment of God, as the justified sinner, David is directly the anointed king, "prototype and shadow" of the crucified Christ. (*GS* IV, 318)

Bonhoeffer reads the David stories in the light of the cross. Thereby he sees an analogy between that which happened on the cross and that which happened to David. He can recognize the analogies because he notes—we take up again the metaphor of light—that the light which goes out from the cross is reflected in the David stories: As God judged Jesus Christ on the cross, even so he judged David the sinner. He is the one who dealt with Christ and David in this fashion (*GS* IV, 320) —and therefore deals with the church of Jesus Christ in 1935 in such a way. In any case, Bonhoeffer ventured to make that claim. Concerning the announcement of judgment on David by Nathan, Bonhoeffer says:[130]

David shed innocent blood, "therefore the sword shall never depart from your house" (II Sam. 12:10). David has broken up the marriage of another person, therefore his wives will be desecrated by other men. One will be punished in the same way he sins. Through David's sin the sword comes eternally upon his head. . . . David's house will be punished by the sword, which comes again and again from David's house and tears to pieces the people of God. . . . The struggle between the violence, which carries the sword, and the church of God is announced and remains "eternally." David's seed, Christ and his church, will be struck by the violence of the sword, but though this sword punishes and slays the body, it does not destroy the promise. Rather—and that is the wonder of the godly punishment—the sword which is set against the house of David brings life and promise to the church

130. Because of the importance of the following sentences, this very lengthy quotation is included.

again. The crucified Christ arises, the church under the cross, under the chastisement by the sword, receives new life. Thus the full grace of God is included in David's punishment. Hence by his act of judgment upon the house of David, God acknowledges his promise. . . . And 12:11: from David's own house the disgrace shall arise, from his own house one shall arise who will desecrate David's body with his wives (see 16:22). From the church of the Messiah itself the son, Absalom, shall rise up and profane the church before the world in broad daylight. The dishonoring of the church of God comes from within. Absalom is the shadow of all those who up to the present as sons of the church were the desecrators of the church. And they must do their terrible work by virtue of the threatening promise of God, but woe to him by whom this work takes place. He will bring himself to judgment and ruin; he enslaves himself. Absalom remains hanging by his hair in the tree and receives death. The sword as the lasting threat to the duration of the house—the desecrator from within—is the judgment of God for David's sin. (*GS* IV, 313 f.)

This exposition is an illustration for a statement made in Bonhoeffer's lecture "Making New Testament Texts Relevant for Today," which was delivered just two months before this Bible study. There Bonhoeffer asks: Is it not "amazing that we need only to exposit a text clearly, keenly, and objectively and it becomes relevant for today?" (*GS* III, 314). It is inevitable to see in the house of David the guilty, embattled and battling Evangelical Church in Germany, to see in Absalom the German Christians, and to hear the promise of the courage and consolation for the vicars of the Confessing Church for whom the Bible study was delivered. He dares to see God's present action in that which the church, a church "under the cross," experiences in its time, namely, the *judgment* of God upon the church through which the church shall receive new life. The shadow of the crucified Lord falls not only backward upon

David but forward upon "the church under the cross." This is what Bonhoeffer proclaimed in his Bible study on Old Testament texts. He led, so to speak, a discussion between three partners: the church in which he lived, the crucified Lord, and the David stories. The church can enter into the discussion with these stories only by way of and through the mediation of Christ, but they also have something important to say to the church: God judges his church in the present with the goal of renewal.

This interpretation of Bonhoeffer is not only the high point in the Bible study "King David" but also a high point in all his Old Testament interpretations. With this idea he is already a step beyond an understanding of the Old Testament in the light of Christ; such an understanding is only the necessary presupposition for making the Old Testament relevant for today and through this process Bonhoeffer aided in an understanding of God's contemporary deeds.[131]

131. In our opinion, what H. W. Wolff says about the goal of a typological interpretation Bonhoeffer achieved in that interpretation. "God's dealings in Israel and in Jesus of Nazareth are witnessed to and known, and through them we are challenged to proclaim God's acts for ourselves and for our work, not in a way that is objectively of universal validity, nor, on the other hand, subjective and optional, but as a valid aid for each of the corresponding types of the kerygma for each corresponding hour" ("Das Geschichtsverständnis der alttestamentlichen Prophetie," *PAH* 330, fn. 14; Eng. tr., J. L. Mays, *Old Testament Hermeneutics,* 1963, 346, fn. 14). This correspondence is not by chance, because Bonhoeffer, as is shown in Chapter III. D.2, later in this work, in some passages of the Bible study "King David" comes close to what H. W. Wolff and others intend by typological interpretation. According to R. Grunow, Bonhoeffer's interpretation of the Scripture during the church struggle was "loaded with a candid prophetical impetus, which through an exclusively 'church' attitude sought to turn the community of Jesus in the direction of a new obedience, to a new seriousness about the word of the Scripture" (*MW* I, 62). Two thoughts from an article by U. Luck, "Herrenwort und Geschichte in Matt. 28:16–20" (*EvTh* 27 [1967], 494–510), can clarify this opinion of Grunow's. We mention Luck's statements as preparation for Chapter IV (see fn. 421). Regarding the early Christian prophet, Luck says: "Inspired by the spirit he interprets the present of the community in the light of the action of God which takes place in proclamation. Inspired by the spirit he intimates: that which now occurs is the work of the Lord himself. . . . Therefore the church is erected on the foundation of the apostles and prophets (Eph. 2:20)—not only apostles as proclaimers of the message and legitimate teaching, but also

It is necessary to return again to the marginal note already mentioned,[132] which Bonhoeffer made in relationship to his discussion of the Bible study. This note can be correctly understood only when we grasp the important function of the Old Testament for Bonhoeffer's proclamation. Therefore we are going to quote it completely:

> 2. The Old Testament must be read in the light of the incarnation and crucifixion, that is, the revelation which has taken place for us. Otherwise, we are left with the Jewish or heathen understanding of the Old Testament. (*GS* IV, 320)

Bonhoeffer speaks of a Jewish and heathen understanding of the Old Testament. He does not expand on what that means. He had indicated in the introduction to *Creation and Fall,* however, what he might mean by heathen understanding: It is the historical-psychological understanding of the Bible, which, for example, can see in the Yahweh of Genesis nothing more than merely Yahweh, but not the God of the entire Bible.[133] The Old Testament is then, we can continue, only one among many other documents from early Oriental religious history. It is merely the report of a past religion. "Jewish understanding" is more difficult to describe. According to H. W. Wolff, it implies a "complete absolutizing of the law," by which the

---

prophets, because that which currently took place in the community was of central significance for the comprehension of the work of the Lord. That which takes place within the concrete community is conjointly the foundation of theological insight" (Luck, *loc. cit.,* 503 f.). In the excerpt already cited, Bonhoeffer attempts to understand that which happens to and in the community which the vicars represent. Luck continues: "Drawing inference from history about God's action has always been a dangerous procedure. This danger can be obviated only if that inference is made in such a manner that the cross is the sign for the effectiveness of the Lord in the community." His obedience to death upon the cross "is at the same time the body of Christ's law of life" (Phil. 2:5–11). (Luck, *loc. cit.,* 505 f.) Bonhoeffer's proclamation is to the "church under the cross" and he is calling her to simple obedience of "discipleship."

132. See above, Chapter III.A, B.3.
133. See above, Chapter II.4.

saving acts of God are concealed.[134] Bonhoeffer aims at an understanding other than the Jewish and heathen understanding of the Old Testament; one that is mediated through the incarnation, crucifixion (and resurrection)[135] of Jesus Christ. This is the revelation which has taken place for us. At the same time this indicates that the Old Testament does not contain—directly—any revelation which has taken place for us.[136] Fun-

134. H. W. Wolff, *PAH* 151 f. However, in this way only one side of the Jewish understanding of the Old Testament is indicated. In our opinion, in speaking of such an understanding, above all, the significance of the suffering of the Jewish people as the suffering of God's servant in Isa., ch. 53, as expressed by Schalom Ben-Chorin and Martin Buber (more cautiously), may not be overlooked (Schalom Ben-Chorin, "Jüdische Fragen um Christus," *Juden, Christen, Deutsche*, ed. by H. J. Schultz, 1961, 146 f.; M. Buber, "Der Glaube der Propheten," *Werke*, Vol. II: *Schriften zur Bibel*, 1964, 483 f.). This side of the Jewish understanding of the Old Testament is in close harmony with the interpretation of the Old Testament we have discussed in Bonhoeffer. In both instances the action in question is proclaimed to the hearers as God's action. There are other considerations based on the Old Testament expressed by Schalom Ben-Chorin which belong to the Jewish understanding of the Old Testament. Namely, because the world is still "a totally unredeemed world," Jesus of Nazareth cannot be the redeemer in the sense of the Old Testament (*loc. cit.*, 141–143). In *WE*, Bonhoeffer comes to see the bodily, earthly dimension of the Old Testament anew; see below, Chapter III. E.2.a and c. These aspects of the Jewish understanding, however, do not exclude those mentioned in the text. Compare H. J. Kraus, who says of Buber's interpretation of the prophetical message that one thought may play a subordinate role, which is of fundamental importance for a Christian interpretation of the Old Testament: the prophetical word entails judgment and salvation without man's doing ("Gespräch mit Martin Buber," *EvTh* 12 [1952/53], 73). In addition, compare M. Buber, "Prophetie und Apokalyptik," *Werke*, Vol. II, 927–942. Also H. W. Wolff asks Buber, "Where then is Yahweh, who is proclaimed as so invariably personal, as the One who acts, who speaks, who is coming?" ("Zur Hermeneutik des Alten Testaments," *PAH* 152; Eng. tr., 172). We shall see in Chapter IV that these important views of Old Testament proclamation (judgment and God as one who acts), in large measure the Jewish interpretation of the Old Testament, can be taken into consideration by an interpretation of the Old Testament which delineates even partially Bonhoeffer's lines of thought.

135. See above, Chapter III.B.2.

136. In addition, compare the following sentences from *GL* on what Bonhoeffer considers to be the significance of reading the Biblical books consecutively. "We become a part of what once took place for our salvation. Forgetting and losing ourselves, we, too, pass through the Red Sea, through the desert, across the Jordan into the promised land. With Israel we fall into doubt

damentally everything takes place for the sake of the nations (Gen. 12:3),[137] but actually everything takes place for the sake of Israel, which in the Old Testament period was the only one elect of all the generations of the earth (Amos 3:2). Only in Christ have they become fellow citizens of the saints and members of the household of God (Eph. 2:13, 19). If I want to interpret the Old Testament as the Word of God, then I must understand it in the light of Christ, because I can speak of God only on the basis of his revelation and Jesus Christ is the revelation (*E* 55/155). Only he can make the Old Testament speak to us as the Word of God. For that reason there is for us no direct access to the Old Testament. Christ stands between us and the Old Testament. On the one hand, through him the Old Testament witness is lifted out of the past and protected from heathen understanding; on the other hand, it does not need to be understood primarily as a summons to

---

and unbelief and through punishment and repentance experience again God's help and faithfulness. All this is not mere reverie but holy, godly reality. We are torn out of our own existence and set down in the midst of the holy history of God on earth" (*GL* 43; Eng. tr., John W. Doberstein, *Life Together*, 1954, 53). Therefore, does the Old Testament contain revelations that have taken place directly in our behalf? These sentences and that comment stand in a certain contradiction; however, it must be pointed out that the goal of these sentences (as already stated clearly in the last sentence, then further developed by Bonhoeffer with the emphasis on the *extra nos* of our salvation) is determined by the pastoral *Sitz im Leben* of this writing. Against every persistent and incipient danger of self-concern in a life together Bonhoeffer asserts: "It is in fact more important for us to know what God did to Israel, to His Son Jesus Christ, than to seek what God intends for us today. . . . Our salvation is 'external to ourselves.' I find no salvation in my life history" (*ibid.*, 44; Eng. tr., 54). In 1944, however, Bonhoeffer is no longer able to identify the Christian community quite so directly with Israel. In his "Die erste Tafel der zehn Worte" ("The First Tablet of the Ten Commandments") he explains that that which belongs to Israel as a political people is not obligatory for the Christian church (*GS* IV, 600). The difference existing between these and the sentences from *GS* will engage us in another form at a later time (see below, D.3.b).

137. Compare H. W. Wolff, "Das Kerygma des Jahwisten," *Gesammelte Studien zum Alten Testament*, 1964, 345–373, especially 351 f. It is one of the main ideas of F. Mildenberger in his work, *Gottes Tat im Wort. Erwägungen zur alttestamentlichen Hermeneutik als Frage nach der Einheit der Testamente* (1964), that the "goal of God's action in Israel is that this people should become a witness to the living reality for the nations" (69).

action; that is, it does not need to be understood in a Jewish way. In the three-way discussion mentioned above, the Old Testament becomes the partner that points out God's contemporary action to the church of Christ via Christ, who is the third partner in the conversation. "Via Christ" means that if he were not resurrected, then the God of the Old Testament would be dead and could not be witnessed to today as the living One. Therefore the Old Testament must be read in the light of Christ.[138]

There remains to be discussed in the last part of this work what may only be intimated at this point. The manner in which Bonhoeffer interprets II Sam., chs. 11 to 19, can aid in understanding his thoughts about the "world come of age" from *Letters and Papers from Prison*. The Old Testament can become to an even greater degree, as has already been the case with Bonhoeffer, a partner in the discussion that he conducts during the last years of his life, the discussion between Jesus Christ and the world in which he lives.

2. *The Offensive Stories of the Old Testament (Second Sunday in Advent, 1943)*

F. Imholf, who has already been mentioned, responded to the publication of a part of the Bible study "King David" in the *Junge Kirche* of February 15, 1936,[139] in a cutting manner. His critique stands in line with A. Rosenberg and Dr. Krause for whom the offensive stories of the Old Testament provided enough material in order to attack it from the standpoint of the "moral and ethical feeling of the German race" (*GS* II, 292).

Bonhoeffer engaged himself once again with these stories of

138. Compare O. Weber: "It is elementary to the New Testament message that Christ is the *telos* of the law and only he who believes in him will be justified. From the outset we can have no *Israelite* relationship to the Old Testament, and therefore should seek no *Israelite* understanding of this book. We have one relationship to the Old Testament . . . only in Christ!" (Weber, *Grundlagen der Dogmatik*, Vol. I, 332).

139. Second lecture, "Der messianische König" (II Sam., chs. 2 to 7), *JK* 4(1936), 157–161.

the Old Testament in a letter from prison. In the letter from the Second Sunday in Advent, 1943, he writes:

> Why is it that in the Old Testament men tell lies vigorously and often to the glory of God (I've now collected the passages), kill, deceive, rob, divorce, and even fornicate (see the genealogy of Jesus), doubt, blaspheme, and curse, whereas in the New Testament there is nothing of all this? "An earlier stage of religion? This is a very naïve way out; it is one and the same God. But more of this later when we meet. (*WE* 93/113; Eng. tr., R. Fuller, *Letters and Papers from Prison* 1971, 157)[140]

What more might Bonhoeffer perhaps "later and orally" have said?[141] That is indicated to us by the Bible study "King David." As the first note to the study, Bonhoeffer had written above it:

> 1. The God of the Old Testament is the Father of Jesus Christ. The God who appears in Jesus Christ is the God of the Old Testament. He is the triune God. (*GS* IV, 320)

Bonhoeffer says it more briefly in the letter: ". . . it is one and the same God." One notes from the context that Bonhoeffer is very cautious in judging and laying aside the offensive stories of the Old Testament as "earlier religious stages." He is aware of his previous decision.[142] Since this sentence is

140. This citation forms the conclusion of a longer statement on the Old Testament which will be analyzed in Chapter III.E.

141. This may be attempted in keeping with Bonhoeffer only if we see those sentences in the light of his other thoughts and remaining Old Testament interpretations. In these latter sources we find the "material" upon which we perhaps "should build" here. When one considers the questions treated in the letter, that excerpt is fragmentary. Bonhoeffer himself no longer answers them. At this point his desire can be fulfilled that the fragmentary aspects of his life should be seen as reflecting the whole of his plan and thought and . . . the material out of which it was made and was to be made. According to Ott, an interpreter of Bonhoeffer must be aware of this "fragmentary character" of his work and on its basis derive the principle of recognizing the "material" and the "whole" (*op. cit.*, 57).

142. See above, Chapter II.2.

found in that letter as well as in the Bible study, it is natural to assume that Bonhoeffer could have had in mind in the letter the method of interpretation that he employed in the Bible study.

As the third note to the study, he had maintained in 1935:

> 3. The men and stories of the Old Testament are not moral prototypes but witnesses of the election and promise of God. The Old Testament witnesses to God's free, merciful, and wrathful action with his people, not moral example. (*GS* IV, 320)[143]

On the basis of this, Bonhoeffer proceeded with the interpretation of II Sam., chs. 11 to 19. Perhaps these two sentences are what he would have expanded upon later.

We can go one step farther, however. In the Bible study he did not remain at this point where he said of the David stories that God's actions in them were more important than the actions of man. Rather, he designated David as the "shadow and prototype" of the crucified Christ, as II Sam., chs. 11 to 19, reveal him to us. He came to such a conclusion because he read those stories in the light of Christ. It is possible that he might have stressed "later and orally" that we would need to read these stories also in the light of Christ.

In order to clarify what that means for these stories we must cite a few of them about which Bonhoeffer could have been thinking.

We find many stories in the Old Testament in which lying is not done "to the glory of God," but in which there is no reprimand of the liar. For example, it is not the lying Abraham

143. H. Vogel, "24. The Bible is not concerned with honorable and pious men, not with heroes or saints, but with God and his praise and his way of salvation for us lost men" ("Kreuz und Hakenkreuz," *ZZ* 11 [1933], 203. In *Das Alte Testament und der evangelische Religionsunterricht* (1934), G. Schmidt says that the Old Testament is not concerned with the glorification of piety or moral examples, but it "reports the real encounter between real men and the real God" (7 f.).

but the ignorant Pharaoh who is punished (Gen. 12:10–20; 20:26). Not only the patriarchs lie, but also the prophet Jeremiah consents to a proposal of Zedekiah not to tell the truth to the princes (Jer. 38:24 ff.). One can say of Jacob's acts of deception that they took place to the glory of God, because God blesses the deceiver, but of course not without judging him (Gen., ch. 32). But God never expressly condemns Jacob's deception. It is often reported in the Old Testament that killing was committed at God's command, and hence to his glory: the execution of the ban under Joshua, the victories of the judges and David. In order to appease God, Ezra commanded those of mixed marriage to divorce (Ezra, chs. 9 f.). The incestuous deed of Lot's daughters (Gen., ch. 19) is reported just as simply as the behavior of Tamara, who seduced her father-in-law to commit adultery (Gen., ch. 38). And in the genealogy of Jesus, Rahab the harlot is found.

Bonhoeffer had understood II Sam., chs. 11 to 19, in the light of the crucifixion and resurrection, but this kind of interpretation could be transferred to only one of the stories discussed, the story of Jacob. Jacob is similar to David in that he as both elect and guilty is judged by God. God punished both of them for their sins. However, their sins do not need to be an offense for whoever reads everything that is written about them in the Old Testament. To the contrary, that something of David's error and punishment is reported shows the uniqueness of the Old Testament as opposed to other Oriental royal accounts. As those judged by God, Jacob and David reflect the light of the crucifixion. For this very reason other stories are offensive where nothing of the punishment of God is reported, and in a few of them offensive deeds do indeed take place to the glory of God.

In the second note to the Bible study Bonhoeffer had said that the Old Testament, among other things, must be read in the light of the incarnation. It is certain that Jesus Christ as the incarnate, crucified, and resurrected Lord is exceedingly important for him. In the *Ethics* he writes of his view of the incarnate Lord:

Ecce homo!—Behold the God who has become man. . . .
God loves man. God loves the world. It is not an ideal
man that He loves, but man as he is. . . . What we find
abominable in man's opposition to God, what we
shrink back from with pain and hostility, the real man,
. . . this is for God the ground for unfathomable love. . . .
God becomes man and . . . makes no distinction at all
in His love for the real man. (*E* 75 f./16 f.; Eng. tr., 71)

On the basis of these ideas it may be suggested that what
Bonhoeffer "later and orally" wanted to say is to be found
in the area of an understanding of those offensive stories
in the light of the incarnation. Such an understanding
recognizes that the real man who lies, deceives, kills, and
commits adultery is loved and "accepted" by God (*GS*
III, 385); it presumes to understand why they have a place
in the Old Testament and are not an "earlier religious
stage" in contrast to the highly developed ethic of the
New Testament, but are rather a witness to the action
of God, the One God throughout the entire Holy Scripture.
Jesus Christ, the incarnate, justifies the place of these
stories in the Old Testament. Therefore, the Old Testament is for us also the book of Christ.[144]

144. Only with these thoughts can one grasp what Bonhoeffer might have
said later. We do not wish to confirm the thesis of the work in this way, but
wish to do justice to Bonhoeffer. His thought guarded against classification of
those stories as "early religious stages." In our opinion only with the help of
a Christological relationship can one conclude what he wanted to say. For
example, in assuming the same presupposition—one and the same God—
P. Althaus arrives at almost exactly that which Bonhoeffer specifically rejects.
Althaus speaks of a "childish stage" of Old Testament faith, upon which
community with God and earthly gifts are inseparably intertwined. Through
God's upbringing we should grow out of this child's stage. "But faith deals
with one and the same God at both the child's stage and the manly stage"
(*Die christliche Wahrheit*, 1962[6], 196 f.). The "child's stage" is extremely close
to the "early religious stage," because both are stages out of which one grows.
On this passage see below, Chapter III.E.5.

3. "Christological" Interpretation of the Song of Songs
(June 2, 1944)

If we understand the stories of the Old Testament in which the human element is so plainly mentioned in the light of the incarnation of Christ, then we neither need to set them aside nor bashfully camouflage the Old Testament before those for whom these stories give welcome cause to attack the Old Testament.

In the letter of June 2, 1944, Bonhoeffer engaged himself with another section of the Old Testament, the Song of Songs, which along with his description of the human element is not far removed from the offensive stories of the Old Testament:

> While you're in Italy I shall write to you about the Song of Songs. I must say I should prefer to read it as an ordinary love song. That is probably the best "christological" interpretation. (*WE* 172/213; Eng. tr., 315)

It is not unusual that Bonhoeffer wanted to read the Song of Songs as an ordinary love song. Others before him had done the same.[145] But his reason is astonishing: It is the best "christological" interpretation. In the traditional sense this

---

145. W. Rudolph names Herder, Döpke, Reuss, Magnus, and Budde (*KAT* XVII, 2 [1962], 99). In the early church Theodore from Mopsuestia understood the Song of Songs as an ordinary love song and wanted it taken out of the canon for that reason (D. Lerch, *RGG*[3] III, 431). Vischer belongs to those who feel that the Song of Songs should have its place in the canon as an ordinary love song, not allegory. Like Bonhoeffer, he sees a relationship between the Song of Songs, understood in this way, and Christ, who "here obviously has not come to bring a solution but to fulfill and to bring again what is corrupted and lost" ("Das Alte Testament als Gottes Wort," *ZZ* 5 [1927], 393). Barth, who rejects any spiritualization of the Song of Songs and requires of an "honest interpretation" that it gladly recognize the Song of Songs as a collection of genuine "love songs in a primitive sense," stands very close to Bonhoeffer (*KD* III, 2, 354). As evidence that these songs, like Gen. 2:18–25, belong in the Old Testament, Barth mentions that writers of this poetry had "*another* . . . *covenant* in mind," namely, that of God with Israel. From the standpoint of this covenant, the bond between man and woman was to be seen and . . . taken seriously in a most positive light" (*ibid.*, 359, see also 361).

interpretation means that the Song of Songs allegorically is based on the relationship of Christ to his church or to the believer.[146] Therefore, Bonhoeffer had set "christological" in quotation marks perhaps because he was consciously in opposition to that interpretation. However, the word "christological" does not appear only because Bonhoeffer wanted to point out some paradoxes with it; rather, it had a deeper meaning. The "christological" interpretation of the Song of Songs means to understand them in the light of the incarnation.[147]

Bonhoeffer had already established a relationship between the Song of Songs and Christ in an earlier letter to his friend (May 20, 1944). There he writes about the love between husband and wife, and how—beside that *cantus firmus* of a real life, namely, love for the sake of God and his eternity—earthly love can resound as the contrapuntal theme. And a more passionate, sensuous, and ardent love than that pictured in the Song of Songs cannot be imagined. That *cantus firmus* and this counterpoint "are 'undivided and yet distinct,' in the words of the Chalcedonian Definition, like Christ's divine and human natures" (*WE* 156/193).

That is precisely the situation, however, through the incar-

146. The Christian allegorization carried out by Origen goes back to the new interpretation undertaken by the synagogue (D. Lerch, *RGG*³ III, 430).

147. What Ott has said, again from the perspective of the whole of Bonhoeffer, about the sentences on the Song of Songs is valid; namely, that he "has experimented in his theological thought." Therefore an interpreter of Bonhoeffer must understand his style. This means that one may not take each one of his sentences to be intended as conclusive, upon which a system may be built and into which each one may be fitted (*op. cit.,* 58). If we attempt here to understand that fragmentary and experimental statement of Bonhoeffer from the standpoint of his Christological concept, which is at the basis of his theological thought, then we do it consciously without submitting to the danger of systematization. Rather, we accede to the *other* claim of Ott that "if one thinks he encounters contradictions in Bonhoeffer's statements, . . . he may not reach a decision on discrepancies in Bonhoeffer's thought merely on the basis of that impression" *(ibid.).* It is precisely a superficial comparison of Bonhoeffer's statements on the Song of Songs and Ps. 58 (see above, Introduction, sec. 1 and Chapter III. D.3.b) that could tempt one to think he has discovered such a discrepancy. While we understand that passage from *WE* from the standpoint of the incarnation, we seek to grasp the "inner uniformity" of Bonhoeffer's thought *(ibid.).*

54

nation of God in Christ. In Bonhoeffer's *Ethics,* concerning God's action in the incarnation for the sake of mankind one reads:

> Jesus Christ, the man—this means that God enters into created reality. It means that we have the right and the obligation to be men before God. (*E* 139/183; Eng. tr., 131.) Only through the incarnation of Christ do we have the right to call others to the natural life and to live the natural life ourselves. (*E* 154/94; Eng. tr., 145)

That we are created man or woman belongs to our human existence. We have the right and the obligation to live out this human existence in recognition of the need to face one another, to be with one another and to count on one another. The Song of Songs shows us how facing one another can be realized in the realm of love between man and woman. Jesus Christ, the man, empowers us to that end. He makes the Old Testament valid for us at this point. Therefore, it is the book of Christ for us.

Since Bonhoeffer understood the Song of Songs in the light of the incarnation, he read it like an ordinary love song.[148] Hence this understanding may be called a Christological (without quotation marks) interpretation to the extent that it

148. H. Schulte understood that statement of Bonhoeffer on the "Christological" interpretation of the Song of Songs with the aid of his idea about the difference between John the Baptist and Jesus from the letter of July 21, 1944. "Just like the Song of Songs, Jesus stands for unabbreviated human life, which does not permit any curtailment of life in this world for the sake of the glories of the life to come—the same Jesus who must allow himself to be reproached as a "glutton and drunkard" (Matt. 11:19). ("In den Tatsachen selbst ist Gott. Die Bedeutung des Alten Testaments für die christliche Verkündigung nach D. Bonhoeffers letzten Briefen," *EvTh* 22[1962], 446 f.) However, if one wishes to do justice to Bonhoeffer, it is not sufficient to establish, as does H. Schulte, only one analogy between the Song of Songs and Jesus. To understand the Song of Songs from the standpoint of the incarnation requires much more consideration. H. Schulte examines only the last letters, and the phrase in question originated from Bonhoeffer's understanding of the Old Testament from the standpoint of Christ in the year 1935. That the understanding of a statement from 1944 is made possible with the help of a statement from 1935 becomes more important in Chapter III. D.3.b.

takes into account the fact that Jesus Christ is the center of the entire Old Testament. For that reason this interpretation does not need to be put immediately into the "cabinet of theological rarities," which, according to D. Lerch, equates the history of the interpretation of the Song of Songs with "meaningful history."[149]

4. *The Old Testament as Witness of God's Acceptance, Judgment, and Renewal*[150]

Bonhoeffer did not approach the interpretation of the Bible on the basis of exegetical presupposition, but on one of faith that God is the One God of the entire Bible.[151] This presupposition determined his understanding of the Old Testament as did nothing else.[152] Can such a presupposition do justice to the Old Testament?

A similar question arises when we state clearly the presupposition of the thesis that the whole Bible, consequently the Old Testament also, is the book of Christ. Bonhoeffer arrived at this presupposition by way of an opinion originating with Karl Barth, namely, that God revealed himself alone in Jesus Christ.[153] If one adheres to the uniqueness of the revelation of God in Christ, and at the same time wants to interpret the Old Testament as the Word of One God throughout the entire

149. D. Lerch, *RGG*[3] III, 431.

150. Because Bonhoeffer's heritage "is still present among us as legacy and obligation," according to Ott, his thoughts must be presented "on two levels" today. Besides their interpretation, the additional work on the questions that concern us and concerned him must be linked to the interpreter's own systematic consideration. In points 1 to 3 in our interpretation of Bonhoeffer we have pursued a path which he traveled only briefly. Now the attempt at a "systematic consideration" should be undertaken, but nevertheless along the lines of Bonhoeffer.

151. See above, Chapter II.2.

152. See esp. Chapter III.C.2.

153. "God revealed himself in 'once-ness' from the year one to the year thirty in Palestine in Jesus" ("Concerning the Christian Idea of God," New York, 1931, *GS* I, 105). Compare also the presentation of the basic position of Barth by Bonhoeffer in the lecture "The Theology of Crisis and Its Attitude Toward Philosophy and Science" (1931, *GS* I, 111 ff.) and Bethge, " 'The Barthian' in New York" (*DB* 195–198).

Bible, then the task of understanding the Old Testament as the book of Christ is a logical necessity. But can one do justice to the Old Testament with such a pattern of logic?

From a biographical point of view Bonhoeffer was first influenced decisively by dialectical theology during 1924 and 1925, and only subsequently came to the Bible during 1931 and 1932. He encountered it with dogmatic assumptions, so that the danger of a dogmatic confinement of the Bible was likely with him. It is noteworthy that he began to read it not in accordance with his own opinion but contrary to it.[154] The prior judgment, however, that God revealed himself alone in Christ remained unquestionable for him.[155]

We are convinced that this prior judgment together with the other—One God throughout the entire Bible—does justice to the Old Testament. We have already indicated that the understanding gained from the second notation to the Bible study "King David"—that in the Old Testament no direct revelation has taken place[156] for us—is in accordance with the Old Testament witness of the exclusive election of Israel. God has revealed himself directly to us only in Christ. Therefore we enter the Old Testament only through Jesus Christ, insofar as we want to understand the Old Testament as the Word of God.

Christ's mediation of the Old Testament for us need not be a forced justification. In the three examples cited above, the witness of the respective texts themselves is taken into account by Bonhoeffer. The fornication and manslaughter by David, the offensive humanness of Abraham and of one of Rachel and Lot's daughters need not be concealed, and the description of the passionate, sensuous, and ardent love in the Song of Songs need not be allegorized. To the contrary, all of this must be brought into the light if these texts are to be understood in the light of Christ. Only then can one recognize how God has acted in the crucified and resurrected Lord as well as in the

154. See above, fn. 89 and 91.
155. Only one testimony, "And the revelation of God is Jesus Christ" (1939/40, *E* 55/155).
156. See above, Chapter III.C.2.

David of II Sam., chs. 11 to 19; how he has acted in the incarnate Lord and for man, whose humanness is described so realistically for us in the Old Testament. With the last example it becomes clear that only in relation to Christ is the Song of Songs able to say what it was not allowed to say for so long.

In a similar way the prior judgment that God is One God throughout the entire Bible does not force the Old Testament into a form inappropriate to it. To the contrary, from Bonhoeffer's beginning onward the understanding of the Old Testament in the light of Christ on the one hand agrees with the witness of the Old Testament in its wholeness, and on the other hand it is faith's pre-judgment to its understanding.

Bonhoeffer defined the One God more closely than the One who loves us in Jesus Christ in that he accepts us in the incarnation, judges us in the crucifixion, and renews us in the resurrection.[157]

According to the second note to the Bible study "King David," Bonhoeffer wanted to interpret the Old Testament in the light of the incarnation, crucifixion (and resurrection). Is the "revelation which has taken place for us" intentionally so defined by him here? One presumes so. At one point in the Bible study itself he read several stories in the light of the crucifixion and resurrection, while at another the Christological concept is extremely fruitful for him.[158]

If one reads the Old Testament in the light of the incarnation, crucifixion, and resurrection, there is a recognizable relationship between Bonhoeffer's three viewpoints of interpretation by which the love of God is more closely defined for him, and between the three main points of the way along which God has led his people according to the witness of the Old Testament. First he accepted this people, elected and delivered it from Egypt (Deut. 7:7 ff.); then he judged it because in its election it became guilty (Amos 3:2); finally, he created a new

157. See above, Chapter II.3.
158. Especially clear in *E* IV and in the sections "The Despiser of Men," "The Successful Man," "The Idolization of Death."

people for himself (Jer. 43:18 f.).[159]

The following conclusions result from Bonhoeffer's early statements: There is One God throughout the entire Bible whose action in Christ and upon Israel is related, the destiny of Jesus Christ is a repetition of the destiny of Israel, the Old Testament is the witness of God's accepting, judging, and renewing love. It is profitable to think through them thoroughly.[160] That does not take place in this work, but they are referred to, since they contribute to the understanding of Bonhoeffer's controversial ideas in *Letters and Papers from Prison.*

According to G. Gloege (1934), the church had to express its opinion on the renunciation and conquest of the Old Testament. Under the presupposition that the entire Bible is the place "where God intends for us to find him," Bonhoeffer set out in conquest of the Old Testament in his interpretation. In the interpretations and fundamental discussions examined up to this point he accomplished his purpose, because he understood the Old Testament in the light of Jesus Christ. The result of such an understanding is the realization that the Old Testament as the book of Christ is made valid for us through

159. Compare W. Zimmerli, "Ezechiel, ein Zeuge der Gerechtigkeit Gottes," *BEvTh* 24(1956), 37–61; C. Westermann, "Das Verhältnis des Jahweglaubens zu den ausserisraelitischen Religionen," *Forschung am Alten Testament,* 1964, 202 f.; on a single text (Ps. 80), H. J. Kraus, *BK* XV, 1, 1961², 560.

160. The thesis of the complete correspondence of the Old and New Testaments must be developed and clarified in a threefold consideration. On the one hand, a consideration of each of the three main conclusions, especially the third. Does it take place within the Old Testament, or as Mildenberger phrases the question: Is it only to be understood as an announcement of a new act of God, which finds its realization only in Christ (*op. cit.,* 64, compare also 52–64: Election as "Beginning" and "Judgment," 64–68: The Basis of Hope)? On the other hand, that thesis must be developed and clarified by a consideration of the attempts already available and with the help of the concept of "analogy" to determine the relationship between both Testaments, as understood by C. H. Ratschow (*Der angefochtene Glaube,* 1960², 72 ff.); H. W. Wolff (*PAH* 140–180); W. Eichrodt ("Ist die typologische Exegese sachgemässe Exegese?" *PAH* 205–227); Von Rad (*Theologie des Alten Testaments,* Vol. II, 376 ff.); and Mildenberger (*op. cit.,* 78–83). Finally, the concept of salvation history must be discussed. See Mildenberger, *op. cit.,* 12 f.

him and belongs to him. That the Old Testament belongs to Christ is verified by the realization, which somewhat transcends Bonhoeffer, that the Old and New Testaments witness to the accepting, judging, and renewing love of God.

D. "CHRIST IN THE OLD TESTAMENT"

In Bonhoeffer's Old Testament interpretation one recognizes a double movement, which a few Old Testament specialists consider appropriate to Biblical interpretation.[161] We have examined the movement in the first direction, namely, the understanding of the Old Testament in the light of Christ; nevertheless, we do not turn immediately to the other: the understanding of the New Testament in the light of the Old Testament. Rather, we turn first to the theme "Christ in the Old Testament," which guides us to a final clarification of the first movement. That is primarily because of chronology. Apart from a few exceptions in *Creation and Fall* (*SF* 18, 120), Bonhoeffer considers how and that the New Testament is to be understood in the light of the Old only after he has presented his "Contribution to the Problem: Christ in the Old Testament."[162] The Old Testament interpretations from 1935 to 1940 contain his contributions to that problem.[163] From 1932 to 1944 he explored the double movement we have mentioned, but it is clear from our study that only from 1940 onward did he pursue the movement in the second direction.

Bonhoeffer wanted to make a contribution to the discussion of the problem of "Christ in the Old Testament." From the time of Vischer's "call to alarm,"[164] there arose a dispute,

161. See above, Chapter III.A.

162. That should be his Bible study "King David" (*GS* IV, 294). Only here does Bonhoeffer use the formulation "Christ in the Old Testament."

163. Primarily the following sources will be drawn upon: see List of D. Bonhoeffer Sources, numbers 13, 14, 20, 25, 28, 30. In these and the other sources from this period the concern is not only "Christ in the Old Testament."

164. That is what H. J. Kraus calls Vischer's *CAT* (see Kraus, *op. cit.*, 389).

which had been carried on vigorously for many years, but which during the time of the beginning of the church struggle was directed to the Old Testament, especially in regard to the sense in which the Old Testament is a witness to the revelation of God *in* Jesus Christ.[165] In placing this theme at the center of a new consideration of the Old Testament, Vischer bade the church reflect on the matter by looking at the Old Testament.[166] On this question Bonhoeffer was a very "close ally" of Vischer and Vischer an ally of Bonhoeffer.[167]

What does Bonhoeffer mean by the small word "in"?[168] The phrase "Christ in the Old Testament" is indeed short, but what it means is not immediately clear. Like certain words from *Letters and Papers from Prison,* it can be branded and misused as a slogan. The judgments of C. Westermann, W. Rupprecht, and H. Pfeiffer that Bonhoeffer interpreted Old Testament texts "directly"[169] or "strictly christologically,"[170] in certain respects are not to be rejected, because they contain an element of truth. Nevertheless we would warn against collectively disposing of Bonhoeffer's Old Testament interpreta-

165. See above, on the first page of Chapter III, the judgment of Von Rad. The phrase "Christ in the Old Testament" is used for the first time, in the literature utilized for this study, by O. Weber in *Die Auslegung der Heiligen Schrift als theologische Frage* (1934), 56. Vischer makes use of it in *Das Christuszeugnis des Alten Testaments,* Vol. I; however Herntrich does not use it in his discussion of Vischer's book in *MPTh* 32(1936), 183, 185. It is found a number of times in H. Hellbardt's "Die Auslegung des Alten Testaments als theologische Disziplin," *ThBl* 16(1937), 136–138. Barth employs it in *KD,* Vol. I, 2, §14, 2: the time of anticipation (1938); however, the exact words occur only once on p. 79.

166. Herntrich, *MPTh* 32, 178.

167. See above, Chapter I.3.b. For "discussion of Wilhelm Vischer and *CAT,*" compare Nicolaisen, *op. cit.,* 150–174. A number of times in these pages he cites Bonhoeffer, who, in addition to Vischer and Hellbardt, may "not remain unmentioned" here (*ibid.,* 161). Nicolaisen draws on *SF* and "The Reconstruction of Jerusalem . . ." (*ibid.,* 223).

168. Lecture from July 31, 1935, "Christ in the Psalms."

169. C. Westermann, *Verkündigung des Kommenden,* 1958, 180; W. Rupprecht, *op. cit.,* 372.

170. H. Pfeifer, *Das Kirchenverständnis D. Bonhoeffers. Ein Beitrag zur theologischen Prinzipienlehre,* dissertation, Heidelberg, 1963, manuscript, 107.

tion from that period on the strength of such judgments.[171]

In order to come to a relevant, collective judgment of Bonhoeffer's Old Testament interpretation at this time it is necessary, above all, to consider a lecture that he delivered on July 31, 1935, at Finkenwalde: "Christus in den Psalmen" ("Christ in the Psalms") (1). The thoughts developed in this lecture differ from those which Bonhoeffer later expressed explicitly on the question of what he meant by the word "in." The Bible study "King David," delivered only two months before, gives other answers to this question (2).[172] They appear again in later interpretations, while those from July, 1935, are not developed further. That generalized judgments are inappropriate is illustrated by the Bible study "The Restoration of Jerusalem According to Ezra and Nehemiah," from April, 1936 (3), and by the sermon on Psalm 58 (4).

1. Lecture, "Christ in the Psalms" (July 31, 1935)

In this lecture, delivered before the brothers of Finkenwalde and the theological students of the Confessing Church,[173] Bonhoeffer maintained: In contrast to all other prayers Christian prayer is *not direct;* rather, it is "mediated prayer, mediated through Christ, the mediator." He who is our brother prays before the throne of God for us as our intercessor. He makes

171. It is inappropriate to generalize those judgments, since they are based only on particular interpretations of Bonhoeffer (Westermann discusses the sermon on Ps. 42; Rupprecht [*op. cit.*, 372, 381] refers to the Bible study "King David"; Pfeifer [*op. cit.*] to "King David," "The Reconstruction of Jerusalem . . . ," and *The Prayerbook of the Bible*); it is also inappropriate to overlook this period of Bonhoeffer's, and to make his understanding of the Old Testament a polemic against Vischer, as K. H. Nebe wishes to do. Nebe says: "In Bonhoeffer we understand that the Old Testament is not to be regarded as the shadow of the New. It has its own independent message. It does not consist in the fact that Christ is proclaimed everywhere, as Vischer among others intends it, rather in things which the New Testament partially presupposes and partially necessarily needs as support" (Nebe, *op. cit.*, 205.) This judgment results from a consideration of *WE* and isn't just pulled out of the air. Nevertheless, it is one-sided, like the others. On Westermann, see fn. 194.

172. On this Bible study, see above, Chapter III.C.1.

173. *DB* 497.

the prayer his own that is prayed in his name daily "in eternal intercession." Therefore, only the prayer in the name of Jesus Christ reaches God. To pray in the name of Jesus Christ, however, is no formula, but designates the circumstance of prayer. Our prayer is bound "to the man Jesus Christ, his life, death, and resurrection, . . . to the spoken Word of God" (*GS* III, 296 f.). Because we have the Holy Scripture as the Word of God, Christian prayer is bound to the Holy Scripture. If it is to be a proper Christian prayer, it must therefore be "the Word of God, that is, prayer of the High Priest Jesus Christ" (*GS* III, 297). This demand does justice to the Psalter, to the prayers of the community and Holy Scripture, in other words God's Word.[174] Nothing else is meant here "than that Christ himself is the one who offers the prayer of the psalms and that we repeat and pray these prayers in the name of Jesus Christ" (*GS* III, 297).[175] Thus we have to understand and join in praying the psalms as the prayers of Jesus Christ in his community or the prayers of the community in the name of Jesus Christ. For that reason we need no longer ask how *we* can pray the psalms in which all the godliness and ungodliness of the community are articulated, if Christ is the one who prays the psalms. The question resulting from all this, however, is how the entire Psalter can be understood as the prayer of Jesus Christ (*GS* III, 297).[176]

In the introduction to *Creation and Fall,* Bonhoeffer had stressed that theological interpretation of the Bible understood it as the book of the church. This assumption is its

174. In the first four points of his lecture Bonhoeffer had agreed to this double character of the psalms (*GS* III, 497).

175. Thus Christian prayer is mediated through Christ not only because he brings our prayers before God but also because that which he mediates as our prayer is bound to him.

176. The ideas referred to up to this point are found with certain modifications in *GL* 35 ff. and again in *The Prayerbook of the Bible* (*GS* IV, 544–547). They are also presented by Grunow (*MW* I, 72–76). He does not concern himself with the phrase "Christ was in David" (see above, Chapter III. D.2); compare "Jesus Christ is the 'I' of the Psalms, because he has prayed the psalms and brought them before God" (*ibid.,* 76). But Bonhoeffer also says, because Christ was in David!

method and this method complies with the thoughts cited up to this point from his lecture. He saw the Psalms, which are a part of Holy Scripture, as the prayerbook of the community (the *Sitz im Leben* for this lecture and the following contributions on the psalms is the daily psalm prayer in the preaching seminar!); he said what the essence of the prayers in the church of Christ is, and thus came to the conclusion that Christ himself is the one who prays the psalms. But that did not settle the questions which resulted from the exegesis of the psalms. Bonhoeffer only drew nearer to them.

He continued in his lecture: With the question of how the entire Psalter can be understood as the prayerbook of Jesus Christ, we are brought to the old and decisive questions regarding the "I" in the psalms. Who is the one praying? Bonhoeffer knows how important this question is and that its answer determines "whether we get bogged down in the orthodox interpretation of the Old Testament—as it is represented somewhat by Hengstenberg—that is, whether we have to set the dogmatic thesis of verbal inspiration over against the textual-critical and historical interpretation of the Old Testament, or whether we are in the position to take up the critical method and place it in the service of a theological interpretation." The viewpoints of an orthodox interpretation are mentioned: (1) This position postulates that the "I" of the psalms is "the voice of Christ in his Old Testament community"; (2) the Biblical assertions of authorship are authentic; (3) in the Psalter there is no ungodly prayer (*GS* III, 298).

In any case one must admit that Bonhoeffer wanted something other than a new version of the orthodox interpretation of the Old Testament. That will be clearer in the following sentences of the lecture, in which he assesses this type of interpretation and historical-critical research.

The protest of historical-critical research against the orthodox interpretation not only was right on the basis of the common, scientific, factual research, but it was *theologically* justified. Historical-critical research attacked the "sanctification of the Bible" maintained by the orthodox interpretation instead of the sanctification of the God of the Bible. Once there was agitation against the orthodox position, everything in Old Testament research was upset. "We stand at the end of this epoch and we can no longer turn back. The question is: What is a theological interpretation of the psalms according to the conclusion of historical theology?" (GS III, 299).[177] Bonhoeffer considered historical theology to be finished, but not textual and literary criticism. "There remained room for them, and their right was not to be infringed" (GS III, 300). They have presented us with the knowledge of the full historicizing of revelation, but cannot dispute the right of a "theological interpretation" of the Old Testament.[178] We accept the result of textual and literary criticism (regarding the psalms that means that it has taught us to see the human motive, the human godliness and ungodliness, the temporal aspect of the "I" in the psalms), "but another sign qualifies this result and this sign is Christ. The world in the Psalter remains what it is: world. However, God enters the world. Christ is in the middle among the righteous and the enemies in this world . . . but Christ among the righteous and the enemies means Christ crucified . . . Christ in the psalms: that means the crucified Christ in the psalms" (GS III, 310).[179]

177. The following citations are not direct citations from Bonhoeffer, since he only outlined the last two and a half points of his lecture (GS III, 299); rather they are from the transcript of the lecture by Bethge.

178. Nicolaisen (op. cit., 161) sees "the real concern of Bonhoeffer, Vischer, and Hellbardt" as that of going beyond the unobliging statements of religious science on the Old Testament to give to historical-critical research its proper place as a *science which assists* theology, and not to be content with its results as the final and only possible *theological* statements on the Old Testament. So far as Bonhoeffer is concerned, this opinion is somewhat too positive, because it is based only on the lecture of July 31, 1935, in which, in addition to all the relativizing of historical-critical research, its *theological* justification is unavoidably emphasized by Bonhoeffer. That was not the case later on.

179. According to the transcript (GS III, 300), Bonhoeffer certainly said more on his main points. Whether or not the *real* Bonhoeffer can be heard in the transcription is shown in the important sentence, "But God enters this world." That is Bonhoeffer's theme. Compare SF 33; GS III, 105; E 139/83, 154/94, 207/60; and J. Weissbach, *Christologie und Ethik bei Dietrich Bonhoeffer*, ThEx NF 131(1966), 18.

As already stressed above, Bonhoeffer wanted something other than a new but unchanged version of orthodox interpretation. So far as this interpretation was concerned he decided that he did not consider the assertions of authorship genuine and did not close his eyes on the ungodly passages in the psalms. There is, however, still another difference and it lies in the question of the presence of Christ in the Old Testament about which both Bonhoeffer and orthodox interpretation speak. According to Bonhoeffer, the latter views this presence as "the voice of Christ in his Old Testament community," but he views it as "Christ the crucified *in the Psalter.*" For the orthodox interpreters, Christ is in the persons who prayed the psalms, but for Bonhoeffer, Christ is present in the words of the psalms. In the psalms there was a confirmation of the presence of Christ *at that time,* but now Christ is present *today* when the psalms are prayed in his name by his community.[180] Then nothing else can be intended with the sentence than that Christ, the sign, takes precedence over textual and literary criticism.

As for the question of the "I" in the psalms in his lecture, Bonhoeffer took care not to get bogged down in the orthodox interpretation. He strove for a theological interpretation of the Old Testament, which did not allow the results of textual and literary criticism to go unconsidered, because this criticism is theologically justified.[181] In so doing, Bonhoeffer did justice to an appeal of G. von Rad, which, in his contributions to the discussion during those years, was concerned with the proper Christological interpretation of the Old Testament,

180. In this way one arrives at a possible interpretation of the sentence in which Bonhoeffer describes the orthodox interpretation. "The orthodox thesis *postulates* that the 'I' of the psalms is the voice of Christ in his Old Testament community" (*GS* III, 298). Does he want only to criticize the *postulating* or also the content of the postulate with this sentence? His answer to the question concerning the "I" of the psalms clearly shows that he also rejects the content of the postulate.

181. According to this, the parentheses in the introduction of *SF* (see above, Chapter II.4) would mean that Bonhoeffer took for granted the philological and historical analysis of a text.

namely, that one not attempt to arrive at the Old Testament's witness of Christ by overlooking historical-critical research.[182] Bonhoeffer also complied with another appeal of G. von Rad. In *Fragen der Schriftauslegung im Alten Testament* (1938), Von Rad spoke of a temptation afoot at that time in regard to the Old Testament's witness of Christ and the presence of Christ in it. It was the attempt to speak of a "personal presence" of Christ in the Old Testament, that is, that Christ was "in Isaac," "in David," "in the one who prayed Psalm 22." Such a presence of Christ in the Old Testament, however, cannot be accepted, because it leads to a misrepresentation of the Old Testament witness. Of a "real presence" of Christ in the Old Testament it can be said only that Christ along with "the actual subject of the witness at the time" is within the scope of a text.[183]

Everything appears to intimate that Bonhoeffer in his lecture of July, 1935, was driving at a presence of Christ in the Old Testament in the sense of Von Rad's "real presence" (1938). What he intended in this lecture may not be overlooked if one wants to reach a comprehensive judgment about his Old Testament interpretation at that time; even if it is only a beginning which he exposed here and did not expand further,[184] but rather abandoned the same year in the Bible study "King David" (Oct., 1935).

2. *"Christ was in David" (Bible Study "King David,"* Oct. 8–11, 1935)

Bonhoeffer conducted this Bible study at Finkenwalde at a meeting of the Pomeranian Brethren of the Confessing

182. G. von Rad, "Das Christuszeugnis des Alten Testaments. Eine Auseinandersetzung mit W. Vischers gleichnamigem Buch," *ThBl* 14(1935), 249 f.; "Sensus Scripturae Sacrae duplex? Eine Erwiderung," *ThBl* 15(1936), 31 ff.; *Fragen der Schriftauslegung im Alten Testament,* 1938, 7 ff.

183. Von Rad, *Fragen der Schriftauslegung im Alten Testament,* 7 ff.

184. In the lecture he did not carry through this assessment, since as examples for the psalms in which "Christ is in the midst of the enemies and righteous in the world . . . as the One foreseen," he mentions the three psalms, Ps. 2, 16, and 10, whose Messianic significance is disputed by the textual and literary criticism.

Church. It has already become clear how important its *Sitz im Leben* is,[185] and that must be kept in view along with that which now is presented and in part criticized. With his Bible study, Bonhoeffer wanted to lead toward the "proper reading of the books of Samuel" (*GS* IV, 294). It is probable that "proper reading" means theological interpretation, which understands the books of Samuel as part of the entire Holy Scripture, which witnesses to the One God who has revealed himself in Christ.[186] "At the same time" the Bible study is a "contribution to the problem: Christ in the Old Testament." This contribution should interest us especially at this point.

In a "preliminary theological remark" Bonhoeffer cited "the New Testament and prophetic witness of David" (*GS* IV, 294–297).[187] He wanted to take it seriously in his interpretation of the David stories, that is, David is "in his person, his office, his word, and his history to be understood as" one "in whom Christ dwelt according to the New Testament. David is important only insofar as he is a witness of Christ, not for himself, but for Christ and thus for the church" (*GS* IV, 297). Next to the statement that Christ dwelt in David according to the New Testament, Bonhoeffer put other assertions: "The office and kingdom of Christ are typified in David" (*GS* IV, 295); David is the "prototype and shadow" of the Messiah.[188]

The portion of the interpretation in which Bonhoeffer understood Christ as the "prototype and shadow" of Christ has been discussed in part already. David as the justified sinner, as II Sam., chs. 11 to 19, pictures him for us, is the "prototype and shadow" of the crucified Christ (*GS* IV, 311–318).[189] In a similar manner Bonhoeffer interpreted the anointing of David,

185. See above, Chapter III.C.1.
186. Compare the first note, *GS* IV, 320.
187. See the New Testament passages in fn. 129, and in addition the following passages from the Old Testament: II Sam., ch. 7; Isa. 9:7; 11:1; 55:3; Jer. 30:8,21; 31:15; Hos. 3:5; Zech. 12:8.
188. Indirect New Testament evidence is Heb. 8:5; 10:1.
189. See above, Chapter III.C.1.

his pursuit by Saul, and his entry into Jerusalem.[190] He always saw represented in that which happened to David that which happened to Christ. Since the God of the Old Testament is the Father of Jesus Christ and the one who appears in Jesus Christ, analogies in the action of this One God are identifiable, for the Old and New Testaments witness to the occurrence of such action in David and Christ. That he is in both instances the One God is illustrated in striking accord: through the one Spirit of God, David and Christ are anointed to their office; both are tempted to set up their kingdom through their own power; both enter Jerusalem in lowliness and meekness.

In a few passages of his Bible study, however, Bonhoeffer saw not only an analogy between that which takes place with David and Christ, but more. In David's fight against Goliath and in his victory over him, David is not only the "prototype and shadow" of Christ, since immediately after the anointing he steps into the fight against enemies of God's people, a fight which he led unarmed and in which he depended solely upon God, but "David conquers Goliath as the one anointed to messianic kingship, as the prototype and shadow of Christ. It is Christ's victory in him. Hence, Christ was in David" (*GS* IV, 298). With these last sentences Bonhoeffer established why David conquered Goliath. He proceeded similarly with the exposition of I Sam. 22:2. David is not "the head of a band of robbers who in his need sides with desperadoes as others do"; "throughout the Biblical witness he is at all times and in all places the anointed of God. Christ is in his loins." Therefore, he is "the companion of sinners, the friend and confidant of the troubled and burdened" (*GS* IV, 301).

"Christ was in David." What does that mean? Has Christ become incarnate in David? Do we have to understand this as a parallel statement to the New Testament "Christ in you, in me" (Rom. 8:10; Gal. 2:20)? Is that possible?

190. I Sam., ch. 16—*GS* IV, 297 f.; I Sam., chs. 22; 24 f.—*GS* IV, 300–304; II Sam., ch. 6—GS IV, 304–306.

Von Rad has reacted to the following sentences from Bonhoeffer's "theological preface": "David knows himself as the one through whom Christ should come into the world, and only through this promise, Christ being the fruit of his loins, is he sustained on the throne. . . . Through the promise he knows already of the resurrection" (*GS* IV, 295).[191] Von Rad reacted with these words: "Who can understand that?"[192] Likewise we cannot make comprehensible the statement that Christ was in David. On the one hand, we can only determine that Bonhoeffer did not speak in this statement about "Christ in the Old Testament," as he attempted it in his lecture on the psalms from July 31, 1935. His statements there are to be interpreted in the direction of a "real presence" in the sense of Von Rad. But here a "personal presence" is under consideration; for Bonhoeffer, Christ is in David. Von Rad warned against making such a statement.[193]

On the other hand, in a certain respect the following question can be answered: What may have motivated Bonhoeffer to abandon in October, 1935, the way already opened up in the lecture of July 31, 1935?[194] That may have resulted from his acquaintance with the writings of H. F. Kohlbrügge. W. Rott,[195] who worked with Bonhoeffer from the end of April, 1935, as the study supervisor of the preaching seminar, brought the reformed, Rhineland books of Kohlbrügge and

191. Cited by Von Rad.
192. Von Rad, *ThBl* 15(1936), 32.
193. Von Rad, *Fragen der Schriftauslegung im Alten Testament*, 14.
194. In Westermann's opinion the close relationship of Bonhoeffer's view of the Christological significance of the Psalter to that of Vischer determined the course of the sermon from June 2, 1935, on Ps. 42 (*GS* IV, 391–399; Westermann, *PAH*, 180). On that basis it might appear that Bonhoeffer had *never* followed any other course than the one of Oct., 1935. However, one must differentiate between a Christianization of an Old Testament text that has not been carefully thought through, as is the case in that sermon and in the Old Testament sermons before *SF*, and the idea of why and how one can pray with the words of the Old Testament in a Christian manner. Sources for such considerations are available only after July 31, 1935. But for Bonhoeffer the daily praying of the psalms took precedence over working out these problems.
195. Bethge's letter to this author from Feb. 6, 1967.

Geyser with him. These reformed interpretations were little known to Bonhoeffer, according to Rott. He made this statement about them: "Yes, we should be able to stand upon the Word in this manner." Kohlbrügge's interpretation of the Old Testament attracted him.[196] It is also possible that Bonhoeffer was influenced by Kohlbrügge on the question of "Christ in the Old Testament," because a few, in part surprising, parallels between Kohlbrügge and Bonhoeffer's Bible study are identifiable.

(a) According to Kohlbrügge, his interpretation through Jesus, the evangelists, and the apostles is obligatory for the interpretation of the Old Testament.[197] In his interpretation of the David stories, Bonhoeffer wanted to take seriously the New Testament witness of David (*GS* IV, 294–297).

(b) In a sermon on Matt. 2:17 f. Kohlbrügge said that Jeremiah "carried Christ around in him," that Christ "was in him."[198] Bonhoeffer said, "Christ was in David" (*GS* IV, 300).

(c) Since the prophet Jeremiah carried Christ around in him,

196. W. Rott, "Ihm fiel immer etwas ein," in *Begegnungen mit Dietrich Bonhoeffer*, 1966², 105 f. A. de Quervain reports that "at the beginning of the 1930's and during the years of the church struggle" both theology and congregation on the lower Rhine kept Kohlbrügge extremely busy ("Kohlbrügge und das Erbe Calvins," *EvTh* 25[1965], 263).

197. H. F. Kohlbrügge, *Wozu das Alte Testament? Anleitung zur richtigen Schätzung der Bücher Mosis und der Propheten*, 1846, 1855³): "A careful examination of the books of the so-called 'New Testament' with sole regard and reference to the so-called 'Old Testament' for the solution of this task is always the most appropriate approach. This would be all the more helpful and up to date since today, as the key to understanding the problem is lost, the opinion seems to become more and more dominant that the law and the prophets belong to ancient times and have no relationship to our own" (7). "For the purpose of Scriptural interpretation one must put himself in the place of the apostles and the first Christian community." "Here there is no middle-of-the-road position. Either the Lord, his apostles, and the first Christians interpreted the writings of Moses and the prophets in completely the wrong way, that is, granted that they themselves did not understand them and that they deceived others, or we have to understand and interpret these writings very simply as they are, without taking away from or adding to them. If one rejects the latter option, he must realize what one does with the Lord and his apostles and that he is destroying the basis of the Christian faith and Christian hope at its foundation" (134 f.).

198. H. F. Kohlbrügge, *Der verheissene Christus. Sieben Predigten*, 1853, 64.

according to Kohlbrügge he lived not "for himself" but for "Christ and his community." The thoughts of murder with which the king and priests hedged him about were not "against the person of Jeremiah," but "against Christ, who was in him."[199] For Bonhoeffer, David was "important only insofar as he is a witness of Christ, not for himself, but for Christ and for the church of Christ" (*GS* IV, 297).

(d) According to Kohlbrügge, the signs of the prophets were executed "through the faith of Jesus, through faith in his mercy, therefore through him. . . . What each one did was his work."[200] According to Bonhoeffer, the victory of David over Goliath was "Christ's victory in him. Hence, Christ was in David" (*GS* IV, 300).

On the basis of these parallels one can surmise justifiably that Bonhoeffer had made use of Kohlbrügge's interpretations for his Bible study. The agreement on important points is too striking for one to suppose Bonhoeffer's independence from Kohlbrügge. Historically, however, that can only be speculated. Furthermore, it is no longer possible to establish if and when Bonhoeffer read the writings of Kohlbrügge in which the parallels here presented are found, as well as which of Kohlbrügge's books Rott brought to Finkenwalde.[201] In like manner the question must remain unsolved as to whether Bonhoeffer had used for his Bible study the *Collegium Biblicum* of A. F. C. Vilmar which was highly regarded at Finkenwalde.[202] This question arises because there are also surprising parallels

199. *Ibid.*
200. Kohlbrügge, *Wozu das Alte Testament?* 63.
201. Bonhoeffer had become acquainted with Kohlbrügge earlier. In *AS* in concurring with Kohlbrügge, he cited and referred to the Kohlbrügge's *Das 7. Kapitel des Briefes Pauli an die Römer,* 1839, 117, 119, 127. Rott mentions no specific time for his report (*loc. cit.*, 105 f.). Since he died at the beginning of 1967, it was impossible to procure any information from him. Bethge could only report that not until June 24, 1935, did they have their books "properly" set in order at Finkenwalde. (Letter to this author, June 6, 1967.) In the remainder of the Old Testament sermons of Kohlbrügge and Geyser cited in Bibliography III, no parallels to Bonhoeffer's interpretations, as quoted, are found.
202. Rott, *loc. cit.*, 106.

between Vilmar and Bonhoeffer's Bible study, if not quite similar to the instance of Kohlbrügge's influence on the question of "Christ in the Old Testament."[203]

203. The influence of Vilmar appears to be evident in one passage. On II Sam. 7:19b, Bonhoeffer asks (phrases reflecting Vilmar's influence are, for instance, "and that according to the law of man," "according to the manner of a *man*, Lord, Lord") whether God is not worshiped here in awe and reverence, because he will fulfill his promise in the incarnation (God become man), whether this is not a vague allusion to the night of Christ's birth. He cites Luther's marginal note without comment and without an indication of the source: "That is, you speak with me of such an eternal kingdom where no one can be king, but one who is God *and man*, both my son and king forever and ever, which is alone possible for God" (*WADB* 3, 319). Vilmar not only interprets this text, as does Kohlbrügge (*Der verheissene Christus*, 34 f.), as one "of the first vague indications of the incarnation of the Son of God" but cites Luther's gloss *without* indication of the source as well (Vilmar, *Collegium Biblicum. Des Alten Testaments zweiter Teil*, 1882, 168 f.). Moreover, there are still a few other passages in Vilmar upon which Bonhoeffer could have drawn for his interpretation:

(1) On I Sam. 22:1-5 Vilmar writes, "That is, of course, the greatness in David that he did not arbitrarily seize that which God had bestowed on him, but patiently waited until it was his turn" (*ibid.*, 140). Compare also *GS* IV, 302.

(2) On David's polygamy Vilmar remarks: "David's sexual sin continues and is in constant growth. But the sin of man does not reverse God's grace. We may not forget that the persons of the Old Testament are only examples of the unmerited grace of God, and they are not the models of Christian sanctification" (*ibid.*, 164). Compare also *GS* IV, 320, third note.

(3) According to Vilmar's interpretation, II Sam., ch. 11, takes into account "David's security because he now found himself in full possession of sovereign authority over the heathen, which had not existed in Israel up to that time, and because he considered his position secure from a human point of view. Such security leads to the most severe of sins; then the power of temptation is always nearest" (*ibid.*, 172). Compare also *GS* IV, 311.

H. Schmidt's question as to whether "Bonhoeffer's positive appraisal of the Old Testament does not go back to Vilmar's influence" (*MW* IV, 83, n. 11) can only be answered "Yes" with qualifications. Bonhoeffer probably made use of Vilmar only after he had long since made his own appraisal of the Old Testament.

A brief word about the parallels under consideration between Bonhoeffer's Bible study and the interpretation of the David stories in Vischer's second volume of *CAT*. The question of a dependence should be raised the other way around, namely, whether Vischer possibly used Bonhoeffer's interpretation, since Vol. II of *CAT* appeared in 1942. Vischer interprets the stories of the anointing of David, Saul's enmity against David, David's escape over the Kidron with the allusion that "the essential events of the David stories repeat themselves and terminate a thousand years later in a peculiar manner" (*CAT*,

After the establishment of this probable dependence of Bonhoeffer on others in his Bible study, we return once more to the circumstances indicated in the first parallel between him and Kohlbrügge, because it substantiates the following criticism of Bonhoeffer's interpretation initiated here. Is the practice of interpreting the Old Testament in the light of the New Testament actually authoritative for us today? That cannot be answered with a simple Yes or No. The problem focused upon by this question is many-sided. This question is considered also in the discussion which W. Vischer's *Das Christuszeugnis des Alten Testaments* initiated.[204]

On the basis of Bonhoeffer's first note to his Bible study it may be concluded: "The God of the Old Testament is the Father of Jesus Christ. The God who appears in Jesus Christ is the God of the Old Testament. He is the triune God" (*GS* IV, 320). The identity of the God attested to in the Old and New Testaments was for Bonhoeffer the fixed presupposition of a Biblical interpretation. Hence, for the New Testament the God of Israel is the God of Jesus Christ; we need only mention the classical passage, Heb. 1:1 f., for our problem. Here the most particular interpretation, which the Old Testament finds in the New, is designated as the New Testament's inherent, basic conception of the Old Testament.[205] This basic conception of the New Testament, however, is also decisive for our interpretation of the Old Testament today.[206] Yet the interpretation of particular Old Testament passages in the New Testament cannot be authoritative without examination. We are alienated from such interpretation by historical-critical re-

Vol. II, 223, 200 f., 217, 270). In those stories also Bonhoeffer had seen represented in what happened to David what would happen to Christ (*GS* IV, 297 ff., 317). Vischer also interpreted other stories in this way.

204. Compare Nicolaisen, *op. cit.*, 163.

205. Von Rad, *Fragen der Schriftauslegung*, 6; compare Galley, *op. cit.*, 46, "Old and new (i.e., salvation events) are comparable, because Paul . . . compares the deeds of *One* God or man with one another."

206. Von Rad, *Fragen der Schriftauslegung*, 14; Herntrich, *MPTh* 32 (1936), 188. For a contributor to the discussion on the hermeneutic of the Old Testament after World War II, compare Eichrodt (*PAH* 212).

search, which has taught us to see the comprehension of the Old Testament texts themselves in a way unknown to the New Testament witnesses.[207] For Bonhoeffer, however, after October, 1925, this alienation no longer existed. On July 31, 1935, he still maintained another opinion: historical criticism possesses a theological justification; a theological interpretation must take into account its results. But now he could remind the professors, who criticized him because of his church-struggle-oriented Bible studies, "that before the first historical-critical and history of religion interpretation there had been legitimate interpretation." For him, historical-critical research had been an intrusion.[208] Therefore it could be laid aside; therefore he could be attracted by an interpreter such as Kohlbrügge, because he stuck "to the Word," while Kohlbrügge himself labeled the method which called the close relationship of the Old and New Testaments more and more into question on the basis of historical-critical research a "wanton method."[209] During the church struggle, opposition to historical-critical research increased greatly and Bonhoeffer stood within this stream of thought at that time. In the opinion of Von Rad and Herntrich, Vischer also belonged to this opposition.[210]

In order to do justice to Bonhoeffer the *Sitz im Leben* of the

207. Compare Eichrodt, *PAH* 213.

208. Rott, in *Begegnungen mit Dietrich Bonhoeffer*, 106. See also the reports of Gollwitzer and Von Rad, in *ibid.*, 112 and 141.

209. Kohlbrügge, *Wozu das Alte Testament?* 134 f.; Barth sees him assuming the position of a very "strict, . . . mechanical teaching of inspiration" (*Die protestantische Theologie des 19. Jahrhunderts*, 1961, 586 f.). Compare also Kraus, *op. cit.*, 221.

210. On Vischer, see Von Rad, *ThBl* 14(1935), 249 ff., 15(1936), 30 ff.; Herntrich, *MPTh* 32(1936), 182. Also Hellbardt must be mentioned here, because according to the report of Gollwitzer (in *Begegnungen mit Dietrich Bonhoeffer*, 112), Hellbardt's "Confession transjordania" (in *Theologische Aufsätze. K. Barth zum 50. Geburtstag*, 1936, 164 ff.) was for him and Bonhoeffer an "example of the actuality of the Old Testament." On Hellbardt's position on historical-critical exegesis see his article "Die Auslegung des Alten Testaments als theologische Disziplin," *ThBl* 16(1937), 136–138, and the answer of Eichrodt, "Zur Frage der theologischen Exegese des Alten Testaments," *ThBl* 17[1938], 73–87). Compare also Nicolaisen, *op. cit.*, 163 f.

Bible study "King David" must be observed. Bonhoeffer did not deliver an academic lecture, rather a Bible study for vicars of the Confessing Church! Old Testament interpretation in this context was not neutral, but took place in view of the opponent for whom the Old Testament could no longer be "the book of the church." This opponent had to be repulsed. Von Rad could admit readily that Old Testament specialists were not able to write a book such as Vischer's *Das Christuszeugnis des Alten Testaments.* [211] However, this book in particular had given to so many the courage to preach from the Old Testament. It even motivated Old Testament science to ask itself, What is the task of theological science?[212] The historical-critical research of the Old Testament had given enough ammunition to the opponents, against whom the Confessing Church had to fight, to make it impossible for it to be "the book of the church." In this situation it was not surprising that Vischer made use of Luther, and Hamann and Bonhoeffer made use of Kohlbrügge and Vilmar; that both of them and others reached back to the interpretation of the Old Testament in the New. Everyone could be an ally who accepted the basic conception of the Old Testament inherent in the New Testament, namely, that the God of the Old Testament is the Father of Jesus Christ.[213]

In order for a relevant evaluation of Bonhoeffer to be successful, it is necessary to refer to three points which hang together.

(a) In the "theological preface" Bonhoeffer brought up the New Testament witness of David, because he wanted to interpret the Old Testament David stories in its light. In the second notation to the discussion on the Bible study, however, he decided that we have to read the Old Testament in the light

211. Von Rad, *ThBl* 14(1935), 254.
212. Nicolaisen, *op. cit.,* 173.
213. Compare the opinion of Herntrich on Vischer: "The significance of Vischer's book is that here the interpretation of the Old Testament, determined by the witness of the New Testament and by the resumption of this witness through the reformation," is established (*MPTh* 32[1936], 177).

of "the revelation which has taken place for us" (*GS* IV, 320). The revelation which has taken place for us—incarnation, crucifixion, and resurrection—is in any case something other than the New Testament witness of David![214] Indeed, he bears witness to it, both are not to be separated, but the testimony of the revelation which has taken place for us and the New Testament witness of David are to be differentiated. Consequently Bonhoeffer can be criticized with his own assertions. The key to the understanding of the Old Testament in the note just described is to be found already in the New Testament, vividly represented in the Emmaus story, in which the resurrection opens the Old Testament to the disciples (Luke 24:32).[215] This key belongs also to the New Testament's basic conception of the Old Testament which is decisive for us. We have alluded to the fact[216] that from the viewpoint of the notation (we see it in the context of Bonhoeffer's other statements about the incarnation, crucifixion, and resurrection) a fruitful path to the understanding of the Old Testament can open up.

(b) Bonhoeffer followed this fruitful path in his Bible study and certainly in the exposition of II Sam., chs. 11 to 19, which we have designated as the high point of the Bible study but not of it alone.[217] In this section the unintelligible expression "Christ was in David" is nowhere to be found. But David is understood as the prototype and shadow of Christ, so that one

214. From the lecture "Re-presentation of New Testament Texts" (Aug., 1935) compare the following sentences in which Bonhoeffer clearly states, even though in another context, the difference between the witness of the New Testament and him to whom it bears witness, Christ: "The New Testament is . . . witness, it is nothing itself, but bears witness to something else; it has no value in itself, but only as a witness to Christ, . . . it reaches beyond itself, its statements and words are . . . true and eternal and holy, . . . only insofar as they bear witness to Christ. . . . The entire New Testament . . . is to be interpreted as witness—not as . . . a textbook" (*GS* III, 315).

215. Compare Galley, *op. cit.*, 17, 58, and P. Stuhlmacher, "Theologische Probleme des Römerbriefpräskripts," *EvTh* 27(1967), 378 f., according to whom Paul used and interpreted the Old Testament from the standpoint of Christ.

216. See above, Chapter III.C.4.

217. See above, Chapter III.C.1.

can ask whether Bonhoeffer comes down close to the questionable phrase "Christ in David." In any case, it seems clear that with the assertion about David as the "prototype and shadow" of Christ, which also is inferred indirectly from the New Testament, Bonhoeffer has remained within the designated framework of the New Testament's basic conception of the Old Testament. That is to say, since the God of the Old Testament is the God of the New Testament, correspondence in the action of this God will be evident as witnessed to by the Old and New Testaments. Moreover, it is noteworthy that in the exposition of II Sam., chs. 11 to 19, Bonhoeffer further pursued a course that he had followed in the Gideon sermon on Estomihi (Quinquagesima) Sunday in 1933 and in the sermon on "Moses- und Aarons-Kirche" ("Moses' and Aaron's Church") from May 28, 1933: God's New Testament people see represented in what he brought to pass with his Old Testament people what he can bring to pass with them.[218] Hence, not only through the encounter with Kohlbrügge did Bonhoeffer become a proclamation (typological) oriented interpreter of the Old Testament.[219]

With his assertion that "Christ was in David" has he not only further pursued the course, which he had chosen previously in

218. *GS* IV, 109–117, 123–129; the Gideon story "a fairy tale like others also? Whoever speaks in this way has not understood that Gideon lives and that the Gideon story repeats itself daily in Christendom" (115).

219. It is also valid then, if not established fact, that Bonhoeffer was acquainted with the interpretation of Ps. 51 by Kohlbrügge in which the latter established a relationship between the resurrection of Jesus Christ and what happened to David after his sin. "David is struck by the power, which lies in the resurrection of Christ, so that he is courageous and cries for mercy that he not perish in his abandonment and not be smothered in his death which hovers over him." Also David was to experience anew this grace (i.e., of the Lord) in all its power and glory in a specific way and was to be made certain of the merciful promise of Christ (made to him long ago) in a way that he would remember it; so that it might be his merciful promise, in such fashion that he might come to know not only the reconciliation but also the power of the resurrection of Christ in the midst of distress, as he previously may not have known it" (*Gott sei mir gnädig! Ein Wort des Trostes und der Zucht für Arme und Elende nach Anleitung des 51. Psalms*, 1855, 4, 16).

Creation and Fall in 1932/33, when in like manner he interpreted Gen. 1:1 f. as though it were the discourse of the resurrection itself (*SF* 18)?[220] We have already stated a lack of understanding in regard to this interpretation. Bonhoeffer did not actually become interested in the question of "Christ in the Old Testament" merely through the acquaintance with Kohlbrügge. It will become apparent that Bonhoeffer did not enlarge on one of his own points of departure (July 31, 1935).

(c) In the sermons from 1933 already mentioned and also in the exposition of II Sam., chs. 11 to 19, Bonhoeffer interpreted the Old Testament "typologically." In the "theological preface" he discusses the matter without utilizing the concept itself, when he states that David is Christ's representation in word and image. Thereby "a special level of relationship of the Old Testament to the New Testament is revealed" (*GS* IV, 297). Examples for it have already been cited.[221] They show that Bonhoeffer was moving toward a typological interpretation represented by G. von Rad, H. W. Wolff, and W. Eichrodt.[222] Typological exegesis proceeds from the essential correlation of the Old and New Testaments in the mutual possession of the revelation of God.[223] It seeks to grasp

220. See above, Chapter III.B.3.
221. See above, Chapter III.D.2.
222. Von Rad, *Theologie des Alten Testaments,* Vol. II, 375–387; Wolff, "Zur Hermeneutik des Alten Testaments" (*PAH* 140–180); "Das Geschichtsverständnis der alttestamentlichen Prophetie" (*PAH,* esp. 327 ff., fn. 14); Eichrodt, "Ist die typologische Exegese sachgemässe Exegese?" (*PAH,* 205–226). In our opinion the last, in spite of its cautious limitation of Von Rad, can be included with these.
The differentiation between word witness and image witness in Bonhoeffer reminds one of J. C. K. von Hofmann, who in his *Biblische Hermeneutik* (1880) differentiated between the context of the deed revelation of God and that of his "word revelation," so that on the one hand he exalts "the theological understanding of the Old Testament account of history" (163–173), and on the other hand "the theological understanding of the Old Testament salvation proclamation" (173–188). In the fall of 1936 Bonhoeffer procured this book (*DB* 642). That is a year after the Bible study "King David." Of course, an earlier acquaintance with it is possible.
223. Eichrodt, *PAH,* 212; Wolff, *PAH,* 167.

the text as clearly as possible according to its inner Old Testamental meaning.[224] Above all, it reminds the exegetes of the Old Testament of the "consideration of the relevant context," namely, of the New Testament,[225] and in so doing seeks to establish an unmistakable "structural analogy" between the saving action of both Testaments.[226] Its goal is to point to the "realization of salvation throughout a history which is formed from the same divine common purpose in the Old Testament and in the New Testament community,"[227] or to lead "to the 'proclamation' interpretation of the Old Testament."[228] The interpretations of Bonhoeffer mentioned thus far belong fundamentally within this incompletely described[229] framework,[230] even if some things militate against it.[231]

In summary and at the same time moving to the next point, it can be said that on the question of "Christ in the Old Testa-

224. Von Rad, *Theologie des Alten Testaments*, Vol. II, 383; Eichrodt, *PAH*, 213; Wolff, *PAH*, 163.

225. Wolff, *PAH*, 162, fn. 81; Von Rad, *Theologie des Alten Testaments*, Vol. II, 377; Eichrodt, *PAH*, 223.

226. Von Rad, *Theologie des Alten Testaments*, Vol. II, 373.

227. Eichrodt, *PAH*, 221.

228. Wolff, *PAH*, 167.

229. Above all, the typological interpretation fails to allow for a cyclical understanding of time, as Bultmann supposes (*ThLZ* 75[1950], 47 ff.); instead, a linear understanding of time, which sees history as striving for a goal under God. Hence the relation of the types is one of intensification and perfection (Eichrodt, *PAH*, 205 f., 214 f.; Von Rad, *Theologie des Alten Testaments*, Vol. II, 382, 399; Wolff, *PAH*, 327).

230. Compare Grunow, "The studies and sermons of Gerhard von Rad and Hans Walter Wolff follow the same path, which Bonhoeffer had in mind" (*MW* I, 65). Compare also the third section, "Der Vollzug typologischer Interpretation," by Wolff, *PAH*, 163–180, at the close of which he considers Bonhoeffer's thoughts on the Old Testament from *WE* and suggests that the "Old Testament helps eschatological existence in this world," if we interpret it typologically (180); see below, Chapter III.E.5 and Chapter IV.

231. For example, the interpretation of the escape of David over the Kidron brook (*GS* IV, 317) which Bonhoeffer brings into relationship with Jesus' going over this brook on the night before his crucifixion. Grunow (*MW* I, 71) calls this interpretation "the utmost extremity," which Bonhoeffer "risks in this respect"—but especially the statements of Bonhoeffer about "Christ in David"; we "can say no more, the historical David" is "a prototype of Christ" (Von Rad, *Theologie des Alten Testaments*, Vol. II, 384).

ment," in his Bible study "King David" of October, 1935, Bonhoeffer abandoned the course indicated in the lecture of July, 1935, and followed another which is not practicable for us, because it relativizes historical-critical research too much and speaks of a "personal presence" of Christ in the Old Testament. Each of these points should now be more closely examined, with a look at two additional interpretations of Bonhoeffer. Therefore, here as well it will be possible to arrive at a discriminate judgment regarding Bonhoeffer, which in addition to all criticism suggests that he belongs to those who reclaimed the lost Old Testament for the German Evangelical Church.

3. Bible Study "The Reconstruction of Jerusalem According to Ezra and Nehemiah" (April 21, 1936)[232]

Bonhoeffer delivered the Bible study on Ezra and Nehemiah during a meeting of the first course at Finkenwalde. It goes back to a sermon, no longer extant, from January 21, 1936, on the Sunday following the conference of the Pomeranian Confessing Church pastors and vicars in Bredow, when there arose a severe argument over the position on the Pomeranian Church Committee formed on December 27, 1935. During the meeting in April, Bonhoeffer delivered the paper "Zur Frage nach der Kirchengemeinschaft" ("On the Question of the Church Community") (GS II, 217–241). Both paper and Bible study alike are a warning not to acknowledge the authority of the church committees, but to follow the adopted course.

Furthermore, Bonhoeffer proceeded in his Bible study: God, who has judged his people, awakens his people who go their own way alone, alone on the strength of his call and of their own free will, without acquiescing to the world's bid to assist in the building of the church, indeed consciously taking upon themselves the consequences of the rejection of the

232. On the *Sitz im Leben* of this Bible study and its criticism, compare *DB* 567 ff., 587 ff., and 597 ff.

world's assistance; that is, prepared to be politically suspicious. God awakens his people, who consciously devote themselves to obedience to the Scripture and the Word of God and consciously accomplish the purification of the community through the strict discipline of the church. The conclusion of the Bible study reads:

> The church is one then and now. The paths along which God leads his church are always the same, through judgment and punishment and destruction the community hears anew the call of God and his promise. But where God's promise is understood and taken seriously, there will be the church. Where a community is ready to have nothing more than the Word, there it stands before God as the community of justified sinners. Finally, the following must be considered: "and since our enemies heard that, all heathen were afraid, those who were round about us and the courage escaped them; then they observed that this work was of God." (*GS* IV, 335)

This Bible study was published in the *Junge Kirche* of July 18, 1936. It was not long before a refutation appeared. On August 4, 1936, Friedrich Baumgärtel, the Greifswald Old Testament scholar, completed the preface to his work *Die Kirche ist Eine— die alttestamentlich-jüdische und die Kirche Jesu Christi? Eine Verwahrung gegen die Preisgabe des Alten Testaments.*[233] He attacked Bonhoeffer severely: "If Bonhoeffer's manipulated method of interpreting the Old Testament succeeds in the church, the Old Testament will be surrendered and lost to the church."[234] He saw the goal of the Bible study as the realization that the church then and now is one.[235] Bonhoeffer came to this realization because he interpreted the Old Testament "arbitrarily." He had in view one picture of the church today and found words and situations in Ezra and Nehemiah that "recall many

233. See also the exchange of correspondence between Baumgärtel and Baumann, *GS* IV, 336–343.
234. Baumgärtel, *Die Kirche ist Eine,* 17.
235. *Ibid.,* 5.

things in this picture." We may grant that particular passages are fruitful, "but it is impossible . . . to seek out a row of singular passages on the basis of arbitrary interpretation and combine them with a properly constructed picture of the 'church at that time,' which is well ladened with the picture of the ecclesiastical structure which one carries in his own heart."[236]

Baumgärtel's criticism is justified insofar as Bonhoeffer actually had sought out singular passages. For example, on the basis of Ezra 1:4; 6:4,8; 7:6,15 f. and 8:25, Baumgärtel can say with reason that the community of God does not reject foreign aid; "rather, one effectively makes use of this aid."[237] Bonhoeffer rests one-sidedly on Ezra 8:22. Baumgärtel is right when he determines on the basis of Ezra 1:1 ff.; 6:3 ff.; 5:14; 7:26 that the foundation of the church at that time "took place in alliance with the power of the state."[238] Bonhoeffer rests one-sidedly on Ezra 4:3. Baumgärtel is also right when he attacks Bonhoeffer because in the entire Bible study nothing is said about the fact that the church, "whose foundation was laid in the days of Ezra and Nehemiah, became the church of the Pharisees and scribes, who brought Jesus Christ to the cross."[239] Bonhoeffer is one-sided!

We must agree with Baumgärtel that Bonhoeffer arbitrarily interpreted the Old Testament and therefore surrendered it when it concerned the exegetical-dogmatical question regarding the identity of the church at that time and today. But this is not his concern. The statement that the church then and now is one, against which the attack of Baumgärtel arose, was not the goal, but *only* the presupposition of his Bible study. And this presupposition is Biblical! Bonhoeffer did not want to bring about a new exegetical-dogmatical understanding for those participating in the meeting, who like himself were distressed by the question of how the Confessing Church in Pom-

236. *Ibid.*, 16.
237. *Ibid.*, 6.
238. *Ibid.*, 7 f.
239. *Ibid.*, 13.

erania should pursue its course in the spring of 1936. Rather, he wanted to communicate to them the realities of God's will; he wanted to proclaim to them what they should *do*. For Bonhoeffer, proclamation did not consist in carefully weighed and considered teaching, which is as general and nonobligatory as possible, but in the imparting of Biblical words and their interpretation, which are carefully selected in view of concrete situations, not with the goal of assisting the hearer to reach an opinion about past events, but to move him toward the simple action of the Word heard in the present.

Did Bonhoeffer surrender the Old Testament? Yes, if one looks at the Old Testament only as the object of historical-critical research. No, to the contrary: he won it anew for the church, if one views this Bible study according to H. J. Kraus as witness to what is "the actual culmination of theological reflection about the Old Testament," namely, its discovery as the book "of the wandering people of God who are moving through idolatry and judgments but who as they go their way may always hear and heed the voice of the living God anew."[240]

240. Kraus, *op. cit.*, 393. We agree with the opinion of Bethge that this Bible study "is both right and wrong at the same time. It does not withstand examination in a Biblical historical context, but its homiletical assertions stand, namely, that the church is not escaping judgment and is not able to find its truth in any meaningful restoration, rather only in the independent renewal of its faith" (*DB* 600). The problem arising here, since proper historical-critical exegesis and proper homiletics have a certain relationship to one another, requires its examination. Baumgärtel would like to differentiate theological and ecclesiastical-political statement and says that in his writing he is concerned "only with the theological matter" (Foreword). Yet, at that time it did not work. Baumgärtel himself senses it when he writes: "What depressingly lays hold of me is the feeling that this incomprehensiveness has to do not only with an antithesis to 'scientific' comprehension" (14), but, we might add, with an antithesis which arises out of its diverse position on the Confessing Church. On "rivalry" between Greifswald and Finkenwalde during the church struggle, see *DB* 497, 500 f. and 600 f. On Baumgärtel's position during the church struggle, see his self-appraisal in his "Wider die Kirchenkampflegenden," 57 f.

4. *Sermon on Psalm 58 (July 11, 1937)*

In spite of all criticism, Bonhoeffer was not deterred from interpreting the Bible as he had done in the Bible study discussed here. An additional example of such interpretation is his sermon on Psalm 58, which would not have originated, according to Bethge, if he had not considered anew "a risk in the transition from the exegesis to the sermon."[241]

Bonhoeffer begins his sermon with the words: "Is this frightful psalm of vengeance our prayer? May we pray like this?" He ends with the sentence: "Thus we have learned to pray this psalm" (*GS* IV, 414, 422).[242]

A treatment of this sermon must call attention to the steps that lead to this goal:

(a) First of all, the answer to the initial question is completely clear. We cannot pray this psalm, not because we are too good, however, but because we are too sinful and evil (*GS* IV, 414).

(b) Only a guiltless person can pray this psalm. Since Jesus Christ, the guiltless one, was in David, David could pray this psalm (*GS* IV, 414 f.).

(c) We do not accuse, Jesus Christ does. We are among the accused (*GS* IV, 415).

(d) Jesus Christ accuses because human beings are treated unjustly by unjust and incompassionate judges, who clear the way for deeds of violence: Psalm 58:2 f. (*GS* IV, 415 f.).

(e) The perfect innocence sees into the depths of malice (Ps. 58:4): Satan has already taken hold of his own in the womb (*GS* IV, 416).

(f) The godless are like deaf snakes who cannot hear the voice of the magician. Their ears are deaf to the mercy of God, their mouths do not speak for the law of God: Psalm 58:5 f. (*GS* IV, 417).

---

241. *DB* 600. Bethge adds also the Judas Sermon (*GS* IV, 406–412) and the meditation of Ps. 119 (*ibid.*, 505–543).

242. The page numbers in the text in parentheses are from *GS* IV.

(g) This understanding leads to prayer. God is implored with terrible desires for vengeance upon his enemies (*GS* IV, 417 f.).

(h) We should learn two things from that. First: in the presence of the enemies of God we can only pray to God, who alone has power over the enemies. Second: whoever prays to God for vengeance waives the right to his own vengeance.

(i) Therefore the only one who can pray this psalm is he who has given up all claim to the gratification of his own desire for vengeance.

(j) David breaks out in unmeasurable jubilation and describes in rapid pictures the quick end of the godless: Psalm 58:8–10.

(k) Because verse 11 concerns God alone and his justice, one may not be turned aside by it (*GS* IV, 419).

(l) "Whoever shrinks back from this joy over the vengeance of God and over the blood of the godless does not yet know what happened on the cross": here the wrath of God is fulfilled in the death of the Godless One upon the cross.

(m) Jesus Christ alone, as the one who bears the vengeance of God, may ask forgiveness for his enemies (*GS* IV, 420).

(n) Whoever comes to this Jesus Christ will not encounter the wrath and vengeance of God, but the vengeance of God will befall whoever does not come.

(o) God's judgment on the godless is carried out alone in the cross of Christ (*GS* IV, 421).

(p) We can join in praying this psalm in thanks for the pardon bestowed in the cross of Christ with the supplication that all enemies be brought under the cross of Christ and with the desire that the day of judgment draw near.

A rather full rendition of the sermon has been provided because its criticism must be extremely discriminate and therefore will necessitate one's coming back to it again and again. (1) In it Bonhoeffer moves very near to an orthodox interpretation but in spite of that it may not be designated as belonging in such a category; (2) a criticism that J. Fichtner has made on the psalm interpretation of Bonhoeffer[243] is correct at certain points but at others incorrect; (3) surprisingly here in this sermon the uniformity of Bonhoeffer's thought will be seen.

(1) On July 31, 1935, Bonhoeffer mentioned three viewpoints of an orthodox interpretation of the psalms: *(a)* It postulates that the "I" of the psalms is the "voice of Jesus Christ in his Old Testament community"; *(b)* the Biblical assertions of authorship are authentic; and *(c)* in the Psalter there is no ungodly prayer (*GS* III, 298).[244]

For Hengstenberg, whom Bonhoeffer cites as representative of such interpretation, the second and third viewpoints prove correct. According to him, David wrote eighty psalms besides forming pairs and cycles of psalms.[245] In his view the vengeance psalms are not ungodly, because they do not speak of a vengeance "which the offended individual seeks and carries out as such," but of "recompense in the service of God."[246] Bonhoeffer says the same thing. (See above, h and i.) Therefore, Hengstenberg interprets Psalm 58:11 f. in such a way that these verses are only for metaphorical understanding. When Saul fell upon his sword, it was the vengeance of God. "Then

243. J. Fichtner, "Vom Psalmbeten. Ist das Beten aller Psalmen der christlichen Gemeinde möglich und heilsam?" *Wort und Dienst, Jahrbuch der Theologischen Schule Bethel,* 1952, 38–60.

244. See above, Chapter III.D.1.

245. E. W. Hengstenberg, *Commentar über die Psalmen,* Vol. IV, 1852², 559 f. Hengstenberg defends David as the author of Ps. 58 in the following manner: the judges, who are spoken about in this psalm, are not the usual unjust judges who are unjust out of self-interest, rather they are judges who are driven by hate. However, during "the time of Saul" David was not handed over to such an unlawful court of justice when he was pursued by Saul (*ibid.,* Vol. III, 1851², 99 f.).

246. *Ibid.,* Vol. IV, 635; compare also 640: "In the psalms of vengeance we do not have before us the unintentional and careless effusions of subjective feelings, rather they are as a whole from the outset for use in the sanctuary (holy place); the singers enter with lucid consciousness as interpreters of the sacred feelings of the congregation, as organs of God to enoble their feelings. They return what they have received in the highest and purest hours of their lives."

David bathed his feet in the blood of the Godless One."[247] In his *Commentar über die Psalmen (Commentary on the Psalms),* however, there is not to be found a single passage which would permit the viewpoint that understood the "I" of the psalms as the voice of Jesus Christ in his Old Testament community. Following tradition he understands the customary psalms as Messianic.[248] Consequently, on this question Bonhoeffer is more orthodox than Hengstenberg![249] While Hengstenberg endeavors to show that David could indeed pray this psalm because he had to deal with unjust judges, the problem is "resolved" for Bonhoeffer in that Christ was in David.[250]

In spite of that, it would be wrong not to express the opinion concerning Bonhoeffer's interpretation of Psalm 58 that it is more orthodox than Hengstenberg. Particularly at verse 11 (see above, k and l), which is decisive for Bonhoeffer, his interpretation is much less metaphorical than Hengstenberg's. God's vengeance has fallen upon a truly Godless One, whose blood actually is spilled; the statement of Psalm 58:11b is metaphorical only insofar as it remains an illustration.[251]

247. *Ibid.,* Vol. III, 107.
248. Summary in *ibid.,* Vol. IV, 647–652.
249. In Kohlbrügge's interpretation of Ps. 51 (see above, fn. 201), on the other hand, there is a passage which comes very close to Bonhoeffer's thought that David could pray the psalm because Christ was in him. "If David were not discovered in Christ, and had not seen the salvation of Christ in all its fullness in the spirit of Christ, he could not have prayed this psalm" (Kohlbrügge, *Das 7. Kapitel des Briefes Pauli an die Römer,"* 20 f.)
Above all, Bonhoeffer's predecessor, Luther, understood the psalms of vengeance as prayers of Christ. Compare *WA* III, 192, 300; XIX, 552–615; XXXVIII, 39 (Ps. 58 as a prayer of Christ against the Jews). In *The Prayerbook of the Bible,* Bonhoeffer cites Luther seven times. In the meditation on Ps. 119, he cites him six times: *GS* IV, 547, 551, 552, 557, 560 f., 563, 569, 510, 512, 518, 523, 532, 533. A comprehensive examination of the Luther-Bonhoeffer relationship must take into account all these passages.
250. The statement that Christ in David prays the psalms is amplified in *The Prayerbook of the Bible,"* 1940, *GS* IV, 548. In *GL,* 1938, it is not found; only this, "Jesus Christ has prayed the psalms; it has become his prayerbook for all times. . . . Jesus Christ prays the psalms in his congregation" (36).
251. "God's wrath is extinguished and the blood of the just, in which we bathe ourselves, gives us a share in the victory of God. The blood of the

88

Bonhoeffer begins his exposition in a more orthodox way than Hengstenberg, but he concludes quite differently because he interprets the psalm with the crucified Godless One in view.[252] From that viewpoint he presumes to put Psalm 58 under the claim of Jesus Christ and his community.[253]

(2) J. Fichtner considers that to be a forbidding presumption. He was not acquainted with Bonhoeffer's sermon on Psalm 58, but comes to terms only with Bonhoeffer's thoughts on the vengeance psalms in *Gemeinsames Leben* (35–40; *Life Together*) and in *Gebetbuch der Bibel* (*GS* IV, 566 ff.; *Prayerbook of the Bible*), but his arguments also are pertinent for the sermon on Psalm 58. His criticism may be summarized as follows: in the vengeance psalms "a mirror is held up before us," in which we should see which dangers threaten all human prayer, namely, the spirit of retaliation. The spirit of these psalms conflicts with the "Spirit of Jesus Christ" (Luke 23:34). They are found at a "stage" where we Christians may no longer remain in prayer.[254] Therefore Fichtner cannot agree with Bonhoeffer's argumentation (*GL* 38) that because Christ is the one who prays these psalms, we, as members of the body of Jesus Christ, may pray them.[255]

It is interesting that in his sermon Bonhoeffer cites exactly the same word of Jesus that is specified by Fichtner as proof that the vengeance psalms contradict the Spirit of Christ: Luke

---

Godless One has become our redemption, it makes us pure from all sin" (*GS* IV, 421).

252. Compare the final sentence on the psalms of vengeance in *The Prayerbook of the Bible*. "Hence the crucified Jesus teaches us to pray the psalms of vengeance correctly" (*GS* IV, 568).

253. This sermon is partially the expansion of the lecture from July 31, 1935, according to which God enters the world of the Psalter, which remains as it is, so that Christ is in this world among the righteous and hostile. "Christ amid the righteous and hostile means, however, Christ, the crucified. This is intended in the double sense: (1) as the One chosen for the cross by God and (2) as the One nailed to the cross by men, One rejected by righteousness and unrighteousness" (*GS* III, 301).

254. Fichtner, *loc. cit.*, 59 f.

255. *Ibid.*, 45.

23:34. The context in which Bonhoeffer used the word of Jesus is as follows:

> In the hour of the fulfillment of God's vengeance on the Godless One in our psalm, Jesus Christ the innocent prays: Father, forgive them, for they do not know what they do (Luke 23:34). He who bore the vengeance, he alone could plead forgiveness for the godless; he alone then has made us free from the wrath and vengeance of God. He has brought his enemies forgiveness and no one may pray in the same way before him. He alone may do so. (*GS* IV, 420)

Both use the same word of Jesus and come to different conclusions. Both proceed from the viewpoint that Christ has no direct relationship to the psalm, but that it is mediated through Christ.[256] Both understand the vengeance psalm in the light of Christ the teacher; Bonhoeffer, in the light of Christ the *crucified*. Indeed, we can understand the vengeance psalms merely as a reflection of false human prayer if we view them only in the light of the teaching of Jesus independent of the cross. A psalm such as Psalm 58 is so obscure that the light of the teaching of Christ cannot illuminate it (as the Word of God). The light of the cross must fall upon it in order that it may be illuminated, or, more tersely expressed, it is not enough (insofar as we do not want to eliminate this psalm as an early religious stage which has been taken over) that Jesus Christ only steps *between* it and us or that we understand it only in his light (which is the assumption here), but Christ must enter into it.[257] Through such a statement the phrase "Christ in the Old Testament" acquires meaning. Bonhoeffer's sermon on Psalm 58 exemplifies the kind of exposition of the Old Testament in which, according to G. von Rad, "that which belongs to the Old Testament is dragged with vehemence directly into the light of Christ and it is then as if Christ himself

256. For Bonhoeffer, see above, Chapter III.D.1; Fichtner, *loc. cit.*, 40.
257. Compare above, fn. 253.

steps into the Old Testament event, fulfilling it and at the same time having it proceed from him."[258]

The justification for placing Psalm 58 under the claim of the crucified, Godless One is not affected by Fichtner's objections. On another point, however, one must agree with him. Bonhoeffer means not only that Christ lays claim to this psalm for himself, but also that he lays claim to it for his community. "Thus we have learned to pray this psalm." Fichtner stresses that we must differentiate between the proclamation of the psalms and the prayer of the psalms.[259] Hence, if we want to join in praying this psalm, as Bonhoeffer describes at the end of his sermon (see above), then we must consciously achieve a new interpretation. We can join in praying the words of the psalm only if we are conscious of another dimension of its meaning. The question is whether or not we have such a freedom in relation to the Bible that we can say what this psalm says with other words which require no completely new interpretation, if Christ lays claim to it. In the sermon everything that Bonhoeffer asserted can be enlarged upon, but to be conscious of everything in praying is an excessive demand and an unnecessary, difficult imposition. Therefore, Fichtner's objection is acceptable.

(3) By putting Psalm 58 under the claim of Christ and his church, Bonhoeffer dared to experiment. On the basis of it Bethge has shown that Bonhoeffer's interpretation tended "to experiment with how the canon of the Christian church taken seriously could become effective in connection with the interpretation of the Old Testament." It was a very necessary ex-

258. Von Rad, *Theologie des Alten Testaments,* Vol. II, 399 f. That we here characterize Bonhoeffer's interpretation with a phrase of Von Rad's and in other places point to Bonhoeffer's proximity to Von Rad is based on the fact that Von Rad himself says that today he would better understand Bonhoeffer's concern, which he could not understand at all at that time without giving up his own concern for the justification of historical-critical research (in *Begegnungen mit Dietrich Bonhoeffer,* 141). In the lecture of July 31, 1935, Bonhoeffer also had not yet renounced this justification; his sermon on Ps. 58 is partially an expansion of this lecture.
259. Fichtner, *loc. cit.,* 40.

periment, but just an experiment, because later he "experimented in an entirely different way"[260] without a lot of new orientation and without prior hermeneutical clarifications. In another place Bethge is of the opinion that Bonhoeffer's Christological interpretation of the Old Testament is only transitory.[261] C. Westermann considers Bonhoeffer's sermon on Psalm 45 a "direct Christological interpretation" and then remarks that "according to his last notes it is safe to assume that it was exactly here that a change started to take place in his thinking."[262] According to H. Schulte's opinion, in *Letters and Papers from Prison* there is to be found neither a customary Christological interpretation of the Old Testament which understands it as direct or indirect prophecy pointing to Christ, nor "a typology."[263] W. Rupprecht and K. H. Nebe, who only examine one period of Bonhoeffer's Old Testament interpretation, come to entirely different judgments regarding his attitude toward W. Vischer.[264]

Consequently Bonhoeffer in the stages of his thought development appears to show different faces also as an interpreter of the Old Testament. *Letters and Papers from Prison* contains no statements about the "Christ in David." Here he interprets the Song of Songs Christologically as a ordinary love song, while in 1940 he understands Psalm 45 in the usual Christological manner, as did Hengstenberg,[265] as the "song and the prayer of the love between Jesus, the king, and his community which belongs to him" (*GS* IV, 558). In *Letters and Papers from Prison* the main point to him is to understand the New Testament in the light of the Old Testament, which he rarely had done up to that point.

Nevertheless, with these examples no "completely differ-

260. Letter to this author from Nov. 12, 1966. Compare Ott, *op. cit.*, 57 f.; see above, fn. 147.
261. *DB* 968; see above, fn. 113.
262. *DB* 180.
263. H. Schulte, *EvTh* 22 (1962), 442.
264. See above, fn. 6.
265. Hengstenberg, *Commentar über die Psalmen*, Vol. II, 1850², 401 ff.

ent" experimentation can be proved. How, however, had Bonhoeffer changed? We believe that changes occurred not in the fundamentals but only in the incidentals. Bonhoeffer always understood the Old Testament as the book of Christ. That can be shown by a comparison of the sermon on Psalm 58 with two comments on the Old Testament in *Letters and Papers from Prison* and with his thoughts on the "world come of age."

(a) In the letter from the Second Sunday in Advent, 1943, in which Bonhoeffer says something about the Old Testament which he had not said up to that point,[266] appeared the sentence: "Only if the wrath and vengeance of God on his enemies (as attested in the Old Testament) remains a reality can our heart be somewhat touched by forgiveness and love of enemy" (*WE* 92/113). The sermon on Psalm 58 is an expansion of this sentence, which, if we want to understand it in keeping with Bonhoeffer, is comprehensible only in relation to Christ. And that means actually *only* in the light of Christ. The Christ, whom the vengeance and wrath of God strike, forgives his enemies who have crucified him. In both instances Bonhoeffer's intention is directed against every attempt to diminish the Old Testament to an "early religious stage."[267] Hence, in 1942 Bonhoeffer did not experiment in a way that was "entirely different" from the way in 1937.

(b) We have attempted to understand Bonhoeffer's statement about the Song of Songs in *Letters and Papers from Prison* as follows: he reads it as an ordinary love song and interprets it Christologically; and on the strength of that we showed that such an interpretation (among others) was achieved with the help of a statement by Bonhoeffer from the year 1935.[268] Yet this interpretation does not stand in complete contrast to the

266. See below, Chapter III.E.5.
267. This opposing viewpoint, which Bonhoeffer had in mind on the Second Sunday in Advent, 1943, is also the viewpoint of his critic Fichtner, for whom the psalms of vengeance remain at a level on which Christians no longer may pray. See above, Chapter III.D.4.(2).
268. See above, Chapter III.C.3.

sermon on Psalm 58, in which Bonhoeffer, as in other interpretations from this period, interprets the Old Testament in certain respects both typologically and in the "usual Christological manner." Hence, in 1944 Bonhoeffer understood the Song of Songs as claimed by Christ just as he understood Psalm 58 in 1935. There is no fundamental difference in the conclusion or in the path to the conclusion: he understands both texts in the light of Christ. That he reads Psalm 58 in the light of the crucified Lord, but the Song of Songs in the light of the incarnate Lord, according to our interpretation, should not conceal the essential agreement, rather only confirm that from October, 1935, onward Bonhoeffer himself pursued his own course in the interpretation of the Old Testament, namely, "the Old Testament must be read in the light of the incarnation and the crucifixion." In 1944 he let the interpretation of the Old Testament in the light of the incarnation come more strongly into its own.[269] Therefore, in 1944 he no longer needed to interpret the Song of Songs as he had interpreted Psalm 45 in 1940 in a traditional Christological manner. This change is very noticeable; nevertheless, it is only incidental insofar as Bonhoeffer only came to the traditional Christological interpretation, in which he is partly more orthodox than Hengstenberg (for which several passages in the *Prayerbook of the Bible* have just been cited[270]), when the fundamentals of an interpretation of the Old Testament to which he always held fast were already clear to him. Thus, once again there is no "entirely different" experimentation!

(c) Also, as one looks at Bonhoeffer's thoughts on the "world come of age," which above all have led to the conclusion that the Bonhoeffer in *Letters and Papers from Prison* is very different from the one of the earlier works,[271] if one compares them with the sermon on Psalm 58 a fundamental agreement can be determined. In both instances Bonhoeffer's thinking

269. Compare above, fn. 147.
270. See especially the statements on the "Christ in David" (*GS* IV, 548 f.).
271. See especially H. Müller, *Von der Kirche zur Welt,* 357 f.

proceeds from the crucified, Godless or God-abandoned One. He is the reason why Bonhoeffer recognizes that Christ has laid claim to Psalm 58, which belongs to the psalms that, in the opinion of many, stand completely apart from the Spirit of Christ; and it is the same Christ who moves him to recognize that Christ likewise has laid claim to the world become godless, which in the opinion of many has fallen away from God and Jesus Christ. Just as Psalm 58, in which the vengeance of God is called down upon the godless, belongs to Jesus Christ, so does the godless world because God's vengeance was called down on him as the Godless One and he was abandoned by God. Figuratively speaking: Bonhoeffer experiments with the same method but on different subject matter. Therefore, the result of the respective experiments can only be judged as appropriate to Bonhoeffer when one does not stick to the subject matter but examines the method and it is the same in both instances. It might have been expected that the principal statement on the thesis of this work would result from the treatment of Bonhoeffer's contributions "on the problem: Christ in the Old Testament." The Old Testament quite easily could be the book of Christ if Christ were to be found *in* it. However, because the *in* in part remains questionable— "Christ was in David"—we have not made that statement. Our position has been strengthened by the examination of the Bible study on Ezra and Nehemiah. On the one hand, because of the problematical position Bonhoeffer takes in the study, which we have established, especially regarding historical-critical research, it remains part of a questionable problem, since in both instances Bonhoeffer reaches back to a method of interpretation that is not permissible for us. On the other hand, however, as church-struggle-related interpretation, the Bible study both in essence and in the period in which it was written belongs together with parts of the Bible study "King David" and the Old Testament sermons of 1933. In view of these interpretations it follows that the Old Testament is the book of Christ for Bonhoeffer because the present action and the concrete will of God can be proclaimed to the community of Christ.

The phrase "Christ in the Old Testament" acquires for us only a plastic meaning: it is not enough to understand the vengeance psalms only in the light of Christ, rather Christ must *step into* them. At the basis of this metaphor lies the idea that Bonhoeffer sees the vengeance psalms fulfilled in the crucified Lord. From this viewpoint it is possible for Bonhoeffer's statement about the Old Testament as the book of Christ, in contrast to the result established in section C, to take on a new nuance. To understand the Old Testament in the light of Christ leads to the understanding that it is made valid for us by Christ and belongs to him. Bonhoeffer recognizes again and again that nothing from the Old Testament has to be excluded when it is brought into relation to Christ. Also Jesus Christ the crucified lays claim to the vengeance psalms which are more offensive than the excessively human stories and the Song of Songs. Hence, the Old Testament belongs in its entirety to him. "Christ in the Old Testament" means then that the Old Testament as the book of Christ belongs *totally* to this Christ because the *entire* Old Testament is fulfilled in him.

E. THE UNDERSTANDING OF THE NEW TESTAMENT IN THE LIGHT OF THE OLD TESTAMENT

In his letters from prison Bonhoeffer comes to an interpretation of the Bible in which the second direction of the "double movement of a reciprocal understanding"[272] above all is evident, the movement from the Old to the New Testament. He had already carried out this movement in *Creation and Fall*,[273] but now it gains wider treatment.[274]

272. See Von Rad, *Theologie des Alten Testaments*, Vol. II, 387; see above, Chapter III.A.
273. See above, Chapter III.B.(2).
274. In the introduction we mentioned that the chronological arrangement sometimes points to an objective arrangement. To the latter arrangement

In the first seven months of his imprisonment he had "read through the Old Testament two and a half times and learnt a great deal" (*WE* 76/93; Nov. 18, 1943).[275] It may be assumed that *what* he learned can be found at least in part in the letter to his friend dated the Second Sunday in Advent, 1943.

> My thoughts and feelings seem to be getting more and more like those of the Old Testament, and in recent months I have been reading the Old Testament much more than the New. [1a] It is only when one knows the unutterability of the name of God that one can utter the name of Jesus Christ; [2a] it is only when one loves life and the earth so much that without them everything seems to be over that one may believe in the resurrection and a new world; [3a] it is only when one submits to God's law that one may speak of grace; [4a] and it is only when God's wrath and vengeance are hanging as grim realities over the heads of one's enemies that something of what it means to love and forgive them can touch our hearts. [5] In my opinion it is not Christian to want to take our thoughts and feelings too quickly and too directly from the New Testament. We have already talked about this

belongs the fact that after the introduction of the idea of the movement from the Old Testament to the New Testament, Bonhoeffer first developed this idea in *WE*. Schwarzwäller feels that only under the condition met by Bonhoeffer—that is, "that only in reference to Jesus Christ can the Old Testament legitimately be used in the church"—can the question concerning the canonical validity of the Old Testament in the church (see fn. 112) be raised in such a way so that in moving back into the Old Testament from the standpoint of Jesus Christ the attempt to move forward toward him from the standpoint of the Old Testament is avoided. That does not mean that such lines of movement are no longer to be pursued; to the contrary, they are to be investigated with utmost care.

275. See also *WE* 33/39. Bonhoeffer especially loved Job and the Psalter. Above all, during the imprisonment Jer., ch. 45, became significant: *WE* 53/64 (also Ps. 60:4); 125/154, 163/202, 200/249. Ott begins his book about Bonhoeffer with a presentation of this evidence and writes, "The word of the Bible is somewhat like a key word for the self-understanding of Bonhoeffer's Christian and theological existence in this particularly meaningful final period" (Ott, *op. cit.*, 13).

several times, and every day confirms my opinion. (*WE* 92/112 f.; Eng. tr., 156 f.)[276] One cannot and must not speak the ultimate word before the penultimate. We live in the penultimate and believe the ultimate, don't we?

This first long letter on the Old Testament in *Letters and Papers from Prison* contains important statements. The questions touched on here Bonhoeffer had already discussed from time to time with Bethge. Therefore these sentences which we have before us are the result of prolonged contemplation and numerous discussions. First, they refer to later statements on the Old Testament in the letters[277] and to earlier Biblical interpretations of Bonhoeffer which help us to understand these sentences. Secondly, they imply a position against an open or concealed Marcionite view of the Old Testament. Thirdly, with the final sentences of the letter excerpt cited above he establishes a connection between that which he pursues in the *Ethics* about the "ulimate" and the "penultimate" things and the relation of the Old Testament to the New.

1. a) *The Unutterableness of the Name of God (Second Sunday in Advent, 1943)*

Behind the phrase on the unutterableness of the name of God stand personal experiences of Bonhoeffer which he submitted to careful theological scrutiny. In the letter of November 21, 1943, he had written to his friend about this: "My fear and distrust of 'religiosity' have become greater than ever here. The fact that the Israelites *never* uttered the name of God always makes me think, and I can understand it better as I go on" (*WE* 185/104; Eng. tr., 135).

In connection with the unutterableness of the name of God

276. The numbers are inserted by the author and indicate the arrangement of this section. After a few sentences comes the section on the objectionable stories of the Old Testament treated above in Chapter III.C.2; see below, Chapter III.E.5 for further discussion on this subject.

277. Bethge considers this letter among those which after April, 1944, already state the idea (*DB* 965).

one must consider not only the rewriting of the name of God in the late Israelite period but also the revelation of the name of God in Ex., ch. 3. The name of God was not for the Israelites, as it was for other people, the means of having control over their God. Here as well the texts of the Old Testament are to be mentioned in which the name of God is only rarely uttered, as in the Joseph stories, the Proverbs, and the Song of Songs. Job may be cited as well,[278] for whom the name of God was unutterable for a long time so that he remained firm in the defense against the doctrinarian answers of his friends.

According to Bonhoeffer's view, one must know that God's name in the Old Testament is unutterable for a variety of reasons, if one wants to speak the name of Jesus Christ relevantly. That knowledge is requisite[279] to the proper use of this name. To what extent, Bonhoeffer does not explain. However, in the letter of April 30, 1944, he did say more on the question of speaking relevantly of God and again the Old Testament is mentioned in this context.

b) *Speaking of God "at the Center" (April 30, 1944)*

On April 30, 1944, Bonhoeffer communicated to his friend for the first time the thoughts of the religionless world, the necessary religionless Christianity, and a "secular" proclama-

278. See above, fn. 275.
279. That the understanding of the New Testament message is contingent upon the Old Testament message is stated with W. Kreck's reservation as follows: If we mean that "the New Testament proclamation of Christ finds its legitimate prior understanding in the encounter with the Old Testament," then is not the assertion withdrawn "that the Word of God itself brings its own horizon of understanding? From this perspective, which we attempted to recast in a trinitarian manner, God, the Father, only can be known through his Son Jesus Christ in the Holy Ghost. Therefore, the Old Testament is not concerned with a 'natural theology' so to speak or with an outline of an Israelite philosophy of religion, which could open the way to the gospel. . . . It should indeed be said that the message of Christ gains its horizon of understanding which it itself brings by taking up the witness of the Old Testament and we cannot ignore that if we ask about the reality of the Word of God" (Kreck, *Die Wirklichkeit des Wortes Gottes, ThEx* NF 134[1966], 45). After the citation of Bonhoeffer's letter of the Second Sunday in Advent, 1943, a few remarks on it follow. See below, fn. 314.

tion. "How do we speak . . . in a 'secular' way about 'God'?" —is one of his questions (*WE* 146/180). His answer begins with the confession of the personal experience that he is often reluctant to mention God by name to religious people, while he uses it in front of religionless people "as the occasion presents itself quite calmly and as self-evident." This experience stands in connection with the reports of the letter from November 18, 1943. He sees his reluctance based on the fact that the religious people actually always speak of God as the *deus ex machina* and that is on human boundaries. Since it is questionable to Bonhoeffer whether death and sin are "still real boundaries" for men today,[280] it is also questionable for him to speak of God on these human boundaries. He writes:

> I should like to speak of God not on the boundaries but at the center. . . .[281] As to the boundaries, it seems to me better to be silent and leave the insoluble unsolved. . . . God's "beyond" is not the beyond of our cognitive faculties. The transcendence of epistemological theory has nothing to do with the transcendence of God, God is beyond in the midst of our life. The church stands, not at the boundaries where human powers give out, but in the middle of the village. That is how it is in the Old Testament, and in this sense we still read the New Testament far too little in the light of the Old." (*WE* 147 f./182; Eng. tr., 282)[282]

In view of the last sentence the connection with the letter of the Second Sunday in Advent, 1943, is clear. From the Old Testament we should recognize—that is, according to Bonhoeffer's "religionless" and "secular" interpretation—how we

280. This author's italics. Death and sin are still boundaries, but no longer "real" ones.

281. This sentence could also read: I would like to speak of God not on these boundaries, rather on the real boundaries. "Real" boundary and "in the middle" mean the same thing according to *SF* (see below, fn. 286)!

282. We shall not take into account the sentence on the church. In our view the "that is how it is in the Old Testament" is related not only to this sentence but also to those which precede.

can speak the name of God today.[283] If he means that God "at the center" must be spoken of, he expresses this idea first in the form of a desire: "I should like to speak of God . . ."; but it need not remain a desire, because speaking of God "at the center" means to follow the Old Testament, since God is to be measured in the light of the Old Testament.

Bonhoeffer himself had recognized that in part already in 1932/33 with the interpretation of Gen. 2:8–17 and ch. 3 in *Creation and Fall.*[284] We should let ourselves be addressed by the "old metaphorical language of magic, because *we* are the ones in mind." The metaphor is this:

> In the middle of the garden there stand two trees with particular names connecting them with human existence in a particular way: the tree of life and the tree of the knowledge of good and evil. To the latter is attached the prohibition to eat of its fruit: the threat of death. (*SF* 59; Eng. tr., 50)[285]

Of the tree of life only this is said: *"It was in the middle."* Bonhoeffer interprets the intention in this particular metaphor in the following manner:

283. The difference that exists between the two letters—in one instance concerning the appropriate articulation of the name of *God* and in the other that of the name of *Christ*—is not of great importance, since in both cases the concern is with the kind of speaking of God, who revealed himself in Christ, that is demanded today. The distinction between God and Christ lies in the fact that in the conditional sentence Bonhoeffer speaks of an essential aspect of the Old Testament proclamation, but in the main sentence he mentions the New Testament name.

284. J. Moltmann has already alluded to that. He calls Bonhoeffer's idea that God meets man in the midst of life a "splendid thesis" (*Herrschaft Christi und soziale Wirklichkeit nach Dietrich Bonhoeffer, ThEx* NF 71[1959], 35, fn. 38). Compare also Nebe, *op. cit.,* 60 f.

285. In *SF,* Bonhoeffer only partially recognizes that God must be spoken of "in the middle," because with regard to the contents of the text he sees the real boundary determined by death, which in 1944 along with sin has become questionable as the "real boundary." Bonhoeffer remains firm in the demand for a relevant speaking of God made in *SF* and also in *WE,* but he finds it necessary to renew the contents of the form. The problem of continuity and change in Bonhoeffer's development is here *in nuce* apparent.

The life that comes forth from God is in the middle. This means that God, who gives life, is in the middle. In the middle of the world which is at Adam's disposal and over which he has been given dominion is not Adam himself but the tree of divine life. Adam's life comes from the middle which is not Adam himself but God. (*SF* 60; Eng. tr., 51)

Therefore, first we can speak of God "in the middle" because God is in the middle of the life which he gives.

Secondly: if God speaks to man, then his speech refers to the middle of human life. Then the tree of the knowledge of good and evil, to which the prohibition is attached, "like the tree of life stands in the middle of the garden" (*SF* 61). Adam is addressed by this prohibition both in his freedom and in his creatureliness, the latter because his boundary is shown to him, but his boundary "in the middle," his "real boundary."[286] In other words, God speaks to man in the form of a prohibition and then this prohibition meets man in the middle of his life.

Thirdly: in view of the fallen Adam, who is of important consequence, it is established that one must speak of God "in the middle." The fall of Adam and Eve consists in the fact that they eat from the tree in the middle of the garden. According to Bonhoeffer, this means: "the middle is tread upon, the boundary is transgressed; now man stands in the middle without a boundary" (*SF* 62). It is man who must live out of himself, who is alone, who as such is like God. He has lost his creatureliness, because he has lost his boundary (*SF* 91).[287] Hence, as limitless man "he admits nothing beyond from which anything can be said about him" (*SF* 92; Eng. tr., 73).

286. Compare above, fn. 281. Bonhoeffer interprets the picture of the prohibition in the following manner: "The boundary of man is in the middle of his existence, not on the edge; the boundary which is sought on the edge is the boundary of his condition, of his technology . . . , of his possibility. The boundary in the middle is the boundary of his reality, of his true existence" (*SF* 62).

287. From the standpoint of Bonhoeffer's presupposition this radical statement, so controversial in the history of dogma, is necessary.

In order to become the image of God once again, he must be addressed by God in the middle of his life. God "does so in Jesus Christ, the cross, and the church." In the cross of Christ the limitless man receives a new center (*SF* 120).[288] If God were to speak to man on the fringe of his existence, he would leave man as he is in the middle and would not make, out of him who has become "like God," a man in the image of God.

According to the Old Testament the encounter of God with man is so structured that God meets man in the middle of his life, first because God himself is the middle of his life and secondly because God addresses man in the middle of his life by his prohibition and thirdly because man is only in the image of God if God, and not man himself, stands in the middle of his life. Therefore God must be spoken of as "in the middle of life," and, to be sure, he is the God who is proclaimed to us in the New Testament. This is what the train of thought in the letter of April 30, 1944, is driving at: for an interpretation of the New Testament which keeps in view its witness of God it is necessary to observe *how* the Old Testament speaks of God. The Old Testament prescribes the structures which an interpretation of the New Testament witness of God must follow.[289]

The same conclusion had resulted from the examination of the sentences on the unutterableness of the name of God in the letter dated the Second Sunday in Advent, 1943; Bonhoeffer sees acquaintance with these structures as a presupposition to a relevant utterance of the name.

Yet something else is to be pointed out. Bonhoeffer is concerned with the question of how God can be spoken of today. In the letter of April 30, 1944, some passages give that impression, when he made the situation one-sided on the basis of the

288. In the final sentences of *SF*, Bonhoeffer already reached an understanding of the cross based on Gen. 2:8–17 and 3: Christ on the cross is the new tree of life which stands "in the middle of the world."

289. That means reading the New Testament from the standpoint of the Old Testament. The question about the *content* of contemporary speech about God still is not answered with the answer to the question about how.

proper speaking of God. Since speaking of certain human boundaries may have become questionable, God may no longer be spoken of on these boundaries. Years before, however, Bonhoeffer had followed such judgment with the interpretation of the Old Testament: God may be spoken of only on "real boundaries," which at the same time are "in the middle." From the Old Testament we learn how we can speak relevantly of God.[290] That speaking of God which is appropriate to the Old Testament is also appropriate to the situation only proves again the "actuality" of the Old Testament, which Bonhoeffer experienced with many others in the Confessing Church in the preceding years.[291]

2. a) *The Love for Life and the Earth (Second Sunday in Advent, 1943)*

In the letter of December 15, 1943, Bonhoeffer writes that all he had to finish was his *Ethics,* because an incomparable desire had come over him "not to vanish without a trace—an Old Testament rather than a New Testament wish" (*WE* 97/118; Eng. tr., 163). His astonishment about this, therefore, validated how Old Testament he thought and felt.[292]

290. Compare K. H. Miskotte, *Wenn die Götter schweigen,* 1963, 87 ff., who with regard to Bonhoeffer's idea about man come of age is primarily interested in "the way in which Bonhoeffer, starting from the situation as he sees it, also turns to the Old Testament and points to it when he advocates a 'worldly Christianity.' " Miskotte then cites *WE* 147 f./182 (April 30, 1944) and 182 ff./222 ff. (June 27, 1944). For him it is above all important that "Bonhoeffer too was very close to the insight that the structures particularly of the Old Testament refer to that which is beyond human religiousness" (Miskotte, Eng. tr., J. W. Doberstein, *When the Gods Are Silent,* 1967, 80, 82).

291. In Chapter IV we will once again deal with this significance of the Old Testament.

292. The love between man and woman belongs to the love for life and the earth. On Bonhoeffer's view of the Song of Songs we have already said what is necessary. Here, however, is an additional quote: "It is a good thing that that book is in the Bible, in the face of all those who believe that the restraint of passion is Christian (where is there such restraint in the Old Testament?)" (*WE* 156/193; Eng. tr., 150).—On Jan. 17, 1943, Bonhoeffer became engaged to Maria von Wedemeyer. He was already in prison when the families an-

Bonhoeffer began the section of the letter from the Second Sunday in Advent, 1943, on the Old Testament with the announcement that he had read much more of the Old Testament than the New Testament in past months. For that reason it could have begun to dawn on him that the Old Testament in many passages as opposed to the New Testament proclaims an inherent and independent message. With the statement on the love for life and earth, which is so strong that one might think everything is lost with it, he has spoken out in a characteristically Old Testament manner, which likewise is attested by both friend and foe of the Old Testament.[293]

Bonhoeffer's appraisal of this typical character of the Old Testament, however, differs very much from the appraisal of others, perhaps from that of his opponent in 1936, F. Baumgärtel.[294] Both agree on an essential aspect of the Old Testament. But the agreement actually already ends in the choice of words for the same state of affairs:[295] where Baumgärtel speaks of "Old Testament piety's aspect of being bound to this world" and of the "elementary longing and inordinate desire for life,"[296] Bonhoeffer speaks of *love* for life and the earth. The being bound to this world, according to Baumgärtel, is further a bond which will be "severed," a "barrier" which will be "overcome";[297] the purpose toward

---

nounced the engagement; nevertheless, he was very happy about it (Letter from Tegel on June 6, 1943; *DB* 888).

293. Von Rad speaks of the "highly fenced in this-worldliness" of the Old Testament (*Fragen der Schriftauslegung*, 18); Baumgärtel speaks of the "this-worldly affiliation of Old Testament piety" (*Die Eigenart der alttestamentlichen Frömmigkeit*, 1932, 13 ff.); according to Marcion everything in the Old Testament is "aimed . . . at this world" (Harnack, *op. cit.*, 143, see also 79).

294. See above, Chapter III.D.3. Baumgärtel, *Die Eigenart der alttestamentlichen Frömmigkeit;* compare P. Althaus, *op. cit.*, 1962, §21.

295. Compare Baumgärtel, *Die Eigenart der alttestamentlichen Frömmigkeit*, 15: "With death the bond between man and God shatters"; Bonhoeffer: ". . . only if one loves the earth and life in such a way that everything appears to be lost and at an end with it."

296. Baumgärtel, *ibid.*, 36; this author's italics.

297. *Ibid.*, 114, 103.

which the Old Testament piety strives is somewhat substantially different, namely, the understanding of the prophets that suffering is not abandonment from God, rather just the opposite, because through the suffering God brings man to himself and into his community.[298] The this-worldliness in the Old Testament is severed, but by something which Baumgärtel in another place calls "New Testament sounds, the gospel in the Old Testament."[299] Here he also writes that already quoted sentence: "Thus as Christians we stand in the midst of the Old Testament and like the Old Testament and with the Old Testament strive toward the New Testament."[300] Consequently, according to Baumgärtel if we want to be New Testamental, the this-worldliness must be overcome. To the contrary, according to Bonhoeffer the passionate love for life and the earth is not a bond that must be *broken,* but the condition whereby "one may believe in the resurrection of the dead and a new world." Bonhoeffer comes very near to the sentence just cited from Baumgärtel, that as Christians we stand in the midst of the Old Testament, when he writes: "We live in the penultimate" and that means nothing other than that we live in reality as the Old Testament represents it.[301] However, it is precisely here that the difference between both is clearly recognizable. Baumgärtel says that we strive toward the New Testament. Yet, included in that is a struggle out of the conditions of the Old Testament. Bonhoeffer stresses, on the other hand, that in the penultimate, in the reality presented by the Old Testament, we believe in the ultimate—here: the resurrection of the dead and a new world. The this-worldliness is, for Baumgärtel, the barrier that must be overcome if we are to strive toward the New Testament, but for Bonhoeffer the Old Testament's love for life and the earth forms the barrier within

298. *Ibid.,* 114, 111; compare P. Althaus, *op. cit.,* 196 f.
299. Baumgärtel, "Das Alte Testament," in *Nation vor Gott,* 106.
300. *Ibid.,* 106 f.; see above, Chapter I.2.C.
301. See below, Chapter III.E.5.

which the Christian resurrection hope can alone be properly interpreted and lived.[302]

b) *Blessing and Cross (July 28, 1944)*

Bonhoeffer undertook such an interpretation of the resurrection in *Letters and Papers from Prison* (June 27, 1944). Before it is presented, however, the letter of July 28, 1944, should be discussed. In this letter Bonhoeffer once more comes very near to the thoughts of Baumgärtel and yet once again differs from him very clearly.

> You think the Bible hasn't much to say about health, fortune, vigour, etc. I've been thinking over that again. It's certainly not true of the Old Testament. The intermediate theological category between God and human fortune is, as far as I can see, that of blessing. In the Old Testament . . . there's a concern not for fortune, but for God's blessing, which includes in itself all earthly good. In that blessing the whole of the earthly life is claimed for God, and it includes all his promises. It would be natural to suppose that, as usual, the New Testament spiritualizes the teaching of the Old Testament here, and therefore to regard the Old Testament blessing as superseded in the New. But is it an accident . . . that Jesus restored people's health, and that while his disciples were with him they "lacked nothing"? Now, is it right to set the Old Testament blessing against the cross? That is what Kierkegaard did. That makes the cross, or at least suffering, an abstract principle. . . . It's true that in the Old Testament the person who receives the blessing has to endure a great deal of suffering (e.g., Abraham, Isaac, Jacob, and Jo-

302. In considering "the highly fenced in this-worldliness" of the Old Testament, Von Rad asks: "Musn't it once be made evident that every belief in another world which bypasses God's will for this world is simple disobedience? Only from this viewpoint can we actually receive as a pure gift of God, as free grace, that which God offered and opened up in communion with him in the other world" (Von Rad, *Fragen der Schriftauslegung,* 18 f.; 1938).

seph), but this never leads to the idea that fortune and suffering, blessing and cross are mutually exclusive and contradictory—nor does it in the New Testament. Indeed, the only difference between the Old and New Testaments in this respect is that in the Old the blessing includes the cross, and in the New the cross includes the blessing." (*WE* 204 f./253 f.; Eng. tr., 374)

According to Baumgärtel, the understanding of the prophets is that suffering does not alienate from God, rather leads into his community, the New Testament sound in the Old Testament.[303] To that extent Bonhoeffer stands very close to Baumgärtel. The difference in their views lies in the fact that, first, Bonhoeffer puts health, fortune, and vigor—every expression for the this-worldliness of the Old Testament—under the theological concept of blessing, which is not to be found in Baumgärtel's book, *Die Eigenart der alttestamentlichen Frömmigkeit.* Secondly, it lies in the fact that for Bonhoeffer blessing and cross may not be brought into an exclusive antithesis to one another, while for Baumgärtel the prophetic-New Testamental understanding of suffering is somewhat substantially different from this-worldliness.

c) *Old Testament and Resurrection (June 27, 1944)*

The letter of June 27, 1944, is an expansion of the sentence on the resurrection from the letter of the Second Sunday in Advent, 1943. Bonhoeffer writes:

Now for some further thoughts about the Old Testament. Unlike the other oriental religions, the faith of the Old Testament isn't a religion of redemption. It's true that Christianity has always been regarded as a religion of redemption. But isn't this a cardinal error, which separates Christ from the Old Testament and interprets him

303. Baumgärtel, *loc. cit.,* 111 ff.; even clearer in Althaus, who, for example, calls Ps. 73:23 ff. *theologia crucis* (*op. cit.,* 198).

on the lines of the myths about redemption? To the objection that a crucial importance is given in the Old Testament to redemption (from Egypt, and later from Babylon —compare Deutero-Isaiah) it may be answered that the redemptions referred to here are *historical,* i.e., on *this* side of death, whereas everywhere else the myths about redemption are concerned to overcome the barrier of death. Israel is delivered out of Egypt so that it may live before God as God's people on earth. The redemption myths try unhistorically to find an eternity after death. . . .

The decisive factor is said to be that in Christianity the hope of resurrection is proclaimed, and that that means the emergence of a genuine religion of redemption, the main emphasis now being on the far side of the boundary drawn by death. But it seems to me that this is just where the mistake and the danger lie. Redemption now means redemption from cares, distress, fears, and longings, from sin and death, in a better world beyond the grave. But is this really the essential character of the proclamation of Christ in the gospels and by Paul? I should say it is not. The difference between the Christian hope of resurrection and the mythological hope is that the former sends a man back to his life on earth in a wholly new way which is even more sharply defined than it is in the Old Testament. . . . This world must not be prematurely written off; in this the Old and New Testaments are at one." (*WE* 182 f./225 ff.; Eng. tr., 336 f.)

Consequently according to Bonhoeffer the content of the Christian resurrection hope can be comprehended only when it is in accordance with the Old Testament proclamation. What the other Oriental religions and religions of redemption have to offer in this respect to such a comprehension is inadequate and inappropriate. In spite of that, Christian theology has agreed often enough to what they have to offer. However, because they "try unhistorically to find an eternity after death," a Christianity understood in their light is regarded as a "genuine religion of redemption" in the sense that everything aims at a redemption from the worldly valley of tears in a better life beyond. According to Bonhoeffer, that is not the essential aspect of the New Testament proclamation of Christ.[304] He can say so here, because he does not separate Christ from the Old Testament, rather interprets the Old Testament in the light of Christ, since he belongs to it. Since the Old Testament knows[305] only of historical redemptions, that is, *"this* side of death," the New Testament message of redemption understood in its light is a message of redemption "on earth," in "this world." Only when Christ in view of worldly difficulties and tasks does not take refuge in the eter-

---

304. The entire letter excerpt in our opinion is a polemic against a Marcionite understanding of Christianity. Compare Harnack, *op. cit.*, 17 ff.: "Religion is redemption—in the first and second centuries the hand of religious history stood at this place: no one could be God anymore who was not a savior. The new Christian religion came to this knowledge in a wonderful way and the apostle Paul put it in such a form that he made Christ as redeemer the center of the entire proclamation. However, Paul's idea of God is excessively nurtured by the Old Testament in comparison with his idea of Christ. . . . God is not only the Father of compassion but he is also the inexplicable One, who lives in an unapproachable light, the creator of the world, the author of Mosaic legislation, the sovereign ruler of history, particularly that of the Old Testament, the wrathful and revengeful God, and finally the judge who stands before the door in the great day of judgment." Marcion eradicates this excessive Old Testament orientation: "The Christian concept of God must be determined exclusively and completely by redemption through Jesus Christ. Therefore God cannot and may not be anything other than the Good in the sense of merciful and redeeming love." Marcion's proclamation "of the foreign and good God, the Father of Jesus Christ, who redeems man, who is miserable and totally alienated from him, from bondage to eternal life," "corresponds to the intense yearning and struggle of the time." —Bonhoeffer fought against a Marcionite Christianity, to which his teacher, Harnack, took a liking, by considering the strong orientation toward the Old Testament witness of God as a lasting authority for the interpretation of the New Testament message.

305. Compare E. Brunner (1930): "The prophet and his preaching comprise an aspect of the movement of God toward the world. Yes, toward the world, not away from the world! The movement away from the world, the escape from the world of finiteness into eternity, worldliness and God's impersonal nature, that is the movement of the idealistic and mystical, i.e., of the Greek, religion" (*ZZ* 8, 45). See above, fn. 63.

nal, but as Christ fully enjoys the earthly life, "is the crucified and risen Lord with him, and he crucified and risen with Christ" (*WE* 183/226 f.).

The worldly orientation of the resurrection of Christ does not arise here for the first time in Bonhoeffer's works, but it appears already in the lecture "Dein Reich komme! Das Gebet der Gemeinde um Gottes Reich auf Erden" ("Your Kingdom Come! The Prayer of the Community for God's Kingdom on Earth," Nov. 19, 1932) and in the "Theologische Brief von der Auferstehung" ("Theological Letter on the Resurrection," Easter, 1940).[306] That which is new in 1944 is that Bonhoeffer openly states the reason for this understanding of the resurrection of Christ. Jesus Christ cannot be separated from the Old Testament, for he belongs to it.[307]

Bonhoeffer wanted to substantiate his thoughts later "in detail from the New Testament" (*WE* 183/227; Eng. tr., 337). But nothing of the same has been preserved.[308] He could have substantiated these and others from the New Testament statements which speak of a sending out of the disciples and Paul

306. *GS* III, 270–285, 405–409. "Your kingdom come," prays the congregation, while it looks to the place where it "astonishingly becomes aware of God's deepest 'Yes' to the world," to the resurrection of Christ, by which "the kingdom of God itself comes to us" (*GS* III, 276; see also 277, 283). It is "not an idea of Christ which lives on, rather the bodily Christ. That is God's 'Yes' to the new creature. In the resurrection we recognize that God has not surrendered the earth, but has reconquered it for himself. He has given it a new future, a new promise. . . . Whoever believing says 'Yes' to the resurrection of Christ can no longer run away from the world; however, he also can no longer be possessed by the world, since he has recognized the new creation of God in the midst of the old creation" (*GS* III, 406 f.).

307. Supposedly this foundation exists also for "your kingdom come." In 1932/33 Bonhoeffer interprets Gen., chs. 1 to 3. In so doing, it is generally clear to him, on the one hand, that they deal with God's concern for his kingdom on *earth* (*SF* 25 f.; see below, Chapter IV). On the other hand, he indicates that he prefers to understand the resurrection of Christ from the standpoint of the creation, for we know the power of the resurrection of Christ because of God's creation, because God "remains the Lord" (*SF* 18; see above, Chapter III.B.2).

308. Also in the "Theological Letter on the Resurrection" no New Testament evidence is found in the section "The Resurrection of Jesus Christ Is God's 'Yes' to Creation" (*GS* III, 406 f.).

by the resurrected Lord: Matt. 28:18 ff.; Acts 1:8; Gal. 1:16.[309] The witnesses of Jesus Christ are sent to the people of the world as a result of their function. This sending of the witnesses in contrast to the Old Testament can be the entirely new and intensified reference to life on earth.[310]

The last sentence is an interpretation of the statements of Bonhoeffer by which he, as previously explained, intimately relates[311] New Testament interpretation and the this-worldliness of the Old Testament, the element of Old Testament proclamation which others call a barrier to be overcome (Baumgärtel); and he does so by considering that part of the New Testament message which has led to the mistaken opinion that Christianity is to be understood as a religion of hope

309. Compare W. Marxsen, *Die Auferstehung als historisches und theologisches Problem,* 1964, 20–25, who stresses the close connection between resurrection and mission.

310. Compare A. van Ruler, *Die christliche Kirche und das Alte Testament,* 1955, 49 f. "The Old Testament knows only the 'centripetal mission'; however, the New Testament knows only the 'centrifugal postulate.' " In addition, J. J. Stamm in his discussion of van Ruler's book says that van Ruler "definitely deserves support here" (*PAH* 190).—H. Schulte interprets the letter of June 27, 1944, in this way: "What is then the difference between the Testaments? We may put it this way: while the Old Testament remains in a naive this-worldliness, faith in the New Testament is freed to be this-worldly" (*EvTh* 22[1962], 443). In *SF,* Bonhoeffer already indicated that the reference to life on the earth is heightened through the resurrection in contrast to the Old Testament. The nothingness which is overcome through the resurrection of Christ, in contrast to the nothingness which was overcome through God's Word at creation "in the beginning," is strengthened because it is taken into God himself through the crucifixion (*SF* 18; see above, Chapter III.B.1). Therefore we can conclude that the power which overcomes the nothingness through the resurrection must be greater and more effective than the power which overcomes the nothingness at creation. To present all of Bonhoeffer's ideas about the resurrection would be a task in itself.

311. Compare Grunow: "The 'this-worldliness of Christianity' is based on the Old Testament. The Old Testament receives almost a normative function in Bonhoeffer" (*MW* I, 69). Compare also H.-G. Fritzsche, *Lehrbuch der Dogmatik,* Part I, 1964, 130 f., who before quoting from *WE* 149/184, 204/253, 92/112 f., speaks of the particular Old Testament emphases characteristic of its basic lines of thought, which prevent the dangerous shifts in the basic character of the Christian proclamation. One such emphasis is the this-worldly aspect of the Old Testament which especially concerned Bonhoeffer.

in a better life beyond, and the renunciation of the earth for this hope of resurrection.[312]

3. a) *The Law of God (Second Sunday in Advent, 1943)*

The second sentence from Bonhoeffer's letter from the Second Sunday in Advent, 1943, is a polemic against a conception of the Old Testament which explains it as inferior to the New Testament. That can also be determined in the next two sentences. At the end of that section of the letter Bonhoeffer rises up against an understanding of the Old Testament as an early religious stage.[313] In contrast to all rejections of the Old Testament he explains that Christ and the Old Testament belong together. Christ cannot be separated from it; he belongs to the *entire* Old Testament.[314]

With the sentence on the law of God, which one must acknowledge as being valid if one wants to speak of grace, in my opinion Bonhoeffer turns against E. Hirsch, who is more radical than Baumgärtel in his view of the Old Testament.[315] In 1936—in the second stage of the National Socialist Jewish policy characterized by the Nürnberg racial legislation—in his text *Das Alte Testament und die Predigt des Evangeliums,* Hirsch had championed the following conception of the Old Testament: The Old Testament is *"in its entirety . . .* a document of legal

312. We can expand the idea as he intended it that the radical censure consists in the mission of the witnesses, which wins a primary place in Bonhoeffer's interpretation: the mission of the witnesses is the consequence of the future and promise given to the earth by God through the resurrection of Jesus Christ. (See above, fn. 306.)

313. See above, Chapter III.C.2.

314. Compare Kreck (*op. cit.,* 46 f.), who cites *WE* 92/112 f. and asks whether these words are not to be understood in view of the attack on the Old Testament as the "horizon of understanding of the proclamation of Christ" which was linked to the attack on the one Word of God, Jesus Christ, during the Third Reich. We answer this question of Kreck's affirmatively in the sense that in this passage Bonhoeffer resists the attack on the Old Testament by German Christians and National Socialists, as well as open or hidden theological attacks.

315. The agreement with National Socialism was likewise greater with Hirsch.

religion"; the "Old Testament Jewish religion (including the figure of Abraham, the prophets, and the psalms) has in the *law* its all-determining central point, the Christian religion has it in the *gospel*."[316] Therefore, both Testaments do not stand amicably next to each other, rather in the relationship of antitheses.[317] The "God of the law"[318] does not act the same as the Father of Jesus Christ.[319] Hence, the entire Old Testament is shattered and declared null and void for the gospel.[320] However, since we belong to the gospel only by the experience of the conflict of law and gospel, the Old Testament is necessary in order for the gospel to remain the gospel, for relationship to God requires the illumination of the law. "Because the Old Testament is the most powerful historical opposition to the New Testament, that is precisely the reason it fits in so well as the first part of the Christian Bible."[321]

Such an opponent is difficult to comprehend, because he acts with the consciousness that his analysis of the Old Testament, as declared null and void by the gospel, can put the same Old Testament "into its proper Christian use."[322] With his conception of the Old Testament, however, Hirsch betrays himself as one who has taken over Schleiermacher's judgment of the Old Testament. For him the relationship of Christianity to Judaism, that is, to the Old Testament and to heathenism, is the same.[323] Placing the Old Testament on the same level

316. E. Hirsch, *Das Alte Testament und die Predigt des Evangeliums*, 1936, 26, 76.
317. *Ibid.*, 11, 83.
318. *Ibid.*, 30.
319. *Ibid.*, 25.
320. *Ibid.*, 14, 26, 31, 61, 63, 83.
321. *Ibid.*, 82 f.
322. *Ibid.*, 83, compare also 16.
323. The Christian faith, §12; compare Hirsch: "The relationship of the Old and New Testaments is at the same time prototype of every relationship of human and Christian religion" (*op. cit.*, 12).—The position of Bultmann as concerns the Old Testament is also characterized in the same manner. See his essays "Die Bedeutung des Alten Testaments für den christlichen Glauben" (*Glaube und Verstehen I*, Vol. I 1958³, 313 ff., especially 321) and "Weissagung und Erfüllung" (*ibid.*, Vol. II, 1952, 162 ff., esp. 185; compare also the criticism of Westermann in *PAH* 106 and H. G. Geyer in *EvTh* 24[1964], 213–219). Bonhoeffer rejects the position of Bultmann along with that of Hirsch.

with other religious witnesses makes the fight against Hirsch's analysis necessary. The result is that Hirsch assigns to the Old Testament only the task of "making distinct in a *negative* manner what is appropriate" to the New Testament.[324] Other religions could do that as well!

That sentence evokes opposition from Bonhoeffer, who assigns to the law, which persuades Hirsch to conceive of the Old Testament only as the dark background for the bright light of the gospel, a *positive* meaning with respect to grace: ". . . only when one allows the law of God to be *valid* for him." Consequently it has no significance for grace as *subdued* law, but as *valid* law. It is Jesus who gives it "new power," as Bonhoeffer writes in *The Cost of Discipleship* (*N* 96).

b) *Interpretation of Matt. 5:17–20 in* The Cost of Discipleship

The exposition of Matt. 5:17–20 substantiates the sentence on the law of God in the letter from the Second Sunday in Advent, 1943, just as the sentence itself is a summary of the exposition. Bonhoeffer explains: Jesus gives the law of the Old Covenant new power as God's law, among other things to prevent the misunderstanding of the disciples that no law might be a hindrance to them in the community with Christ, as if the law were declared null and void. That is a dangerous misunderstanding, because with such an idea the disciples would divorce God from his law "in order to exploit God by their possession of salvation."[325] Therefore, one must allow God's law to be valid for oneself in a positive sense in order to be able to speak of the grace of God as well. That the New Testament message is to be understood in the light of the Old

---

That is important for the explanation of Bonhoeffer's criticism of Bultmann; see below, fn. 368.

324. S. Kierkegaard, *Papirer* 11/1 A 151, used by Hirsch as the motto for his book; the author's italics. In one passage in *WE* in relation to the Old Testament Bonhoeffer contests Kierkegaard (204/253 f.).

325. *N* 93–98. On p. 96 Bonhoeffer cites Marcion's changing of the text (according to Harnack, *op. cit.*, 86, the change of text was by Marcion's student) in Matt. 5:17, "Do you think that I have come to fulfill the law or the prophets? I have come to dissolve not to fulfill."

Testament is valid here again. However, such an idea does not permit the view of the Old Testament as the "opposite" of the New, rather as the positive presupposition of the New in order that a relevant interpretation of the New Testament message can be achieved.

c) *Excursus: On the Interpretation of a Few Statements of Bonhoeffer on the Law by K. H. Nebe*

"Christ validates the law of the Old Covenant," writes Bonhoeffer in *The Cost of Discipleship* (*N* 94; Eng. tr., R. H. Fuller, *The Cost of Discipleship,* rev. ed. 1970, 138). What does he mean here by law? First, the answer to this question will make clear why Bonhoeffer in contrast to Hirsch can speak of a lasting, positive significance of the law. We shall pursue this question by discussing K. H. Nebe's interpretation of a few of Bonhoeffer's statements.

Nebe, in his dissertation *Religionlose Interpretation bei D. Bonhoeffer und ihre Bedeutung für die Aufgabe der Verkündigung,* 1961 (*Religionless Interpretation of D. Bonhoeffer and Its Significance for the Task of Proclamation*), says that in this sentence on the law from the letter of the Second Sunday in Advent, 1943, he has found an answer to the question of whether Bonhoeffer knew of a "genuine law" which has taken the place of a false law. He interprets the sentence as follows: Bonhoeffer speaks unequivocally of the genuine law "when he writes about Old and New Testament thought." Without the Old Testament "the meaning of the New Testament word as the last word of grace . . . is not conceivable to us," and he cites the sentence in this connection. When we look at this interpretation of Bonhoeffer itself, it appears to be appropriate. But when we observe how Nebe (1) arrives at speaking of a "genuine law," and (2) the consequences of such for the task of proclamation, his interpretation becomes very questionable.

(1) For Nebe the understanding of Bonhoeffer's thoughts on the law and the gospel is the key to Bonhoeffer's entire theology (see his dissertation, *op. cit.,* 34, 55, 210, 230). Therefore, in Part I, "The Significance of Bonhoeffer's Theological

116

Point of Departure for Secular Interpretation," in the section "The Law and Its Breakthrough in Proclamation," he has brought together the statements of Bonhoeffer on this question in *Sanctorum Communio, Act and Being, The Cost of Discipleship, Life Together, Ethics,* and *Letters and Papers from Prison.* We need deal only with Nebe's interpretation of the passages in question from the *Ethics.* On the basis of these passages Nebe thinks he can establish that Bonhoeffer demands a preaching "which proclaims law and gospel unshortened and unmixed. That is, it is correct proclamation when the genuine law takes the place of the false law and when in this process the genuine gospel in Christ . . . is freed for full operation. If the law is lacking, the gospel becomes the 'law of grace.' " (Nebe, *op. cit.,* 133 f.)

Actually in the passages presented by Nebe from the *Ethics,* Bonhoeffer demands a preaching from law and gospel; for example, "The word of the church to the world can never be anything but law and gospel" (*E* 380/279). In this sentence Bonhoeffer used the "Lutheran formula"—"law and gospel" —just as in three other passages of *Ethics* IV, "Über die Möglichkeit des Wortes der Kirche an die Welt" (*E* 379 ff./279 ff., "On the Possibility of the Word of the Church to the World"), and one could deduce with Nebe that Bonhoeffer means a so-called "genuine law." However, Bonhoeffer never once expresses himself in the passages presented by Nebe about such a law.[326] Secondly, Nebe overlooks

326. *E* 379 f./279, 350 f./257, 323–340/237–248, 244 f./179, 134 ff./80 ff. Where Bonhoeffer speaks of an "alien law," that is where its elimination "through Christ" occurs (*E* 351/258). And when he speaks of the "law of Christ" from which the world may not be alienated, inasmuch as the world should not stand by itself in isolation from the law of Christ (213/65), this law may not be understood as the "real law," as does Nebe, because the "real law," according to Nebe, is broken "in the proclamation." According to Bonhoeffer, however, the law of Christ is not broken but must endure. The *termini* of "real law" and of "false law," which Nebe uses for the interpretation of the passages cited from *E,* may originate (more exact cannot be determined) from Bonhoeffer's interpretation of Matt. 5:17–20 (*N* 97). "Jesus, the advocator of true law, must suffer at the hands of the advocators of the false law. He dies on the cross as a blasphemer, a transgressor of the law, because he has

the fact that when Bonhoeffer speaks of the word of the church as law and gospel he says: "The community recognizes and bears witness to God's love for the world in Jesus Christ as *law and gospel*" (*E* 379/279). One may not consider the order of words here conclusive, because "the order: gospel and law, as well as the other order: law and gospel, is theologically justified and necessary." "In both, however, the gospel is the 'actual' Word of God."[327] Nebe did not take these sentences into consideration.[328]

Nebe must ignore the fact that for Bonhoeffer the word of the love of God for the world is *the* word of the church to the world, because he understands Bonhoeffer's critical statements against Barth in *Letters and Papers from Prison* on the basis of G. Wingren's and H. Thielicke's criticism of Barth's "Evangelium und Gesetz" ("Gospel and Law").[329] Therefore, in Part III where he speaks about "The New View of the Law" in Bonhoeffer he thinks he can establish the following: "Bon-

---

vindicated the true law against the misunderstood false law." Compare Nebe, *op. cit.*, 132.

327. This relativizing of the order (*E* 335/245) makes the following sentence of Nebe impossible: "As shown, Bonhoeffer holds fast to the dominating Lutheran scheme, law-gospel" (Nebe, *op. cit.*, 188). Similarly Nebe adds, "And yet it is somewhat different with him, because he develops a new view of Christ and the law, which in part is considerably influenced by his particular understanding of the Old Testament." But the variations which Nebe sees in Bonhoeffer over against Luther do not do justice to the core of Bonhoeffer's thoughts on the law nor to his thoughts on the influence of the Old Testament.

328. Similarly Nebe utilizes Bonhoeffer's section "The Doctrine of the Primus Usus Legis according to the Lutheran Confessional Writings and Its Criticism" (*E* 323–340/237–248). Nebe draws on only the passages in which Bonhoeffer determines the unity of the threefold use of the law and in which he holds fast to the close relationship between law and gospel also with the *primus usus* (*E* 326 f./239). The following sentences remain unconsidered: "The *primus usus* has its origin and goal in the gospel. . . . Because God has loved man and the world in Christ, therefore there should be order among men and in the world. Because man belongs to God in grace, he should obey him in works" (*E* 334 f./245).

329. In the section "Die neue Sicht des Gesetzes" in Bonhoeffer (Nebe, *op. cit.*, 210–230), Nebe concurs with the critical statements of H. Thielicke (*Theologie der Anfechtung*, 1949) or Wingren (*Die Predigt*, 1955; *Die Methodienfrage der Theologie*, 1957; *Schöpfung und Gesetz*, 1960) in contrast to Barth.

hoeffer does not understand the law in the light of the covenant as does Barth, but with Paul and Luther in the light of the creation" (Nebe, *op. cit.*, 221). Shortly afterward Nebe must indeed admit that the connection between creation and law in Bonhoeffer is made in only a very few passages; nevertheless he claims that the connection is "the silent background of his understanding of the law, because for him it concerns the whole created world" *(ibid.)*.[330] That is to be contradicted. On this question Bonhoeffer is not to be set in opposition to Barth. He must have read carefully Barth's *Evangelium und Gesetz* (1935).[331] What Barth says briefly: "Thus the *law* and the *gospel* are like the tablet in the Ark of the Covenant,"[332] Bonhoeffer expands further in June and July, 1944, when he writes in the essay "Die erste Tafel der zehn Worte" ("The First Tablet of the Ten Commandments"): "In the Ark of the Covenant in which there is the throne of the merciful presence of God lie both tablets enclosed, encircled and enveloped by the mercy of God. Whoever wants to speak of the Ten Commandments must search for them in the Ark of the Covenant and at the same time speak of the grace of God" (*GS* IV, 602). It is certain that Bonhoeffer understands the law as does Barth in the light of the covenant! And it is surely because he has taken the Old Testament statements about the law into consideration. One further illustration. In the "Meditationen über

330. Nebe does not cite the singular and significant proof for such an opinion, which he found in Bonhoeffer. Namely, "The creation and the law are the two great unbreakable ordinances of God, which belong unendingly together, because they were brought about by the same God (Ps. 19)" (*GS* IV, 519, "Meditation on Ps. 119," 1, 1939/1940). However, see below, fn. 333.

331. Bonhoeffer's knowledge of Barth's *Evangelium und Gesetz* may be assumed, since first there was a debate at Finkenwalde from Dec. 18 to 21, 1936, under the direction of G. Ebeling on the question "How Do I Preach the Law?" (*DB* 640), and secondly Bonhoeffer delivered a lecture on the law (ms. is not preserved, *DB* 641) at the end of Aug., 1936, to a fellowship of the Confessing Church. Thirdly, in Dec., 1943, and Jan., 1944, he read *KD*, Vol. II, 2 (*DB* 1102). Furthermore, in a certain sense in 1931 Bonhoeffer had already said what Barth worked out in 1935 primarily in his lecture "Zur theologischen Begründung der Weltbundarbeit" (*GS* I, 140–161, esp. 150 f.).

332. Barth, *Evangelium und Gesetz*, 11, see also 3.

Psalm 119" (1939/40, "Meditations on Psalm 119"), Bonhoeffer answers the question, What is this "law" which is praised in this way? by citing Deut. 6:20 ff. and adds: "That is the answer to the question about the law: God's deed of redemption, God's commandments, and God's promise. No one understands the law of God who does not know of the redemption which has taken place and of the future promise. Whoever asks about the law will remember Jesus Christ and the redemption from the slavery of sin fulfilled in him for man, and will remember God's new beginning in Jesus Christ decreed for all men. The answer to the question about God's law is not a moral philosophy or a norm, rather a fulfilled act of God. . . . God's law cannot be separated from his redemptive action" (*GS* IV, 509; compare also 554). Nebe thinks Bonhoeffer interprets the law as God's way of working in normal, earthly life, and further, that this interpretation could "never be completely lost" "if one holds fast to the Old Testament" (Nebe, *op. cit.,* 209). That is acceptable insofar as law is understood by Bonhoeffer as the law which results from the covenant. But that is not what Nebe means. Therefore his interpretation at this point is a misinterpretation of Bonhoeffer, which could have been avoided if he had taken into account *all* of Bonhoeffer's statements on this theme, but especially the interpretation of Old Testament texts![333] Then he could not have brought Bonhoeffer so easily into opposition with Barth's "gospel and law."[334]

333. Nebe writes in his foreword that *GS* IV, in which the Old Testament interpretations of Bonhoeffer are found and which for our purpose are crucially important, could not be thoroughly studied. That excuses him only in part. The interpretation of the Ten Commandments was just as available to him as *The Prayerbook of the Bible,* both of which were already generally accessible before the appearance of *GS* IV (1961).

334. Nebe discloses the doubtfulness of his own interpretation himself when he writes on p. 11, that Bonhoeffer's thoughts in *N* on the commandment "in our opinion seem to have their origin in Barth's teaching of the gospel and the law, which is above all concerned with the unity of both in Jesus Christ. Bonhoeffer later abandons this line." Yet, on p. 131 one reads: "Here (i.e., in *N*) lies the foundation of Bonhoeffer's teaching on the command of Christ and on all that which he later develops in *E.* It is already clear in *N* that

(2) Proceeding from this misunderstanding, Nebe sets forth the tasks of a proclamation which would carry out Bonhoeffer's intention concerning a nonreligious proclamation. These turn out to be tasks which are exactly the opposite of what Bonhoeffer demands of such a proclamation. Since Nebe sees "proclamation as being concerned with liberation from the power of the law, which is always there" (Nebe, *op. cit.*, 221), it is the task of proclamation today to have a sharp and watchful eye upon the law's harassment of conscience—today it is everything else other than the moral-religious law!—and then without timidity to proclaim the victory over the law which has occurred in the reality of Christ" (*ibid.*, 223). Not only does Nebe say much too little here (among other things, what is to be proclaimed is the liberation from legalities which has occurred in Christ, but Nebe has in mind not only the legalities which men set up but also the "genuine law" which has its basis in the creation), but also things that are wrong. Hence, a proclamation as required here is to the finest detail precisely that which Bonhoeffer rejects! The proclamation with sharp and watchful eyes must track down the "points of harassment" (*ibid.*, 223)—Bonhoeffer rejects such a proclamation, which with the help of existential philosophy and psychotherapy proves to the "man without life's questions" "that in reality he is deeply involved in such questions," in order to make him ready for God to speak to him (*WE* 186/230). Is not a sermon that follows Nebe's method in danger of leading astray from the gospel, if only in the first part of the sermon? According to Bonhoeffer, however, if the church wants to proclaim Christ, it may not speak of him by "temporarily disregarding the gospel" (*E* 380/279), or else the end result is that Christ (as revealed in the gospel) is only an addition. However, Christ is "by no means just an addition" (*WE* 171/211).

Nebe thinks that Bonhoeffer's understanding of "law and

---

the Lutheran teaching of the law remains preserved. Also here it is said that there can be preaching of the Word of God only as law and gospel." In *N* is Bonhoeffer then "Barthian" or "Lutheran"? One would have to decide what "Lutheran" means on the question of "law and gospel."

gospel" is the key to Bonhoeffer's theology. That is correct inasmuch as we actually pay attention to what he said on this question and do not attempt to interpret him with thoughts of other theologians.[335] Nebe considers the *Ethics* a "source of Bonhoeffer's discussion on law and gospel" (Nebe, *op. cit.*, 133). That is also acceptable if we take into account what Bonhoeffer says on this question in the *whole* of the *Ethics*. Hence, it follows that Bonhoeffer sees the love of God for the world as *the* act and *the* Word of God; therefore the gospel is "the actual" Word of God. If we want to press Bonhoeffer into one of the two formulas—either "law and gospel" or "gospel and law"[336]—then only "gospel and law" comes into question. "God gives before he demands" (*E* 160/99).[337] He acts upon men before he calls on them to act. But these formulas them-

335. The question of the law in Bonhoeffer has already been discussed at length. Ebeling says that "non-religious interpretation is distinctive with respect to the law and the gospel." This, however, is criticized by Moltmann. "In my opinion this attempt at classifying Bonhoeffer's interpretation does not get at the heart of its problems" (*ThEx* NF 71 [1959], 40). In turn Moltmann is criticized by Nebe (*op. cit.*, 55). Compare in addition H. Thielicke, "Das Ende der Religion. Überlegungen zur Theologie D. Bonhoeffers" (*ThLZ* 81 [1956], 322) and H. Müller (*op. cit.*, 311 ff.).—An exact presentation of the evidence in Bonhoeffer on the background of his relationship to Luther and Barth among others is necessary. However, there can be no doubt that during his final period Bonhoeffer understood the law from the standpoint of the covenant.

336. Nevertheless, that can occur only hypothetically because Bonhoeffer himself relativizes the sequence. Nebe, however, speaks only of "law and gospel"! The warning against pressing Bonhoeffer's thought into the molds of others must also be taken into account on this question with regard to a comparison between Barth and Bonhoeffer. Our statements about the "Barthian" Bonhoeffer are to be understood with this reservation.

337. This sentence is the foundation of Bonhoeffer's view that in a Christian ethic, which has as its basis the Bible, rights rather than duties must be mentioned first, because the duties are implicit in the rights. Hence, he wants to give the "gospel a place within the framework of natural life" (*E* 161/99). —Bonhoeffer repeats almost word for word a sentence of Brunner's (see above, fn. 63), who in 1930 saw the Old Testament doctrine of God as being different from everything else in the Old Testament and that in the Old Testament the concept of holiness and the concept of compassion and love could not be separated. "God gives before he demands." Further: "The law of God is an element of his sealing of the covenant. . . . First the gift, then the task" (Brunner, *ZZ* 8 [1930], 41 f.).

selves are too formal to describe the nature and manner of the action of God. They deal only with the relationship between the action of God and men. If one wants to define the contents of the action of God as Bonhoeffer sees them, he must adhere to his thoughts on the incarnate, crucified, and risen Lord. Bonhoeffer himself knew that they were important for nonreligious proclamation (*WE* 149/184).

Consequently the part of the Old Testament proclamation which Hirsch denies as belonging to the gospel and understands as invalid—namely, the law[338]—has a binding validity for Bonhoeffer through the interpretation of the New Testament message of grace. The law has this positive significance for him because, like Barth, he understands the Old Testament[339] in the light of God's covenant.

4. a) *The Wrath and Vengeance of God (Second Sunday in Advent, 1943)*

The sentence that God's wrath and vengeance must hang over one's enemies as actual realities if forgiveness and love of enemy are to touch our hearts illustrates Bonhoeffer's position directed against Marcion. Marcion rejected the Old Testament. He saw the God of the Old Testament as the practician of wrath and vengeance in contrast to the good God of the New Testament; therefore the God of the Old Testament was different from the God of the New Testament.[340] In order to be able to resist this opponent of the Old Testament, Bonhoeffer does not attempt somehow to weaken the Old Testament message of God's anger and vengeance. Bonhoeffer sees the Old Testament with this message as having binding au-

338. Hirsch understands the *entire* Old Testament as law.

339. Hirsch means that his understanding of the Old Testament is an "understanding of the Old Testament which is forced upon us today by true exegetes" (*op. cit.*, 26). In addition, see only Wolff, *PAH* 150 ff.

340. "*Alter deus iudex, ferus bellipotens, alter mitis, placidus et tantummodo bonus atque optimus*" (Tertullian, *Adversus Marcionem* I.6); Harnack quotes from the same work, "*irascitur et aemulatur et extollitur et exacerbatur*" (*ibid.*, V.4; Harnack, *op. cit.*, 88).

thority through the interpretation of the New Testament. That which was the basis for Marcion's and his disciples' rejection of the Old Testament is for Bonhoeffer the necessary presupposition for an existential understanding (". . . something can touch our heart") of the New Testament message of forgiveness and love of enemy.

b) *Sermon on Psalm 58 (July 11, 1937)*

Just as the third sentence (from the Second Sunday in Advent, 1943) can be seen as the summary of an earlier Bible study and was explained by the same, the fourth may be seen in like manner. It summarizes the sermon on Psalm 58 from the year 1937, and is explained by it.[341] We saw[342] that Bonhoeffer did not, as did his critic Fichtner, consider the vengeance psalm in the light of Luke 23:34 as sub-Christian. Rather, according to Bonhoeffer, since Psalm 58 is fulfilled in Christ, he prays for forgiveness for his enemies as no one before him, because he bore the wrath and vengeance of God on the cross. Hence, on the basis of this conclusion it has been shown how uniformly Bonhoeffer interprets the Old Testament. One difference consists in the fact that in 1937 he recognized that the entire Old Testament belongs to Christ, but in 1943, that Christ belongs to the entire Old Testament. Perhaps one may even say that the former insight is a prerequisite to the latter.

5. *The Old Testament as Penultimate Word Is Instruction for Our Life in the Penultimate (Second Sunday in Advent, 1943)*

The conclusion to the four sentences discussed reads: "In my opinion it is not Christian to want to take our thoughts and feelings too quickly and too directly from the New Testament." Two sentences later he continues: "One cannot and must not speak the ultimate word before the penultimate. We

341. See above, Chapter III.D.4.(3).
342. See above, Chapter III.D.4.(2).

live in the penultimate and believe the ultimate, don't we?"
These three sentences lead us to the conclusion that the Old
Testament is the penultimate word in comparison to the New
Testament, the ultimate word.[343] Indeed, Bonhoeffer did not
say it quite so clearly, yet it lies along the line which is apparent
in this letter and in the *Ethics* in the section "The Ultimate and
the Penultimate Things" (*E* IV).[344] Just as these three sentences can be better understood in the light of the fourth
section of the *Ethics*, a few statements in that section can be
better understood in the light of the knowledge that the Old
Testament is the penultimate word.

Bonhoeffer pursues the matter in *Ethics* IV and other places
as follows: The justification of sinners by grace and faith alone
is the last word. When Christ comes to men, the ultimate word
takes place: then man believes, loves, and hopes (*E* 128 f./75).
God's ultimate word is qualitative and temporal; qualitative
because there is no word of God "that goes beyond his *mercy*,"
and it excludes any method of "achieving it by one's own way"
(*E* 131/77); it is temporal because "it is always preceded by
something penultimate, . . . a span of time, at the end of which
it stands. . . . There is a time when God permits, awaits, and
prepares, and there is a final time which cuts short and passes
sentence upon the penultimate. . . . Nevertheless the penultimate must not be annulled, rather it *must* remain" (*E*
132 f./78; Eng. tr., 124 f.). Thus Christian life is "the beginning of the ultimate in me, . . . but also always life in the
penultimate" (*E* 150/91).

In *Letters and Papers from Prison,* Bonhoeffer takes up these
thoughts in a somewhat altered manner when he writes: "We
live in the penultimate and believe the ultimate."[345]

It is surprising that what Bonhoeffer said in the *Ethics* about

343. Nebe even says that for Bonhoeffer the penultimate and the ultimate
have their origin in the Old Testament (*op. cit.,* 109).
344. From the 6th ed., 1963.
345. The "also" from *E* is lacking here, namely, that Christian life is "also
always life in the penultimate." Instead it is simply stated, "We live in the
penultimate." ". . . is it not so?" We view this question as rhetorical.

the ultimate and penultimate without alluding to the relationship of the Old to the New Testament describes precisely the relationship of both Testaments to each other as Bonhoeffer sees it. That is clearest of all in the previously mentioned thoughts on the ultimate word as the *temporal* ultimate word. The ultimate word is preceded by "a span of time," "a time when God permits, awaits, and prepares." That is the time of the Old Testament![346] This can be shown also in another of Bonhoeffer's ideas even though at first glance it does not seem to lend itself to supporting his position. Bonhoeffer writes: "The penultimate is not a . . . condition in itself, but it is a judgement which the ultimate passes upon that which has preceded it" (*E* 142/86; Eng. tr., 133). This sentence does not appear to comply with our purpose here, since it looks as if it contains a rejection of the Old Testament, when we refer to the relationship of both Testaments; for then the Old Testament would have no worth in itself. It has worth only because it can be declared valuable from another dimension. The goal of Bonhoeffer's thoughts in the letter from the Second Sunday in Advent, 1943, however, is to win the Old Testament completely for Christ and his church in opposition to all concealed and open rejections and repudiations of it. But if Bonhoeffer himself notes in 1935 that the Old Testament must be read in the light of the revelation that has taken place for us in Jesus Christ or else we are left with the Jewish or heathen understanding of the Old Testament,[347] then this statement is essentially identical with the sentence that the penultimate is only a judgment which the ultimate passes upon that which has preceded it. Without Christ, the ultimate word, the Old Testament has no reality and remains obscure to us. Only through the light of Christ does it begin to become illuminated for us, and indeed, according to Bonhoeffer's understanding in *Letters*

346. Compare Von Rad, *Theologie des Alten Testaments,* Vol. II, 363: In a discussion of the relationship of the Old Testament to the New Testament, the idea of "preparation" returns again and again, since the Old Testament in any case has a preparatory significance.

347. See above, Chapter III.C.1.

and Papers from Prison, so strongly that in its light the New Testament begins to be illuminated.

Now it is no longer surprising in looking at these three sentences of the letter from the Second Sunday in Advent, 1943, that thoughts from the fourth section of the *Ethics* contribute to the understanding of them. Bonhoeffer makes a harsh judgment[348] when he says, "In my opinion it is not Christian to want to take our thoughts and feelings too quickly and too directly from the New Testament." Assuming the identity of the ultimate and the New Testament word, this thought is one-sided when viewed from the standpoint of section four of *Ethics.* Whoever takes his thoughts and feelings too quickly and too directly from the New Testament will be able to solve the relationship between the ultimate and penultimate only in a radical sense which sees "only the ultimate, and in it only the complete breaking off of the penultimate" (*E* 135/80).[349] This solution is just as hostile to Christ as the compromise set over against it. Therefore it is not Christian to want to take one's thoughts and feelings only from the New Testament. Being Christian also involves taking thoughts and feelings from the Old Testament as well.

One idea from the fourth section of the *Ethics,* however, in the light of *Letters and Papers from Prison* is more clearly to the contrary. There Bonhoeffer says "that we must speak of penultimate things" (*E* 133/79).[350] This *must* is justified if the Old Testament is the penultimate word. Together with the New Testament it is the word of the One God, which cannot be set aside if one wants to speak of the God of the Bible and which must be heard by us who live in the penultimate as the penulti-

348. Compare Wolff, *PAH* 180.
349. We must make an additional comment on Hirsch, which can also be evidence here for our view that Bonhoeffer stands in opposition to Hirsch. Immediately following the sentence quoted from *E* IV one reads, with regard to the radical solution mentioned above, "Ultimate and penultimate stand in exclusive opposition." If one replaces ultimate with gospel or New Testament and penultimate with law or Old Testament, the sentence could come from Hirsch!
350. This author's italics.

mate word. The modification shown in *Letters and Papers from Prison,* "we live in the penultimate," as opposed to section four of the *Ethics*[351] is evidently attributed to the fact that Bonhoeffer took the New Testament message more strongly into consideration.[352] The Old Testament leads him to the understanding that Christian life is not only *"also* life in the penultimate" (*E* 150/91), but can be realized *"only* in the fullness of this world"[353] (*WE* 200/248).[354]

In his article "Zur Hermeneutik des Alten Testaments" ("On the Hermeneutic of the Old Testament"), section three, part two, "What Does the Old Testament Mean for the Proclamation of the Church?"[355] H. W. Wolff has considered Bonhoeffer's statements on the Old Testament in *Letters and Papers from Prison* and referred to him on the last page,[356] where he asserts in this context: "The Old Testament aids the eschatological existence of this side of history."[357] A final comment should be made on the title of this section with reference to this sentence. It can be brief. With the interpretation of the four conditional sentences we have already said what the Old Testament proclaims as the penultimate word. In addition, in the neighboring sentences something is also said about that in which life in the penultimate consists. It is the understanding and respect of the unutterableness of the name of God; it is the passionate love for life and the earth; it is the standing under the law of God; it is the experience of the wrath and vengeance of God. In this life in the penultimate, as is shown by the Old Testament as reality, the penultimate word is issued as instruction. The significance of the Old Testament for us is not exhausted by the fact that it is a necessary "aid to understanding" for the proper grasp of the New Testament

351. See above, fn. 345.
352. In addition there is the stronger significance which the incarnate held for Bonhoeffer especially in contrast to *N.*
353. This author's italics in both of the last quotations.
354. Compare above, fn. 312.
355. Wolff, *PAH* 168–180.
356. See below, Chapter IV.
357. Wolff, *PAH,* 180.

but without affecting us further in our *existence;* rather, the message of the Old Testament opens up to us our reality as penultimate reality in which we live and in which we believe the ultimate.

In a few passages in section four of the *Ethics,* Bonhoeffer himself observed this didactic character of the Old Testament. Then with the definition of the content of the "natural" as a realm of the penultimate he referred back to the Old Testament passages three times: (1) Bonhoeffer draws on several passages from Ecclesiastes to illustrate and establish that man possesses a right to bodily enjoyment, because he has his life only "as bodily life" and his body is an end in itself and a means to an end, an enjoyment which is subordinate to no higher end (*E* 165 ff./102 ff.). (2) Bonhoeffer concludes the section that carries the heading "The Right to Bodily Life" after he has come to terms with the problem of euthanasia, with the sentence from Ex. 23:7: "The innocent . . . you shall not slay." In this sentence he sees summarized everything that he has said on the question of the deliberate destruction of innocent life (*E* 176/111). (3) In the third instance he quotes Gen. 2:18 and 23 as evidence that "for the sake of marriage as a whole, one should acknowledge a right to full bodily union as a right which is quite distinct from the right of reproduction, even though essentially it can never be entirely separated from it, the two being closely allied; it is a right that is founded upon the mutual love of the married pair" (*E* 190 f./122; Eng. tr., 179 f.).

In the letter of the Second Sunday in Advent, 1943, Bonhoeffer also indicated to what extent the Old Testament can be didactic for us. He says that his idea that "we live in the penultimate and believe the ultimate" at which "Lutherans (so-called!) and pietists would shudder" has far-reaching consequences, for example, "for the use of the Bible, etc., but above all for ethics." Following these comments comes the section concerning the objectionable stories in the Old Testament, which Bonhoeffer does not want to call an "early religious stage." In what are the consequences "above all for ethics" to be seen? Bonhoeffer himself has drawn them into his essay "Was heisst die Wahrheit sagen?" ("What Is Meant by 'Telling the Truth'?" (*WE* 77/94; *E* 385–395/283–290). This work originated "incidentally" during the first months of his imprisonment, when he read much of the Old Testament. Indeed it contains only one Old Testament citation (Eccl. 7: 24; *E* 393/289), but its origin is indebted to the circumstance that Bonhoeffer was in a similar situation to that of those Old Testament men who lied, killed, etc. Through his cooperation in the resistance movement and through the hearings Bonhoeffer was forced to lie and was ready to kill. He knew from the men of the Old Testament that they did these things "to the glory of God" and from his perspective he knew that it was for "the cause of Christ" that he sat in prison (*WE* 75/92). In this situation the Old Testament gave him not only fundamentally a good conscience for life in this world but also concrete instruction along his difficult way. If in his essay he places so much emphasis on the knowledge of the place where I tell the truth, then that is one of the consequences which he has drawn out of the thoughts of his letter from the Second Sunday in Advent, 1943 (*E* 385/283, 393/389).

We spoke in the introduction of the fact that in Bonhoeffer's Old Testament interpretations a definite direction is to be recognized, for the Old Testament gains more and more importance[358] for him, an importance which finds[359] its deepest and purest expression in the letters from *Letters and Papers from Prison*. Bonhoeffer's way along this path is the way of resistance against the open and concealed attacks on the Old Testament.[360] Meanwhile he grants the Old Testament an authority

358. See above, Introduction, sec. 3.
359. Compare Grunow, "The role which the Old Testament always played in the Scripture interpretation of Bonhoeffer has certainly not remained hidden to anyone who knew him. I must admit, however, that the theological foundation and significance of this role first became clear to me through the letters" (*MW* I, 68).
360. That is the case, e.g., with G. Schmidt, who writes in 1934, "Without the Old Testament there is no understanding of the New Testament and no way to make it understandable, and indeed the *entire* New Testament . . . , in

that is binding on the interpretation of the New Testament,[361] and particularly in its so-called sub-Christian parts he solved the task that was placed before the church then and now: that of reclaiming the Old Testament for the church.[362] The church, which draws its life, thought, action, and proclamation from Christ (*SF* 6), may not surrender the Old Testament. To the contrary, it must take its necessary possession of it, because it is the book of Christ which is made valid by him and belongs fully to him, just as he fully belongs to this book.

peripheral historical matters or in the central theological matters" (*Das Alte Testament und der evangelische Religionsunterricht*, 17).

361. Compare H. Schulte, who summarizes the significance of the Old Testament for Christian proclamation according to the last letters. "But while the Old Testament was justified earlier from the standpoint of the New Testament as far as validity is concerned, since it leads forward toward it, today the interpretation of the New Testament must be well counseled from the standpoint of the Old Testament if it does not want to go astray" (*EvTh* 22, 448). Compare once more (see above, fn. 63) Brunner (1930): "Jesus Christ and the New Testament are not to be understood without the Old Testament. . . . I do not mean that the genesis of the New Testament cannot be understood without the Old Testament, but that the content, the matter, the Word of the New Testament can be understood only in connection with the genesis of the Old Testament" (*ZZ* 8[1930], 33). From here Brunner turns against the "Greek" understanding of the New Testament; see above, fn. 305.

362. Bonhoeffer would agree with Von Rad, who asks whether it is really in that way that one knows so precisely who Jesus Christ was and is, and "only from that vantage point—actually a secondary problem—that one validly determines the proper relationship of the Old Testament to this Christ who has already been made known to us" (Von Rad, *Theologie des Alten Testaments*, Vol. II, 440). According to Bonhoeffer, "Who Jesus Christ was and is" can only be determined from the standpoint of the Old Testament. Even if according to Von Rad the state of affairs were made clearer with that question, the unsettled question, still not dealt with, of the "preservation" of the Old Testament would be answered. (*Ibid.* Compare the sentence of H. G. Geyer in that connection: "The Old Testament is justified in the canon of the Holy Scripture only if it is indispensible to the clear and full truth of the New Testament, that is, if it is positively necessary for the understanding and interpretation of this truth," *EvTh* 25[1965], 210.) As we see it, Bonhoeffer answered the still unanswered question for himself and also for us. His statements on the Old Testament in *WE* lead convincingly to the judgment that in order to know Christ the Old Testament is absolutely necessary.

IV

THE CONTRIBUTION OF THE OLD TESTAMENT TO AN UNDERSTANDING OF BONHOEFFER'S STATEMENTS ON THE "WORLD COME OF AGE"

For a work that concerns itself with Bonhoeffer's appraisal and interpretation of the Old Testament, it seems fitting in summing up to determine what is transient and what is viable for us in his intercourse with the Old Testament. In order to satisfy this task the voices from the Old Testament hermeneutical discussion of past years must be referred to much more than has been done up to now.[363]

It will become clear where Bonhoeffer belongs with his appraisal and interpretation of the Old Testament. He neither grants a greater value to the New Testament as opposed to the Old Testament, as do F. Baumgärtel, R. Bultmann, F. Hesse, and others, nor does he place too much vch value on the Old Testament as does A. van Ruler;[364] rather, both Testaments are of equal value for him, as for G. von Rad, H. W. Wolff, and W. Zimmerli, since both witness to Jesus

363. The literature up to 1962 is found in the bibliography in *PAH* 363–372. Additional literature includes: K. H. Miskotte, *Wenn die Götter schweigen. Vom Sinn des Alten Testaments,* 1963. F. Mildenberger, *Gottes Tat im Wort. Erwägungen zur alttestamentlichen Hermeneutik als Frage nach der Einheit der Testamente,* 1964; H. G. Geyer, "Zur Frage der Notwendigkeit des Alten Testaments," *EvTh* 25(1965), 207–237; K. Schwarzwäller, "Das Alte Testament in Christus," *ThSt*(B) 84(1966); F. Hesse, *Das Alte Testament als Buch der Kirche,* 1966.

364. In our opinion, also Miskotte must be considered here. Just as in the first direction the Lutheran tradition remains alive by solving the relationship of both Testaments through the law and gospel scheme, this takes place in the Reformed tradition, where the law is appreciated even more.

Christ.[365] Therefore only a reciprocal relationship of both Testaments without underrating or overrating one or the other can lead to their relevant interpretation.

We intentionally forgo the direct discussion on the justification of Bonhoeffer's position. We will mention it indirectly when we pursue another question: Can the Old Testament contribute to a better understanding of the final theological ideas of Bonhoeffer? Two things will be achieved with the affirmative answer. First, we shall examine by example. The pros and cons of Bonhoeffer's viewpoint will not be theoretically discussed; rather, we shall attempt to show whether or not the lines that he followed with his appraisal and interpretation of the Old Testament can make the Old Testament come alive anew for us. In this direction we shall examine the prophets, of whom F. Hesse thinks that the proof of their significance "remains mostly of a very theoretical nature. If one becomes engrossed in Bible-reading without guidance in the prophetical books, then most of it will remain foreign to him, if not completely incomprehensible."[366] Alongside the theoretical discussion concerning the right of a certain hermeneutical standpoint, such a standpoint should also be tested in the practice of proclamation. Here, of course, only an introduction to proclamation can be attempted.

Secondly, R. Schulze's challenge to Bonhoeffer's interpretation will be taken into account. According to it, theological consequences may be drawn from Bonhoeffer to the extent "that they are legitimized by the witness of the Scripture."[367] Does Bonhoeffer think according to the Scriptures in his last

365. On the first and third positions compare E. Hübner, *Evangelische Theologie in unserer Zeit*, 1966², 175–193.

366. Hesse, *op. cit.*, 16. Hesse also says of Leviticus, Esther, the Song of Songs, and Chronicles that they are "simply completely foreign" to us (14). With the Song of Songs we have already made a test case with Bonhoeffer that it does not need to remain "completely foreign" to us.

367. R. Schulze, *EvTh* 25 (1965), 698. According to Barth you can expect the "very best" from Bonhoeffer. In the light of that claim (*MW* I, 122), R. Schulze writes: "The 'very best' is engendered in the main line of his interpretations of the prophetical problems willingly or unwillingly *(nolens volens)*. He

letters? Since his appraisal of the Bible is an essential, if not *the* essential, viewpoint of his theology, the question whether the justification of his last ideas can be shown by the Bible must be clarified.

In his letter of May 5, 1944, Bonhoeffer writes: What does it mean to "interpret in a religious sense?" I think it means to speak on the one hand metaphysically, and on the other hand individualistically. Neither of these is relevant to the biblical message or to the man of today. Hasn't the individualistic question about personal salvation almost completely left us all? Aren't we really under the impression that there are more important things than that question (perhaps not more important than the *matter* itself, but more important than the *question!*)? I know it sounds pretty monstrous to say that. But, fundamentally, isn't this in fact biblical? Does the question about saving one's soul appear in the Old Testament at all? Aren't righteousness and the Kingdom of God on earth the focus of everything, and isn't it true that Rom. 3:24 ff. is not an individualistic doctrine of salvation, but the culmination of the view that God alone is righteous? It is not with the beyond that we are concerned, but with this world as created and preserved, subjected to laws, reconciled, and restored. What is above this world is, in the gospel, intended to exist *for* this world; I mean that, not in the anthropomorphic sense of liberal, mystic pietistic, ethical theology, but in the biblical sense of the creation and of the incarnation, crucifixion, and resurrection of Jesus Christ. . . .

I'm thinking about how we can reinterpret in a "worldly" sense—in the sense of the Old Testament and of John 1:14—the concepts of repentance, faith, justifica-

---

sheds illuminating light on the primary problems of theology and proclamation today (!) and labels the sidestepping of them as irresponsibility." This part of the work attempts to delineate Bonhoeffer's "very best."

tion, rebirth, and santification. (*WE* 149 f./183 ff.; Eng. tr., 285–287)

This letter is extremely important.[368] In expressing his opinion about it, Bonhoeffer says that what he has written is more for his own clarification than to enlighten Bethge, to whom it was written (*WE* 150/185). It is the second letter on "religionlessness." The letter of April 30, 1944, stands very close to this letter in regard to Bonhoeffer's comments on the Old Testament.[369] Both are not letters on the Old Testament, but on

368. Perhaps it also has to do with a clarification of Bonhoeffer's criticism of Bultmann. The section of the letter quoted above is preceded by a paragraph in which Bonhoeffer criticizes Bultmann's "demythologizing," because, on the one hand, he "has not gone far enough," and on the other hand, because he curtails the gospel with his assessment in a liberal manner (*WE* 148 f./183, also 178/220). Ebeling treats Bonhoeffer's criticism of Bultmann in this way: Bonhoeffer's reproach "fails to recognize the explicit intention of Bultmann" (*MW* II, 51; see in that section the corresponding quotation of Bultmann from "Kerygma und Mythos I," 25 ff.). This criticism is taken up by A. D. Müller ("Dietrich Bonhoeffers Prinzip der weltlichen Interpretation und Verkündigung des Evangeliums," *ThLZ* 86[1961], 729) and G. Krause ("Dietrich Bonhoeffer und Rudolf Bultmann," *Zeit und Geschichte*, 1964, 450 f.). If, however, Bonhoeffer's criticism is set in the context of the appraisal of the Old Testament by both theologians, there can be no question of Bonhoeffer's failing to recognize Bultmann's intention. Neither G. Harbsmeier ("Die 'nicht-religiöse Interpretation biblischer Begriffe' bei Bonhoeffer und die Entmythologisierung," *MW* II, 74–91) nor G. Krause (*loc. cit.*, 439–460) in their lengthy contributions, nor others who have addressed themselves to the Bonhoeffer-Bultmann problem have agreed with this opinion (see the overview in G. Krause; in addition, H. Ott, *op. cit.*, 100–105). In his position on the Old Testament, Bultmann stands very near Hirsch, whose position is contrary to Bonhoeffer's. See above, fn. 323. For Bultmann the Old Testament is only a negative mirror image of the eschatalogical proclamation of the New Testament (on Bultmann besides Westermann and Geyer see also W. Zimmerli, "Verheissung und Erfüllung," *PAH* 96–99). For Bonhoeffer an interpretation of the New Testament which views the Old Testament from Bultmann's perspective can only be a "typical, liberal reduction process" (*WE* 178/220; compare Harnack). Compare also O. Weber, *Grundlagen der Dogmatik*, Vol. I, 323. In this section proceeding from the interpretation of the letter from May 5, 1944, we will attempt to show how strong the Old Testament background is for Bonhoeffer's theological ideas in *WE*. It need be no coincidence that Bonhoeffer criticizes Bultmann in this letter.

369. See above, Chapter III.E.1.b.

nonreligious interpretation and proclamation. Both only touch on the Old Testament. Yet what is already recognizable in the letter of April 30 is that the allusions to the Old Testament may not be overlooked. What appeared in that letter reveals itself here as well: consciously or unconsciously in his definition of nonreligious interpretation and proclamation Bonhoeffer refers back to realizations which were the result of and confirmed in the exposition of Gen., chs. 1 to 3. In *Creation and Fall* we find the reason why speaking metaphysically and individualistically does not concern the Biblical message. There Bonhoeffer interprets Gen. 1:4a as follows:

> God views his work and is satisfied with it; this means that God loves his work and therefore wills to preserve it. . . . It is the theme of the whole Bible that the thing done, the condition, the embodiment of the will should become deed, that the world is good, that God's kingdom is to be upon earth, that his will be done on earth. (*SF* 25 f.; Eng. tr., 25)

This interpretation is an answer to the question of whether or not justice and the Kingdom of God on earth are the focus of everything that is in the Bible. So far as the interpretation is concerned, the question is only rhetorical. Speaking metaphysically—that is, speech which concerns the world beyond[370]—has nothing to do with the Biblical message which concerns God's kingdom in this world. With Gen. 1:4a the place where the Kingdom of God will be built is determined.

---

370. We agree with the evidence of Ott "that Bonhoeffer uses the word 'metaphysical' in a specific and limited sense" (*op. cit.,* 142). According to Ott, "metaphysical" means that "this world is superseded by the other world, that the existence of an otherworldly God is claimed and that man is oriented toward another world from this world" (*ibid.,* 134). Bethge says: "Instead of this, however, the metaphysical Christian religion provided the world with the kind of transcendence for which it yearned. God became necessary as the superstructure of existence, and religious longing found its goal in a heavenly domain. Hence, metaphysics led the Christian religion astray into thinking statically in terms of two spheres and has forced it to stress one-sidedly its redemptive character" (*DB* 980).

The Old Testament relies on this decision and "guards the Christian message against transcendentalism" (H. W. Wolff).[371]

On the basis of Bonhoeffer's interpretation of Gen. 1:26 f. it is indicated that speaking individualistically also is not appropriate to the Biblical message (*SF* 39–46). Karl Barth praises this interpretation because in it "finally . . . the contents of verse 27 are illuminated, where it . . . actually cannot be ignored that God created man as man and woman."[372] Bonhoeffer takes account of verse 27 by filling the concept of freedom with it, a concept in which he sees expressed that man is created in the image of God.[373] However, it is created freedom, which is differentiated from the freedom of the creator "by the fact that creature is related to creature. Man is free for man. Male and female he created them" (*SF* 43; Eng. tr., 38).[374]

371. Wolff, *PAH* 179; see above, fn. 355.

372. Barth, *KD*, Vol. III, 1, 219. According to J. J. Stamm, before 1940 varied opinions with regard to Gen. 1:26 f. were to be found in Old Testament science: spiritual superiority of man, lordship over the creatures, bodily form of man, expression of the direct relationship between God and man were understood as the Godlikeness of man. After 1940, especially the image likeness in the relationship is emphasized ("Die Imago-Lehre K. Barths und die alttestamentliche Wissenschaft," *Antwort*, Festschrift für K. Barth, 1956, 87 f.). Therefore, no consideration of v. 27! On the discussion of Barth's interpretation and hence implicitly Bonhoeffer's, see J. F. Konrad, *Abbild und Ziel der Schöpfung. Untersuchung zur Exegese von Genesis 1 und 2 in Barths Kirchlicher Dogmatik III 1*, 1962, 177 f.

373. "That God creates in man his image on earth means that man resembles the Creator in that he is free" (*SF* 41).

374. Bonhoeffer summarizes his interpretation of Gen. 1:26 f. in the sentence, "Man's being free for God and other men and his being free from the creatures in his domain is the image of God in the first man" (*SF* 46). In our opinion this interpretation has three roots. The first is the influence of R. Seeberg, who in Bonhoeffer's judgment was the first theologian after Schleiermacher to present the idea of society as belonging to primordial human being, "in his dogmatics under the doctrine of man and his innate spirituality (I §22, 1), and once again brought an important doctrine into theology" (*SC*, 1960[3], 38; see also 235–238). The second root is the understanding of this passage from the standpoint of Jesus Christ; alone and through him do we know about the original man. Since as the message of the gospel we hear that God does not desire to be free for himself, but free for man, our freedom is definitely

Where the Old Testament defines the being of man, it does not see him as an unrelated individual. Therefore the individualistic question in regard to the personal salvation of the soul does not concern the Biblical message.[375] Hence, "the Old Testament protects the Christian message against false individualization" (H. W. Wolff).[376]

Consequently if we want to be clear about Bonhoeffer's presentation of the content and form of nonreligious interpretation and proclamation, we cannot disregard realizations that had arisen in previous years in his exposition of Gen., chs. 1 to 3, or were confirmed by this work. Also in his letter of May 5, 1944, he grants the Old Testament a forcible word for the accomplishment of the program of the nonreligious interpretation. What "nonreligious" and "worldly" mean is determined by the Old Testament.[377] However, the Old Testament can fulfill this function only when it is "nonreligious" and "worldly."[378]

---

a freedom for . . . (*SF* 41 f.; compare *SC* 232–239; *E* 357/262). The third root is that "final consideration" of v. 27.

We could have spoken much longer in Chapter III, section B or C, about the second root, because Bonhoeffer has illuminated here an obscure passage from the Old Testament through the light of Christ. We have forgone that, because within the framework of this work only a brief treatment would be appropriate for the importance of Gen. 1:26 f. and of the literature on this passage. Moreover, the existing problems have already been treated in part by Konrad.

375. If in the phrase "the question in regard to the welfare of the soul" Bonhoeffer understands the soul in a Greek dualistic sense as imprisoned by the body, then he has rejected such an idea as un-Biblical in *SF*. The interpretation of Gen. 2:7 reads: "The man whom God has created . . . is the man who is formed out of earth. . . . His bond with the earth belongs to his essential being. . . . From it he has his *body*. His body belongs to his essential being. Man's body is not his prison, his shell, his exterior, but man himself. Man does not 'have' a body; he does not 'have' a soul; rather, he 'is' body and soul" (*SF* 52; Eng. tr., 46).

376. Wolff, *PAH* 177.

377. Thereby the Old Testament comes to terms with the "worldly" view of the New Testament, as it speaks out fundamentally in John 1:14. On the question of the "worldliness" both Testaments cannot be brought into contradiction. Compare above, Chapter III.E.3.c.

378. Compare Miskotte, *Wenn die Götter schweigen*, 89; see above, fn. 290. See

Bonhoeffer seeks to understand a few central concepts in the Old Testament sense (and in the sense of John 1:14) in order to reinterpret them in a "worldly" fashion. "In the Old Testament sense" means to interpret those concepts in view of God's kingdom on earth and that man lives in relationships.[379] However, an interpretation in the Old Testament sense cannot be exhausted in this manner.

Indeed, that appears to be the case with Bonhoeffer regarding the letter of May 5, 1944. The one fundamental principle of nonreligious interpretation and proclamation ("In the gospel what is above this world is intended to exist for this world") he means "in the Biblical sense of the creation." Thus Bonhoeffer's realizations which prevent a religious interpretation of the gospel are gained from the Old Testament proclamation of creation. The Old Testament, however, embraces more than just Gen., chs. 1 to 3! If this alone were the contribution of the Old Testament to the clarification of the question of nonreligious interpretation, it would be unimportant.[380] Then

also Bethge—whether Bonhoeffer told his fellow Soviet prisoner of the last days of his beloved Old Testament is an open question. . . . He considered this book to be the great witness for the overcoming of the religious" (*MW* I, 22).

379. Already in 1932 both are very closely related for Bonhoeffer. See "His Kingdom Come," *GS* III, 274. Likewise for Brunner in 1930 (see above, fn. 63)—"That the redemption of the world in the kingdom of heaven does not mean the platonic otherworldliness, the idealistic immortality of the soul, but includes the bodily, that the world shall not dissolve but shall be fulfilled—that the same is also meant in the New Testament can properly be understood only on the basis of the Old Testament prophetic hope." And, "God who wants to build his kingdom on earth, . . . is concerned with the whole not only with the individual; with the people and with all individuals insofar as they are members of the whole. . . . God's will is from the outset directed to the community" (*ZZ* 8[1930], 46).

380. That is Nebe's opinion. In "Die neue Sicht des Alten Testaments" he stresses that for Bonhoeffer in contrast to Vischer the Old Testament has its own independent message in the message of creation and of life (Nebe, *op. cit.*, 205; see above, footnote 171). "The first and foundational deed of God (i.e., according to the Old Testament) is the creation" (*ibid.*, 206). To be sure, Nebe does not overlook the rest of the Old Testament's message, but it is considered only very generally: the God of the Old Testament, who is the Creator, may not be forced into a religious corner, because the Old Testament accounts of God's deeds are accounts of his deeds in creation and history. God

Bonhoeffer would have done only what happens with almost all dogmaticians—namely, that they merely take Gen., chs. 1 to 3, into consideration.

It is certainly otherwise with Bonhoeffer. The contribution of the Old Testament to the proclamation he requires is much greater. Directly (June 27, 1944) and indirectly (Second Sunday in Advent, 1943) in connection with nonreligious interpretation he pointed to other parts of the Old Testament, although in the letter of June 27, 1944, he called special attention only to one viewpoint of the Biblical sense of the creation, the redemption in this world, with his reference to Exodus and Deutero-Isaiah. But the letter of May 5, 1944, indicates a possibility of nonreligious interpretation that has occurred in the rest of the letters. Bonhoeffer conceives the one fundamental principle of this interpretation "in the Biblical sense" to be not only "the creation" but also "the incarnation, the crucifixion, and the resurrection of Christ." We have pointed out that Jesus Christ as the incarnate, crucified, and resurrected Lord stands at the center of Bonhoeffer's theology;[381] that in connection with Bonhoeffer's notation we must read the Old Testament in the light of the incarnation, cru-

---

may not be separated from the action of Israelite history. "The Old Testament is always concerned with concrete deeds of earthly life. . . . It has to do with life, the natural and the penultimate" (*ibid.*, 207). We have also stressed that these statements are absolutely an essential aspect of Bonhoeffer's new view of the Old Testament (see above, Chapter III. E.5). We will also attempt to show that through Bonhoeffer the Old Testament can become even more opened up for us, also in the content of its basic proclamation, i.e., God's encounter with Israel in the whole of history, not only the early stage of creation (in addition, see H. Benckert, "Schöpfung und Geschichte," *EvTh* 20[1960], 433 ff., especially 437 f.). In addition, we shall also attempt to show that that proclamation understood in Bonhoeffer's sense—the Old Testament as the book of Christ!—in our opinion is one of the fundamentals of his thought in *WE*. It is not only, as Nebe thinks, Bonhoeffer's understanding of the creation and Christ as the mediator of creation which forms the basis of his thoughts on the non-religious proclamation in the "world come of age" (Nebe, *op. cit.*, 7 ff.). On pp. 115 ff. we have already shown that Nebe's view of Bonhoeffer's understanding of the law in the light of creation instead of the covenant is inaccurate. For further reference to Nebe, see fn. 393.

381. See above, Chapter II.3.

cifixion, and resurrection; and further, that the Old Testament witness as well as that of the New is of God's accepting, judging, and renewing love.[382] These three realizations suggest a direction in which the significance of the Old Testament for the attempt to clarify the controversial thoughts in *Letters and Papers from Prison* can be made clearer than it already is in the letters themselves.[383]

In addition, there are two more viewpoints whose connection with ideas from *Letters and Papers from Prison* has already been mentioned. First, we considered Bonhoeffer's interpretation of II Sam., chs. 11 to 19, as the high point of the Bible study "King David," because in it he proclaims most forcefully that God *judges* his church in the *present* with the goal of renewal. He had arrived at this pronouncement, because he conducted a threefold discussion: the discussion between the church and the Old Testament about and mediated by Jesus Christ.[384] Again in 1944 he conducted another discussion between Jesus Christ and the world in which he lives. The Old Testament as well is already involved in this discussion, but it has even more to say.

Afterward, with definitive remarks on Bonhoeffer's sermon on Psalm 58, we were able to establish a correspondence between the claim laid by the God-abandoned, crucified Lord not only to this psalm but also to the "world come of age."[385] At that point through this correspondence the uniformity of Bonhoeffer's thought was indicated. At this point it should draw our attention to the realization which Bonhoeffer had reached through the interpretation of Old Testament texts: Jesus Christ as the crucified Lord also claims godlessness for himself.

382. See above, Chapter III.C.4.
383. Compare R. Schulze, "Hauptlinien der Bonhoeffer-Interpretation," *EvTh* 25(1965), 699 f. Here Schulze seeks to go beyond Bonhoeffer and points out that the "incarnation, crucifixion, and resurrection are the three points at which the center of the non-religious message is Christologically articulated" (699).
384. See above, Chapter III.C.1.
385. See above, Chapter III.D.4.(3)a.

Hence, we face the question of whether a better understanding of a few of the controversial ideas from Bonhoeffer's prison letters can be achieved on the basis of the conclusions drawn from the Old Testament.

We shall attempt to answer this question by looking at Bonhoeffer's statements on the "world come of age." Two reasons were decisive for the choice of this theme. On the one hand, the first reason has already been discussed—that of understanding the statement in the light of the Old Testament; on the other hand, Bonhoeffer wanted to discuss it in the first chapter of a work he had planned, "Mündigwerden des Menschen" ("Man's Coming of Age").[386]

The attempt of an Old Testament interpretation stems from H. Schmidt.[387] He comes to the conclusion that Bonhoeffer's thoughts on the "world come of age" among others are to be understood in the light of Old Testament wisdom.

H. Schmidt presents the thesis "that Bonhoeffer was not able to solve the problem that obsessed him, that of the relationship of world reality and God's reality, and with the concept of the 'world come of age' he has fallen prey to the misunderstanding of *society attempting to free itself.*"[388] Not only that, but in this way Bonhoeffer has disowned history.[389] He was

386. *WE* 208/257. Compare Bethge in *DB*, who organizes the key concepts world come of age, non-religious interpretation and proclamation, and discipline in *WE* according to the three chapters of "Outline for a Book," and then comments on them and relates them to one another.

387. H. Schmidt, "Das Kreuz der Wirklichkeit. Einige Fragen zur Bonhoeffer-Interpretation," *MW* IV, 79–108. Compare R. Schulze (*EvTh* 25, 696 ff.) with him.

388. H. Schmidt, *MW* IV, 80, fn. 1, 95. H.-R. Müller-Schwefe follows this judgment with a small alteration (*Homiletik,* Vol. II: *Die Lehre von der Verkündigung,* 1965, 225, fn. 9).

389. H. Schmidt, *MW* IV, 95. According to Schmidt, in *SC* Bonhoeffer already disowned history, since he conceived "Christ's presence in history . . . as analogous to the eternal presence of a timeless order" (*SC* 86). To the end he remained "alienated from the thought tradition of the Greek assurance of truth." "Through his nonhistorical, obligatory scheme of world reality and God reality with its ancient-Occidental tradition of the doctrine of two natures, he shut himself off to the end from entering into an understanding of the crisis of tradition. He overlooked the problem of society already made

much more concerned with the innate secret of God's world itself, "without showing a wider interest in the phenomenon of history."[390] "With his attempt to claim a nonreligious world for the Kingdom of God, Bonhoeffer came back to the 'universal Yahweh faith' of Israelite wisdom with its 'absence of salva-

---

apparent through the disclosure of man in his freedom, a society for which the world had become history: a world of a thousand possibilities, of a race for the future, of a system of safeguards against failures, of an open future with its anxiety and yet a field of inescapable duties" (H. Schmidt, *MW* IV, 101 f.). Under the disowning of history H. Schmidt understands the view of the world which grows out of the understanding of the eternal and timeless presence of Christ as an established system of order without the possibility of change and the necessity of responsibility. This claim is incorrect so far as Bonhoeffer is concerned. See "Inheritance and Decay" and *E* VI, "History and Good." On the basis of those passages Schmidt's accusation of Bonhoeffer's disowning of history should become very questionable. This is especially true with regard to the understanding promoted by his historical understanding of responsible existence. Bonhoeffer came into this existence as Christ's disciple (see his own testimony, *WE* 75/92 f.) with the reality about "the cross," a reality he did not sanctify. Compare H. Schmidt, *MW* IV, 100 f.

It is not debatable that Bonhoeffer stands partially in that ancient-Occidental tradition; for example, his four mandates from *E* V have their roots there. Compare J. Moltmann, *MW* III, 63, fn. 11a.

It is also valid, as H. Schmidt states (*MW* IV, 101 f., 104), that in his theological thought Bonhoeffer was very stimulated and influenced by Hegel. The closeness of his idea about the death of God on the cross in *SF* (see above, fn. 120) and about Christ as the example in *E* (see above, fn. 103) to Hegel's philosophy of religion cannot be overlooked. Both of these ideas belong to the foundation upon which Bonhoeffer outlines his conception of the "world come of age." Fundamental here is the Christological scheme of the incarnate, crucified, and risen Lord, a scheme itself which in form recalls Hegel's dialectic and in content recalls some passages in the chapter "Der Gottmensch und die Versöhnung" ("The God-man and the Reconciliation"), from Hegel's philosophy of religion (*Die absolute Religion*, 130–174). This influence of Hegel on Bonhoeffer, however, does not establish a negative judgment about Bonhoeffer's theology! If Hegel's influence on him is a biographical matter, then it is valid likewise that his last theological ideas are more Biblical than they appear at first. For the underlying Christological conception of the "world come of age" we have shown that the idea that God loves the world in the incarnate, crucified, and risen Lord in that he accepts, judges, and renews it is verified by the Old Testament which bears witness to God's accepting, judging, and renewing love. But also, if we allow Bonhoeffer's ideas about the "world come of age" to be rooted in the prophetical tradition, the consequences of such an interpretation of Bonhoeffer move very close to Hegel. In addition see fn. 421.

390. H. Schmidt, *MW* IV, 99.

tion history' and to its 'pathos of knowledge.' "[391] One discovers anew "the unhistorical world consciousness of late Jewish wisdom, but not the understanding of history of the Old Covenant promise of the law and of the prophetic witnesses of history consummated by Jesus Christ."[392]

The light that H. Schmidt sheds on the thoughts of Bonhoeffer on the "world come of age" on the basis of certain parts of the Old Testament makes them clear in his opinion, but only insofar as it is possible better to establish the negative judgment: Bonhoeffer disowns history and falls prey to the misunderstanding of society attempting to free itself.[393]

391. *Ibid.*, 100. In this sentence H. Schmidt quotes Von Rad, *Theologie des Alten Testaments*, Vol. I, 319, upon whose explanation of Old Testament wisdom he collectively relies.

Not far from H. Schmidt stands G. Harbsmeier with his view that Bonhoeffer has in mind essentially "a matter of 'wisdom' " as non-religious interpretation. Therefore, Bonhoeffer is bound to the Old Testament, but not to the wisdom of the Hellenistically stamped wisdom books of the Bible, rather to the entire Old Testament. It may be said that so far as the Old Testament is concerned here, it is more appropriate to speak of a wisdom than a theology as in the case of Paul or John. Bonhoeffer's "special charisma" is his teaching on wisdom (*MW* II, 89 ff.).

392. H. Schmidt, *MW* IV, 107.

393. K. H. Nebe unwillingly supports H. Schmidt at this point as far as his understanding of creation as the basis for Bonhoeffer's non-religious interpretation is concerned. Schmidt sees Bonhoeffer as recalling late Israelite wisdom, which was turned intensively toward the wonder of creation (see Von Rad, *op. cit.*, Vol. I, 448). Nebe supports him although he implicitly takes a position against him, as if Bonhoeffer had made some kind of compromise with the world in *WE* and stressed that Bonhoeffer is much more of a Biblical theologian (Nebe, *op. cit.*, 23 f., 102). Then again he takes the following position: "From the standpoint of the idea of Christ's mediation of creation Bonhoeffer's concept of the world coming of age is grounded and developed within the dominion of Christ" (249). Nebe finds this position acceptable. Nevertheless the positions of both are not completely contrary to each other. Nebe can protect Bonhoeffer from criticism, such as that of H. Thielicke against K. Barth that the latter's scheme of "gospel and law" does not take seriously historical reality, only by setting Bonhoeffer in an anti-Barthian position in opposition to the sources as regards the question of "law and gospel." At one place in his article H. Schmidt also suggests that he bases his criticism of Bonhoeffer on the fact that Bonhoeffer "applied the distinction of law and gospel to the understanding of history as little as did Luther, although it had long been necessary to do so" (H. Schmidt, *MW* IV, 92). We suspect that Thielicke's criticism of Barth is behind this sentence just as with Nebe.

H. Schmidt's attempt is, nevertheless, to be contradicted. Drawing on late Israelite wisdom to explain Bonhoeffer's statements on the "world come of age" is suspect from the beginning, because the Old Testament is used here in a manner inappropriate to Bonhoeffer. If one intends to come to a better understanding of those ideas with the aid of the Old Testament, it is absolutely necessary to draw upon it in keeping with Bonhoeffer's interpretation and with the Old Testament itself.

That means, above all, that one cannot comprehend the Old Testament by overlooking Jesus Christ, as H. Schmidt has done. Bonhoeffer understood the Old Testament as the book of Christ at all times, to the extent that it never became the Word in itself, but always only in relation to Christ. The parts of the Old Testament that come into question as possible participants in the discussion between Christ and the world which Bonhoeffer led in 1944 can be only a *third* partner, because they are only capable of speaking *about* Christ. We must seek the corresponding Old Testament participant through Jesus Christ. In this manner we can observe that Bonhoeffer sees a close connection between the God-abandoned, crucified Lord and the "world come of age" in the letter of July 16, 1944. This letter, along with the one of July 18, is the high point of Bonhoeffer's thought on problems that engaged him. Hence, here it is clear that "Bonhoeffer's understanding of the world's coming of age is neither philosophy nor phenomenology, but an understanding of God, that is, 'theology' " (Bethge).[394] The world's coming of age "leads to a true recognition of our situation before God" and "opens up a way of seeing the God of the Bible." "God himself compels us to recognize it." And it is indeed recognition of God in the crucified Christ: "God lets himself be pushed out of the world on to the cross" (*WE* 194 f./241 f.; Eng. tr., 360). The "world come of age" teaches us to see again the center of the Bible, the crucified, powerless, suffering God, who "wins power and

394. *DB* 973.

space in the world. . . . This will probably be the starting point for our 'worldly interpretation' " (*WE* 195/242).

"Worldly," "nonreligious" interpretation has the recognition of the world coming of age as its theological presupposition, that is, the theology of the cross. Worldly interpretation has to begin here, because Bonhoeffer does not wish to expand it in the "anthropocentric" sense, rather in the "Biblical," that is, theocentric sense.

Consequently the Old Testament's participation in the discussion of the "world come of age" must be sought along the path that goes by way of the crucifixion. Hence, in answer to the question, Which parts of the Old Testament especially "resound" to the "sound" of the cross? this question is already answered.[395] In establishing Bonhoeffer's lines of thought, it followed that the New Testament message of God's judgment which he accomplishes in the crucified Lord corresponds to the Old Testament message of judgment which the prophets proclaimed to the people. For that reason it is not late Israelite wisdom but the prophetic message of judgment which brings the Old Testament into the discussion between Jesus Christ and the world, which alone permits Bonhoeffer's appraisal and interpretation of the Old Testament in consideration of the "world come of age."

This Old Testament message obviously satisfied the two conditions which according to Bonhoeffer are valid for a nonreligious interpretation and proclamation: It is neither "metaphysical" nor "individualistic." What Bonhoeffer says about the message of redemption in Deutero-Isaiah—namely, that it concerns a redemption in *this world* (*WE* 182 f./225 f.)—is also valid for the prophet's message of judgment. Certainly no words need to be wasted on the fact that this message is not "individualistic," because it is, above all, meant for the people.[396]

395. See above, Chapter III.C.4.f.
396. For that reason we do not limit ourselves to the message of judgment of the prophet Nathan to King David (II Sam., ch. 12), which Bonhoeffer has interpreted, although it is precisely this interpretation which has given us not

In order to comprehend the essential viewpoints of the Old Testament message of judgment a thesis, formulated as follows, will be attempted: Amos, Hosea, Isaiah, Micah, Habakkuk, Zephaniah, Jeremiah, and Ezekiel proclaim to the people of Israel, whom God (subject!) has accepted, an entirely new action of God, while they refer to the historical events of their time, which brought about the end of the individual political existence of Israel and Judah as pointing to God's judgment, which would serve the renewal of the people.

Bonhoeffer's statements about the "world come of age" can be reproduced in a thesis similarly formulated: In them he intends to proclaim to his world in which the figure of Jesus Christ had prevailed an entirely new action of God, while he refers to the historical event of coming of age, which means the end of a religious Christianity as it points to God's present judgment, which is to renew the world.

This thesis summarizes Bonhoeffer's statements on the "world come of age," their relationship to "Inheritance and Decay" from the *Ethics*, their intention, and the beginning point of "worldly" interpretation.

(1) Bonhoeffer's thought is oriented toward the relationship of the world to Christ, in which this figure had prevailed.

In the letters of June 8 and July 16, 1944, Bonhoeffer makes an effort to characterize his viewpoint on the historical process. He sketches various stations along the way to autonomy (July 16). He described this development in the *Ethics* in "Inheritance and Decay." Both presentations belong necessarily together![397] Not only can "Inheritance and Decay" fundamentally not be separated from the "world come of age" because this section stands with *Letters and Papers from Prison* under the

only the impetus but also guidance for the solution of the prescribed task.

397. This is contrary to H. Müller, who thinks that Bonhoeffer's "own outline of the history of the Occident from the *Ethics*" falls under his verdict on the Protestant description of history in *WE* (H. Müller, *op. cit.*, 329, fn. 1034), for which the development to world autonomy is the great defection from God and Christ (*WE* 174/216). It is also contrary to Müller's view that the historical perspective in "Inheritance and Decay" is essentially different from that of *WE* (H. Müller, *op. cit.*, 357, 360 f.).

same theme of knowledge of the present Lordship of Christ,[398] but, above all, it has its necessary place among the statements on the "world come of age," because here Bonhoeffer attempts to comprehend in a *positive* manner the *past* history of the European-American world, whose relationship to Christ concerns him in 1944. The world of the people of Europe and America stands "in the midst of Christ's taking form, in a section of human history which He himself has chosen" (*E* 92/30; Eng. tr., 87).[399]

In the light of the prophetic proclamation of justice this attempt is necessary. Just as the Old Testament prophets did not stand in a vacuum, rather proclaimed the present action of God to the *chosen* people, in like manner since Bonhoeffer has the same desire, he cannot and may not forgo comprehending God's past—positive!—history with the world on which the present is based.[400]

(2) On the strength of historical events Bonhoeffer knows what the end of a religious Christianity means. He *begins* the theological discussion under the heading the "Presence of Christ in the World Today"[401] on April 30, 1944, with the conclusion that the time of religion is past.[402] How are the

398. "Inheritance and Decay" is a section from the fragment in which Bonhoeffer imparts to a concrete Christian ethic the task of saying "how Christ gains stature among us here today" (*E* 91/28). In *WE* his concern is "Christ's laying claim to the world come of age" (187/231).

399. This aspect of past history is not mentioned further in *WE*—that is the basis of justification for H. Müller's viewpoint—because here Bonhoeffer one-sidedly saw past history from the standpoint of making God recede from the world, a standpoint which only gradually became positive for him.

400. "Inheritance and Decay" is a necessary point along the way toward *WE*. But never to move from this point would be dangerous; just as dangerous as it would have been if the prophets had limited themselves only to the one-sided citation of Deuteronomy. That is what the false prophets did.—It is self-explanatory that such a viewpoint makes it impossible to disregard or minimize the differences between "Inheritance and Decay" and the "world come of age," but they do not justify H. Müller's criticism.

401. *DB* 971 f.

402. This opinion (*WE* 144 f./178) is acceptable, if one understands under religion that which Bonhoeffer understood. According to Bethge, his concept of religion has the following characteristics: metaphysics, individualism, partiality, *deus ex machina*, privilege, guardianship, and negligibleness (*DB* 979 ff.).

church and theology to relate to this situation? Is their existence threatened by that development, because "the foundation is taken away from the whole of what has up to now been our 'Christianity' " (WE 145/179)? Should they try to save religion as much as possible in order to be able to address at least a few people as "religious"? Bonhoeffer rejects such attempts (WE 145/179).[403]

He sees the development toward religionlessness (June 8, 1944) in connection with the far-reaching development in "the direction of human autonomy" in which he includes "the discovery of the laws by which the world lives and deals with itself in science, social and political matters, art, ethics, and religion . . . without recourse to the 'working hypothesis' called 'God' " (WE 174/215; Eng. tr., 325). This far-reaching development "has in our time reached an undoubted completion." Bonhoeffer cannot recognize "in this development the great turning away from Christ . . . as in the Catholic and Protestant writing of history," rather in an intentional polemic against such judgment labels it with the positive concept of "coming of age."[404] He can use this concept because on the basis of the

---

By *this* religion Bonhoeffer meant in contrast to Barth that man's existence is no longer accompanied by an eternal necessity, but is "rather a historical, transitory, hence perhaps nonrecurring 'Western' phenomenon" (DB 978 f.). On the basis of that Bethge points out that Bonhoeffer "did not sufficiently think through all the consequences of these matters, and the statements which exist here present an open and weak point" (DB 979). Much has already been written about this "point" and has often fed the criticism of Bonhoeffer; nonetheless, it reduces the thesis of the end of religion and the resulting implications(!) to nothing. If one wishes to understand and criticize him somewhat, as did A. D. Müller (ThLZ 86[1961], 738 ff.) with help from Luther's Larger Catechism—that upon which you depend is your God—one loses the possibility of grasping adequately what is meant by that thesis in spite of the weak point and of understanding it as something new.

403. See also the letters of June 8, 30, and July 8, 1944.

404. The first time: "Efforts are made to prove to a world come of age that it cannot live without the tutelage of 'God.' " Hence: "The attack by Christian apologetic on the world come of age I consider to be in the first place pointless, in the second place ignoble, and in the third place unchristian" (WE 175 f./216 f.). Compare Bethge: Bonhoeffer sought the word that "stressed the positive element of the relationship between Christ and the modern world" (DB 974).

worldly proclamation which he already has in view, "which does not presuppose religion to be the condition of faith . . . ," that development is "no longer an occasion for polemics and apologetics"(*WE* 178/221). He has, so to speak, the answer to the new situation already at hand. In the same letter in taking up the concluding question from April 30, 1944—What is Christianity, and who actually is Christ for us today?—he also mentions the theme that concerns him: "Christ and the world come of age" (*WE* 176/218). The fact that the "world come of age" is a positive judgment becomes clearer when on June 30, 1944, he once again formulates and expands "Christ's claiming of the world that has come of age" (*WE* 187/231). Whoever is able to speak of the "world come of age" as being claimed by Christ, for him this world has not fallen from Christ and therefore need not be damned.

The positive character of the concept of "coming of age" will be completely and conclusively clear in the letter of July 16, 1944, which has been previously mentioned in part and which is the high point of the thought development along with the letter of July 18. In it Bonhoeffer admits the development toward the world's coming of age and that it "leads us . . . to a true recognition of our situation before God" and of the God of the Bible. In addition, from the letter it is clear that it is the crucified Lord who claims the "world come of age" (*WE* 194 f./241). These acknowledgments, among other things, are the basis for the sentence in the following letter: "The world that has come of age is more godless and perhaps its coming of age is nearer to God than before" (*WE* 198/246). Bonhoeffer speaks here for the first time of the godlessness of the "world come of age."

So much for the essential statements of Bonhoeffer on the "world come of age."[405]

405. The first one from the letter of June 30, 1944, with which Bonhoeffer summarized his point of departure (*WE* 185/229 f.) is lacking. On the basis of the statement which stands in connection with his rejection of sniffing around for the sins of man, he wanted to suggest that "God should not be smuggled into some last place, but that we should frankly recognize that the

150

(3) Their intention must be seen in the fact that in them he intends to proclaim God's present judgment as his new action which shall renew the world. Bonhoeffer concerns himself with the theological grasp of a problem in the face of which anxious souls ask: "What room is there left for God now?" (*WE* 194/241). Within this problem he sees God at work and namely the God "who wins power and space in the world by his weakness" (*WE* 195/242; Eng. tr., 198). The Old Testament prophets of judgment have proclaimed to what extent a powerless God is powerful. They turned to those who could not recognize God in present events on the basis of the experience of the fathers with him, because they seemed to reveal the power of the Assyrian and Babylonian gods. Even there, however, the prophets saw the action of God who judges his people through the Assyrians, the rod of his anger (Isa. 10:5), and through Nebuchadnezzar, his servant (Jer. 27:6). In the same manner the powerless God, who lets himself be pushed out of the world through the development toward the world's coming of age to the extent that anxious souls can no longer find him, is a powerful God because he accomplishes his judgment upon the world in that development.

In the letter of July 18, 1944, Bonhoeffer describes the "world come of age" as more godless than the world "not come of age." In this manner the means by which God judges the "world come of age" are determined: He judges it through and in its godlessness.[406] It is God himself who allows the world to become more and more godless, but because it is God who does this, the more godless the world is, the closer it is

---

world, and people, have come of age" (*WE* 190/236; Eng. tr., 183). In the last statement from the "Outline for a Book" Bonhoeffer wanted to present "the coming of age of mankind" and "the religionlessness of man who has come of age" (*WE* 208/257 f.).

406. Compare H. Benckert, "Sive Deus sive Jesus," according to whom in atheism in its varied modern forms "the judgment of God" occurs, "God's judgment" takes place (*EvTh* 24[1964], 666). Compare also R. Schulze's criticism of H. Müller, "The disclosure of the godlessness of this world through the cross as *judgment* is something we do not find in Müller" (*EvTh* 25[1965], 689).

to God. We have no evidence, as we have had previously, that Bonhoeffer sees in this action of God his will for renewal. Yet, beyond the intention that God judges, also the statement that God judges in order to renew has its place in this context.[407] Bonhoeffer writes in "Thoughts on the Day of the Baptism of D.W.R.—May 1944":

> The day will come . . . when men will once more be called so to utter the world of God that the world will be changed and renewed by it. It will be a new language, perhaps quite non-religious, but liberating and redeeming—as was Jesus' language; it will shock people and yet overcome them by its power; it will be the language of a new righteousness and truth, proclaiming God's peace with men and the coming of his kingdom. (*WE* 167 f./207; Eng. tr., 300)

Such an expectation is possible only in the assurance that God judges in order to renew.

If this is the intention of the statements about the "world come of age," then the central question is answered by it: since God judges the world in and through its godlessness, it is "formed in the likeness of Him who was abandoned by God and crucified (*E* 86/24),[408] that is, "the presence of Christ in today's world" and "his claim" upon it are recognizable.

(4) If we understand the intention of the statements about the "world come of age" as an indication of God's present action, then it is also understandable why Bonhoeffer chose the recognition of the powerless-powerful God as "the begin-

407. We agree with R. Schulze, according to whom an interpretation of Bonhoeffer at this point must be considered "to strengthen qualitatively the eschatological aspects of *WE*" (*ibid.*, 699). The essential eschatological aspect is, however, this-worldly and historical; compare above, pp. 92 ff.

408. Here in *E* III, "Ethics as Formation," Bonhoeffer has not yet exposed the relationship between the crucified Lord and godlessness; that happens first in *E* VII, "The 'Ethical' and the 'Christian' as a Theme" (314/230). It becomes clear in our study that a stronger relationship between the crucified Lord and the "world come of age" results from these passages. This relationship is expressed well in Bonhoeffer's concepts and ideas in *E* III!

ning point" of "worldly interpretation." It must begin here, because it points toward an *action of God* and this is appropriate to Bonhoeffer's basic principle of nonreligious interpretation, of thinking not in the anthropocentric sense but in the Biblical or theocentric sense. If we interpret Bonhoeffer's statements in this way, then they do not contradict the line of thinking he has pursued in his remarks on the law in the meditations on Psalm 119 and in other passages. There he says, among other things: "If we ask how we can begin a life with God, the Scripture answers that God has already begun life with us long ago" (*GS* IV, 509). Our attempt at interpretation can be paraphrased with the following sentence: "If we ask," in view of the development of the world coming of age, "how we can begin a life with God" (and this question originates in view of that development), the Scripture answers "that God has already begun life with us long ago," because it is he who directs the world in its development toward coming of age and who directs us through its and our godlessness.[409]

It was our goal to understand how Bonhoeffer's statements on the "world come of age" correspond to the Old Testament message of judgment. If this correspondence is to be legitimate, something else definitive and fundamental must be

409. The last sentences are written for the sake of K. H. Nebe. He says that "only on the basis of this doctrine of law and gospel" is it possible for Bonhoeffer "to find and hold on to the new conception of God's relationship to the Word" (*op. cit.*, 137 f.). Under "this doctrine" he understands Bonhoeffer's conception of the law from the standpoint of the creation, not the covenant. Under the "new conception" he understands that God as Creator is at work everywhere (200 f.), because his law "as power is always already there" and "can only be kept through the occurrence of the reality of Christ" (221). We are against the view that should the attempted "new conception of the relationship of God to the world" correspond to Bonhoeffer's statement on the law, one must first look at the historical action of God and ask in which form (acceptance, judgment, renewal) God realizes his love today, which is his action.

Our interpretation *only* approaches a closer definition of the point of origin of the "worldly interpretation." If it is correct must be shown, among other things, on the basis of whether the "worldly interpretation" can be developed upon its foundation. This question, which can be clarified obviously only by discussion of the extensive literature, we leave open.

added; on the one hand, a consideration of H. Schmidt's criticism of the "world come of age" and on the other hand, a consideration of the Old Testament.

(1) On the basis of the assumption indicated here the two rebuttals of H. Schmidt become a closed matter; namely, (a) that with the concept of the "world come of age" Bonhoeffer has fallen prey to the misunderstanding of society's attempting to free itself, (b) and has disowned history.

(a) Contrary to Schmidt, we are of the opinion that Bonhoeffer has submitted to the thought of the Old Testament prophets.[410] The Old Testament substrata are stronger than one thinks. Bonhoeffer himself points out in some instances that his thoughts on nonreligious interpretation are rooted in the Old Testament. This same close attachment can also be determined in the complex of the "world come of age." The inferences that Bonhoeffer made in this direction are not obvious, but they are sufficient to oppose the opinion that he laid down his arms before the godless world and another opinion as well, namely, that with the attempt to claim and win the "world come of age" for Jesus Christ he was able to draw ammunition from the Old Testament.[411]

(b) The Old Testament provided Bonhoeffer with the weapons that reclaimed for the faith of Israel the dimension in which Yahweh had especially revealed himself, the dimension of history.[412] The light which the Old Testament sheds on Bonhoeffer's thought does not permit H. Schmidt's negative opinion (that Bonhoeffer disowns history), rather a very positive one. Bonhoeffer's statements on the "world come of age" reclaimed for faith in Jesus Christ the dimension of *that* history

410. The prophets are even open to the criticism of H. Schmidt, for they were not politicians in the arena of politics, but all too often had to appear like traitors.

411. For that reason Bethge's opinion, "The implications do not originate from a capitulation in the face of the modern, godless world; they come from concentrated immersion in the being and work of the author of our faith" (*MW* II, 100), can be expanded and can entail a still more viable Old Testament principle.

412. Von Rad, *Theologie des Alten Testaments,* Vol. II, 192.

to which the Old Testament witnesses.[413]

According to G. von Rad, there was history for Israel only "insofar and inasmuch as *God* walked with Israel." This "fundamental concept . . . always remained the same."[414] Bonhoeffer's statements on the "world come of age" point in this direction to the extent that God has something to do with the history of the European and American people. His recognition of this world's coming of age is "recognition of God," "a theological phrase," which holds fast to "a proclamation of God concerning a part of history."[415] On the basis of the insight gained from our attempt at interpretation we agree with this opinion of Bethge, for such insight fully confirms his opinion. In seeking to understand the development toward the world's coming of age as God's judgment, Bonhoeffer proclaims God's claim to a part of history. It may be recognized here, as with the Old Testament prophets, that God is the judging Lord of history. The following is closely connected with that.

Once again according to G. von Rad it was an "epoch-making step" when Israel came to the realization that she "established herself, not in one event, but over a *long* period of time, that is, a history preceded."[416] This realization makes the theological justification of the glances back into history in *Letters and Papers from Prison* and in "Inheritance and Decay" *(Ethics)* once again quite clear. At the moment in which Bonhoeffer concerned himself with the question of the "presence

413. The following thoughts are no longer a discussion with H. Schmidt. This would make necessary in addition a clarification of his concept of history beyond what he has laid down in his essay. In our opinion the dogmatic form of the following sentences is justified, because here Bonhoeffer's thoughts are once more judged by the Old Testament.

414. Von Rad, *Theologie des Alten Testaments*, Vol. II; this author's italics.

415. *DB* 973.

416. Von Rad., *Theologie des Alten Testaments*, Vol. II, 119; this author's italics. See also the sentence from a discussion of Von Rad in Leoni, 1963 (Conference on "Word and History. The Old Testament in the New"). "And it is precisely the progression from an intial point of an act of salvation to a linear 'salvation history' which is characteristic of Israel's concept of history" (*EvTh* 24[1964], 167).

of Christ in *today's* world," he concerned himself also with the realization of the way that led to today's world *(Letters and Papers from Prison),* and with the presence of Christ in the world of the *past* ("Inheritance and Decay"). In this way he avoided the danger which, according to H. W. Wolff, is the "greatest of all in our time," the danger of the "separation of the actualization of existence from universal history." And what H. W. Wolff writes about Old Testament prophecy in our opinion also proves correct for Bonhoeffer's statements on the "world come of age": "It addresses men in the irreversible and unrepeatable context of occurrence in which God's discourse with the hearer takes place."[417]

(2) Nevertheless that reference can be made to the significance of the Old Testament, which results from the function, which it fulfills according to our interpretation of the "world come of age."

In the Bible study "King David" (1935), Bonhoeffer, with the help of the Old Testament, arrived at a proclamation of God's *present action.*[418] This is also the goal of his thought in 1944. Since according to the pattern of that Bible study we let the Old Testament take part in the discourse between Christ and the world, we saw that "the proclamation of the acts of God for us and our world *at this time* is challenged by the action of God attested to and discerned in Israel and in Jesus of Nazareth. This insight is not objectively and generally valid, nor is it merely subjective; rather, it is a valid aid for the appropriate hour" (H. W. Wolff).[419] The Old Testament, whose prophetic testimonies insist so much upon God's action in the present, also assists us to gain this insight.

417. H. W. Wolff, *PAH* 338 f.
418. See above, Chapter III.C.1.
419. H. W. Wolff, *PAH,* 330, fn. 4; this author's italics. According to H. W. Wolff, that is the goal of a typological interpretation. H. Schulte's judgment that in *WE* there is no question of a typological interpretation *(EvTh* 22[1962], 222) cannot be accepted without investigation, because the Old Testament background was perceived through typological interpretation. God's judgment on Israel corresponds to God's judgment in Jesus Christ and to present-day judgment.

It does not help us as a book isolated from Jesus Christ, but as the book of Jesus Christ. Therefore, "listening to the Old Testament ensures the true historicity of Jesus Christ, because it not only makes visible the *kairos* of a 'today,' but in addition, a *yesterday* and therefore a *tomorrow* as well" (W. Zimmerli).[420] The Old Testament, which prevents an isolated view in terms of history, does so in view of Jesus Christ. It can make visible the long road of God's history with the world in Jesus Christ.[421]

420. W. Zimmerli, *BEvTh* 24, 84; see also *PAH* 99.
421. H. Schmidt writes that the origin of the "world come of age" goes back to Hegel's analysis of middle-class society "in which the attempt was undertaken for the first time to analyze the phenomenon of the self-emancipating society in order to come to a meaning of the world as history" (*MW* IV, 104). "The Greeks once asked about the *logos* which governs the whole cosmos; similarly, Hegel asked, with the Greeks and thereby at the same time going beyond the Greeks, about the *logos* which governs world history" (*ibid.*, 105). "Threatened by the incalculable events of history he convinced himself of a total rationalization of the sense of history." Also Bonhoeffer remained engrossed in this tradition (*ibid.*, 106).
Our interpretation of the "world come of age" could verify this view. If we widen Bonhoeffer's lines a little further, we arrive at a system of salvation history which can also be accused of a total rationalization of history. We have understood the "world come of age" against the background of the Christological concept which is reminiscent of Hegel's three-stage dialectic and which includes the Old Testament as one of the three stages. From this point we are not very far from the salvation history outline. The Old Testament declares the opening theme to us with God's accepting, judging, and renewing love toward Israel—the Old Testament as penultimate word!—the New Testament declares the main theme with God's action in the incarnation, crucifixion, and resurrection, and the concluding theme is in the history which begins with and follows the New Testament. We find ourselves with the "world come of age" in the second act in which God judges the European-American world as an accepted one in order to renew it. Even though it appears that this system is the presupposition of our interpretation of the "world come of age," its intention is to arrive at a theological understanding between the scylla of a separation of the actualization of existence from universal history and the charybdis of a historical construction. This understanding upholds the proclamation of God on past and present history. That the proclamation of God about the present can take place only on the basis of God's proclamation attested to in the Bible is not overlooked by Bonhoeffer and that makes his attempt so valuable and is at the same time the justification for the recognition of the *long road* of God's history with man. The dangerous, yet necessary conclusion from the history of God's action is permitted alone under the sign of the cross and the call to obedience under the cross; see above, fn. 131

In his interpretation of the Bible, Bonhoeffer accomplishes the double movement, which is seen by a few Old Testament specialists to be appropriate to the Bible of the Old and New Testaments.[422] In continuing Bonhoeffer's line of approach it is clear that the movement actually is *reciprocal*. Bonhoeffer's Christological conception—incarnate, crucified, risen Lord—proves itself fruitful for an understanding of the Old Testament in the light of Jesus Christ. Then the main stations on the road along which God has led his people correspond to that which God in Christ has done and does for the world. Even the viewpoint that opens the Old Testament to us in the overall correspondence to the New Testament contains in itself the viewpoint of a true historicity (yesterday—today—tomorrow). But precisely this viewpoint is confirmed, if we understand it in the light of Christ through the Old Testament, which is full to the brim with history. Bonhoeffer's intimate acquaintance with the Old Testament which he loved and which he *heeded* as the book of Christ is the realization of the sentences from the letter to R. Schleicher:

> The entire Bible is the place where God intends for us to find him. . . . It may be that that is a very primitive matter. But you have no idea how happy one is when he has found his way back from the wrong-directed paths of some theologies to these primitive matters. (*GS* III, 28, 30)

(U. Luck). Bonhoeffer's recognition of the world's coming of age is one of a cross-theology. He himself died as a "witness of Jesus Christ" (memorial plaque in the church at Flossenbürg).

422. See above, Chapter III.A.

LIST OF D. BONHOEFFER SOURCES

1931
1. Harvest celebration sermon, Oct. 4, evening worship; Ps. 63:4; *GS* IV, 17–25

1932
2. Confirmation sermon in the Zion Church, Berlin, March 13; Gen. 32:25–32; 33:10; *GS* IV, 44–50
3. Fragment of a devotional, Dec. 1; Dan. 10:1,2,8,9,15–19; *GS* IV, 144–146
4. Exaudi Sermon in the Kaiser-Wilhelm-Gedächtnis Church, Berlin, May 8; II Chron. 20:12; *GS* I, 133–139

1932/33
5. *Creation and Fall*

1933
6. Final semester worship in the Dreifaltigkeit Church, Berlin, Estomihi, Feb. 26; Judges 6:15 f.; 7:2; 8:23; *GS* IV, 109–117
7. Sermon in the Kaiser-Wilhelm-Gedächtnis Church, Berlin, Exaudi, May 28; Ex. 32:1–7,15,19,30–34; *GS* IV, 123–129
8. First draft of the Bethel Confession, I. On the Holy Scripture, Aug.; *GS* II, 91, 103

159

9. Remembrance Day sermon, London, Nov. 26; Wisdom of Solomon 3:3; *GS* IV, 160–165

1934

10. Evening sermon in the German Reformed St. Paul's Church, London; Prov. 16:9; *GS* IV, 174–179

1935

11. Exaudi sermon, Zingst, June 2; Ps. 42; *GS* IV, 391–399
12. Trinity sermon outline, transcription; Ex. 20:2 f.; *GS* IV, 206–208
13. "Christ in the Psalms," address to the Pomeranian students of the Confessing Church, Finkenwalde, July 31; *GS* III, 294–302
14. "King David," three-hour Bible study in Finkenwalde from Oct. 8 to 11 with the fellowship of Pomeranian vicars; *GS* IV, 294–320
15. Advent sermon outline, transcription; Ps. 50:1–5; *GS* IV, 223 f.
16. Sermon outline, transcription; Isa., ch. 53; *GS* IV, 210–213

1936

17. Epiphany sermon outline; Isa. 60:1–6; *GS* IV, 187–189
18. Memorial service for Mrs. Julie Bonhoeffer in the cemetery chapel in Berlin-Halensee, Jan. 15; Ps. 90; *GS* IV, 456–460
19. Letter to Rüdiger Schleicher, April 8; *GS* III, 26–31
20. "The Restoration of Jerusalem According to Ezra and Nehemiah," Bible study on April 21 on the occasion of the first course at Finkenwalde; *GS* IV, 321–335
21. A teaching plan for confirmation, delivered on the occasion of the second course at Finkenwalde, Oct. 20; *GS* III, 337, 339
22. Outline on the Fourth Commandment, transcription; Ex. 20:12; *GS* IV, 227–229

23. Sermon on the bronze serpent, transcription; Num. 21: 4–9; *GS* IV, 229–231

1937
24. "Temptation," Bible study on the occasion of the first course at Finkenwalde, April 12–17; 1956[3], 14–17
25. Sermon on a Vengeance Psalm, July 11; Ps. 58; *GS* IV, 413–422

1938
26. Confession homily, collective pastorate Gross-Schlönwitz, Dec. 3; Micah 4:9; *GS* IV, 450–452
27. Confession homily, sketch; Prov. 28:13; *GS* IV, 448 f.

1939
28. *Life Together;* 1961[10], 35 ff., 43 f.

1939/40
29. Meditations on Ps. 119; *GS* IV, 505–543

1940
30. *The Prayerbook of the Bible.* "An introduction to the Psalms"; *GS* IV, 544–569
31. Sermon meditations for Christmas (1940?); Isa. 9:5,6; *GS* IV, 570–577

1941
32. Memorial service in Kieckow, Aug. 3; Prov. 23:26; *GS* IV, 578–583
33. Suggestion for talk on the *Losungen* for Oct. 20, 1941; Jer. 16:21; *GS* IV, 583–584

1943/44
34. *Letters and Papers from Prison*

1944
35. Devotional aids for the Bohemian Brethren for Pente-

cost, 1944; Isa. 57:18; Ps. 94:12,13; Gen. 39:23; Ps. 54:6; 34:20; *GS* IV, 588–596

36. "The First Tablet of the Ten Commandments," Tegel, June/July; Ex. 20:1–11; *GS* IV, 597–612

37. "The Death of Moses," Tegel, Sept.; *GS* IV, 613–620

Extant, Unpublished Works

1. "The Various Solutions to the Problem of Suffering in Job," seminar paper under E. Sellin, 1926/27; E. Bethge, *D. Bonhoeffer,* 115

2. Sermon on the Song of Songs 8:6b, Barcelona, 1928; *GS* IV, 630

3. Sermon on Deut. 32:48–52, Havanna, Dec. 21, 1930; *GS* IV, 630

4. Baptismal homily, London, 1934; Josh. 24:15; *GS* IV, 631

5. Baptismal homily, London, May 3, 1934; Ruth 1:16 f.; *GS* IV, 631

6. Outline on Isa. 11:1–9, not reconstructable; *GS* IV, 631

(These sources were not accessible to us.)

BIBLIOGRAPHY I

Selected Works on Bonhoeffer's Appraisal
and Interpretation of the Old Testament

Barth, K. *Kirchliche Dogmatik* III, 1, *Die Lehre von der Schöpfung,* 1945, 1947[2] (218 f., 221, 272, 277 reference to *SF*).

Baumgärtel, F. *Die Kirche ist Eine—die alttestamentlich-jüdische und die Kirche Jesu Christi? Eine Verwahrung gegen die Preisgabe des Alten Testaments,* 1936.

Benktson, B.-E. *Christus und die Religion. Der Religionsbegriff bei Barth, Bonhoeffer und Tillich,* 1967 ("Die Diesseitigkeit des Christentums," 41–45, quotations on the Old Testament from *WE*).

Bethge, E. *Dietrich Bonhoeffer. Eine Biographie,* 1966.

Fichtner, J. "Vom Psalmbeten. Ist das Beten aller Psalmen der christlichen Gemeinde möglich und heilsam?" *Wort und Dienst,* 1952, *Jahrbuch der Theologischen Schule Bethel,* 38–60.

Fritzsche, H.-G. *Lehrbuch der Dogmatik,* Part I, "Prinzipien-lehre," Berlin, 1964 (103 f., quotations from *WE* on the this-worldliness of the Old Testament).

Godsey, J. D. *The Theology of Dietrich Bonhoeffer,* 1960 (table of contents from *SF,* the Bible study "King David," and *The Prayerbook of the Bible,* 119–150, 189–194).

Grunow, R. "Dietrich Bonhoeffers Schriftauslegung," *MW* I, 1955, 1959[3], 62–76.

Hellbardt, H. "D. Bonhoeffer: Schöpfung und Fall. Theologische Auslegung von Genesis 1 bis 3," *ThBl* 13(1934), 110–112.

Kreck, W. *Die Wirklichkeit des Wortes Gottes, ThEx,* NF 134 (1966) (46 f., quotation from *WE* 92/112 f.).

Miskotte, K. H. *Wenn die Götter schweigen. Vom Sinn des Alten Testaments,* 1956, German edition 1963 (87 f., quotations from *WE*).

Nebe, K. H. *Religionslose Interpretation bei D. Bonhoeffer und ihre Bedeutung für die Aufgabe der Verkündigung,* dissertation, Hamburg, 1961, manuscript. ("Die Bedeutung des Alten Testaments bei Bonhoeffer," 108–110; "Die neue Sicht des Alten Testaments," 204–210).

Nicolaisen, C. *Die Auseinandersetzungen um das Alte Testament im Kirchenkampf 1933–1945,* dissertation, Hamburg, 1966 (161 ff., mention of Bonhoeffer in the context of the discussion on W. Vischer).

Pfeifer, H. *Das Kirchenverständnis D. Bonhoeffers. Ein Beitrag zur theologischen Prinzipienlehre,* dissertation, Heidelberg, 1963, manuscript (107, reference to the Bible studies "King David" and "The Reconstruction of Jerusalem . . . ," and *The Prayerbook of the Bible*).

von Rad, G. "Sensus Scripturae Sacrae duplex? Eine Erwiderung," *ThBl* 15(1936), 30–34 (32, quotation from the Bible study "King David").

Rupprecht, W. *Die Predigt über alttestamentliche Texte in den lutherischen Kirchen Deutschlands,* 1962 (372, 381 references to the Bible study "King David").

Schulte, H. "In den Tatsachen selbst ist Gott. Die Bedeutung des Alten Testaments für die christliche Verkündigung nach D. Bonhoeffers letzten Briefen," *EvTh* 22(1962), 441–448.

Westermann, C., ed. *Verkündigung des Kommenden. Predigten alttestamentlicher Texte,* 1958 (150 ff., reprint of Bonhoeffer's sermon on Ps. 42; 180, discussion).

Wolff, H. W. "Zur Hermeneutik des Alten Testaments," *PAH,*

1956, 1963², 140–180 (173 ff., for ideas from *WE* with quotation).

Zimmermann, W.-D., ed. *Begegnungen mit Dietrich Bonhoeffer. Ein Almanach,* 1964, 1965²; essays of W. Rott, 105 f., H. Gollwitzer, 111, G. von Rad, 141.

BIBLIOGRAPHY II

Selected Works on Bonhoeffer's Theology

Essays from *MW* I–IV:

Bethge, E. "Dietrich Bonhoeffer. Person und Werk," I(1959³), 7–25.

———. "Dietrich Bonhoeffer. Der Mensch und sein Zeugnis," II(1956), 92–103.

Ebeling, G. "Die 'nicht-religiöse Interpretation biblischer Begriffe,' " II(1956), 12–73.

Glenthoj, J. "Bonhoeffer und die Ökumene," II(1956), 116–203.

Harbsmeier, G. "Die 'nicht-religiöse Interpretation biblischer Begriffe' bei Bonhoeffer und die Entmythologisierung," II(1956), 74–91.

Moltmann, J. "Die Wirklichkeit der Welt und Gottes konkretes Gebot nach Dietrich Bonhoeffer," III(1960), 42–67.

Müller, H. "Zur Problematik der Rezeption und Interpretation Dietrich Bonhoeffers," IV(1963), 52–78.

Prenter, R. "Bonhoeffer und der junge Luther," IV(1963), 33–51.

———. "Dietrich Bonhoeffer und Karl Barths Offenbarungspositivismus," III(1960), 11–41.

Schmidt, H. "Das Kreuz der Wirklichkeit. Einige Fragen zur Bonhoeffer-Interpretation," IV(1963), 79–108.

Other works:

Hinz, Chr. "Christliche Verkündigung angesichts atheistischer Anfechtung," *MPTh* 51(1962), 26–35.

Krause, G. "Dietrich Bonhoeffer und Rudolf Bultmann," *Zeit und Geschichte*, ed. by E. Dinkler, 1964, 439–460.

Moltmann, J. *Herrschaft Christi und soziale Wirklichkeit nach Dietrich Bonhoeffer*, ThEx NF 71(1959).

Müller, A. D. "Dietrich Bonhoeffers Prinzip der weltlichen Interpretation und Verkündigung des Evangeliums," *ThLZ* 86(1961), 721–744.

Müller, H. *Von der Kirche zur Welt. Ein Beitrag zu der Beziehung des Wortes Gottes auf die societas in Dietrich Bonhoeffers theologischer Entwicklung*, 1961, 1966².

Ott, H. *Wirklichkeit und Glaube*, Vol. I: *Zum theologischen Erbe Dietrich Bonhoeffers*, 1966.

Schulze, R. "Hauptlinien der Bonhoeffer-Interpretation," *EvTh* 25(1965), 681–700.

Thielicke, H. "Das Ende der Religion. Überlegungen zur Theologie D. Bonhoeffers," *ThLZ* 81(1956).

Weissbach, J. *Christologie und Ethik bei Dietrich Bonhoeffer*, ThEx NF 131(1966).

BIBLIOGRAPHY III

Other Literature

Abramowski, R. "Vom Streit um das Alte Testament," *ThR* NF 3(1937), 68 ff.

Althaus, P. *Die christliche Wahrheit*, 1962⁶.

Barth, K. *Der Römerbrief*, Preface to the second edition, 1922.

———. "Das Schriftprinzip der reformierten Kirche," *ZZ* 3 (1925), 215–245.

———. *Die Lehre vom Wort Gottes. Prolegomena zur christlichen Dogmatik*, 1927.

———. *Evangelium und Gesetz, ThEx* 32(1935).

———. *Kirchliche Dogmatik* I, 2, *Die Lehre vom Wort Gottes*, 1938.

———. *Credo. Die Hauptprobleme der Dogmatik dargestellt im Anschluss an das Apostolische Glaubensbekenntnis*, 1935.

Baumgärtel, F. *Die Bedeutung des Alten Testaments für den Christen*, 1925.

———. *Die Eigenart der alttestamentlichen Frömmigkeit*, 1932.

———. "Das Alte Testament," in Künneth/Schreiner, *Die Nation vor Gott*, 1934³, 97–114.

Bea, A. " 'Religionswissenschaftliche' oder 'theologische' Exegese?" *Biblica* 40(1959), 322–341.

Behm, J. *Pneumatische Exegese? Ein Wort zur Schriftauslegung*, 1926.

Benckert, H. "Schöpfung und Geschichte," *EvTh* 20(1960), 433–455.

————. "Sive Deus sive Jesus," *EvTh* 24(1964), 654–669.

Bornkamm, H. *Luther und das Alte Testament,* 1948.

Brunner, E. "Die Bedeutung des Alten Testaments für unseren Glauben," *ZZ* 8(1930), 30–48.

Buber, M. "Der Glaube der Propheten," *Werke,* Vol. II: *Schriften zur Bibel,* 1964, 231–484.

————. "Der Mensch von heute und die jüdische Bibel," *ibid.,* 849–869.

————. "Prophetie und Apokalyptik," *ibid.,* 927–942.

Bultmann, R. "Das Problem einer theologischen Exegese," *ZZ* 3(1925), 334–357.

————. "Ist voraussetzungslose Exegese möglich?" *ThZ* 13(1957), 409–417.

————. "Die Bedeutung des Alten Testaments für den christlichen Glauben," *Glauben und Verstehen,* Vol. I, 1958³, 313–336.

————. "Ursprung und Sinn der Typologie als hermeneutische Methode," *ThLZ* 75(1950), 205–212.

————. "Weissagung und Erfüllung," *Glauben und Verstehen,* Vol. II, 1952, 162–186.

Eichholz, G. "Der Ansatz K. Barths in der Hermeneutik," *Antwort. K. Barth zum 70. Geburtstag,* 1956, 52–68.

Eichrodt, W. "Zur Frage der theologischen Exegese des Alten Testaments," *ThBl* 17(1938), 73–84.

————. *Theologie des Alten Testaments,* Vol. I: *Gott und Volk,* 1933, 1957³.

————. "Ist die typologische Exegese sachgemässe Exegese?" *PAH,* 1956, 205–227.

Frick, H. *Wissenschaftliches und pneumatisches Verständnis der Bibel,* 1927.

Galley, K. *Altes und neues Heilsgeschehen bei Paulus,* 1965.

Gauger, J. *Chronik der Kirchenwirren,* 1935.

Geyer, H. G. "Zur Frage der Notwendigkeit des Alten Testaments," *EvTh* 25(1965), 207–237.

Geyser, P. *Das Panier des Sieges. Predigt nach Jerem. XLVI, 27–28,* 1883.

——. *Nachgelassene Predigten*, Vol. II: *Predigten über das 26. Kapitel des Propheten Jesajah*, 1884.

Girgensohn, K. "Geschichtliche und übergeschichtliche Exegese des Neuen Testaments," *AELKZ* (1922), 626–674.

——. *Die Inspiration der Heiligen Schrift*, 1925.

Gloege, G. "Die Deutschkirche," in Künneth/Schreiner, *Die Nation vor Gott*, 1934[3], 393–415.

von Harnack, A. *Marcion. Das Evangelium vom fremden Gott*, 1921.

Hegel, G. W. F. *Die absolute Religion*, PhB 63(1929), ed. by G. Lasson.

Hellbardt, H. "Die Auslegung des Alten Testaments als theologische Disziplin," *ThBl* 16(1937), 136 ff.

Hengstenberg, E. W. *Commentar über die Psalmen*, Vols. I–IV, 1850/52.

Herntrich, V. *Völkische Religiosität und Altes Testament*, 1933.

——. "Theologische Auslegung des Alten Testaments? Zum Gespräch mit W. Vischer," *MPTh* 32(1936), 119 ff., 177 ff.

Hesse, F. *Das Alte Testament als Buch der Kirche*, 1966.

Hirsch, E. *Das Alte Testament und die Predigt des Evangeliums*, 1936.

Hübner, E. *Evangelische Theologie in unserer Zeit. Ein Leitfaden*, 1966.

von Hofmann, J. C. K. *Biblische Hermeneutik*, ed. by W. Volck, 1880.

Jepsen, A. "Wissenschaft vom Alten Testament," *PAH*, 1957, 227–265.

Kohlbrügge, H. F. *Wozu das Alte Testament? Anleitung zur richtigen Schätzung der Bücher Mosis und der Propheten*, 1846, 1855[3].

——. *Der verheissene Christus. Sieben Predigten*, 1853.

——. *Drei Gastpredigten über Rom. 7,14; Ps. 65,5 und Ps. 45, 14–16*, 1855[3].

——. *Predigt uber Ps. 138,8*, 1855[3].

——. *Sieben Predigten über das dritte Kapital des Propheten Sacharja*, 1855[3].

——. *Sieben Predigten über den Propheten Jona*, 1855[3].

170

————. *Das gnadenvolle Geheimnis des grossen Versöhnungstages nach 3. Buch Mose Kapitel 16,* 1855.

————. *Gott sei mir gnädig! Ein Wort des Trostes und der Zucht für Arme und Elende nach Anleitung des 51. Psalms,* 1855.

Konrad, J. F. *Abbild und Ziel der Schöpfung. Untersuchungen zur Exegese von Genesis 1 und 2 in Barths Kirchlicher Dogmatik III 1,* 1962.

Kraus, H. J. "Gespräch mit Martin Buber," *EvTh* 12(1952/53), 59–77.

————. *Geschichte der historisch-kritischen Erforschung des Alten Testaments von der Reformation bis zur Gegenwart,* 1956.

Luck, U. "Herrenwort und Geschichte in Matt. 28:16–20," *EvTh* 27(1967), 494–510.

Marxsen, W. *Die Auferstehung als historisches und theologisches Problem,* 1964.

Mildenberger, F. *Gottes Tat im Wort. Erwägungen zur alttestamentlichen Hermeneutik als Frage nach der Einheit der Testamente,* 1964.

Miskotte, K. H. "Das Problem der theologischen Exegese," in *Theologische Aufsätze. K. Barth zum 50. Geburtstag,* 1936, 51–77.

————. "Der moderne Dogmatiker als Dilettant und Dirigent," *EvTh* 20(1960), 245–262.

Moltmann, J. *Theologie der Hoffnung,* 1965².

Noth, M. *Geschichte Israels,* 1956.

Oepke, A. *Geschichtliche und übergeschichtliche Schriftauslegung,* 1931.

de Quervain, A. "Kohlbrügge und das Erbe Calvins," *EvTh* 25(1965), 262–273.

von Rad, G. "Das Christuszeugnis des Alten Testaments. Eine Auseinandersetzung mit W. Vischers gleichnamigem Buch," *ThBl* 14(1935), 249–254.

————. *Fragen der Schriftauslegung im Alten Testament,* 1938.

————. *Theologie des Alten Testaments,* Vol. I: *Die Theologie der geschichtlichen Überlieferungen Israels,* 1958²; Vol. II: *Die Theologie der prophetischen Überlieferungen Israels,* 1961².

van Ruler, A.A. *Die christliche Kirche und das Alte Testament,* *BEvTh* 23(1955).

Schalom Ben-Chorin, "Jüdische Fragen um Christus," *Juden, Christen, Deutsche,* ed. by H. J. Schultz, 1961, 140–150.

Schmidt, G. *Das Alte Testament und der evangelische Religionsunterricht,* Schriftenreihe Bekennende Kirche, Heft 13, 1934.

Schmidt, K. D. *Die Bekenntnisse und grundsätzlichen Äusserungen zur Kirchenfrage des Jahres 1933,* 1934.

Schwarzwäller, K. "Das Alte Testament in Christus," *ThSt* (B) 81(1966).

Seeberg, R. *Christliche Dogmatik,* Vol. II, 1925.

Sellin, E. *Das Alte Testament und die evangelische Kirche der Gegenwart,* 1921.

————. *Abschaffung des Alten Testaments?* 1932.

Stamm, J. J. "Die Imago-Lehre K. Barths und die alttestamentliche Wissenschaft," *Antwort,* 1956, 84–98.

————. "Jesus Christ und das Alte Testament. Zu A. A. van Rulers Schrift: Die christliche Kirche und das Alte Testament," *PAH,* 1956, 181–191.

Stuhlmacher, P. "Theologische Probleme des Römerbriefpräskripts," *EvTh* 27(1967), 374–389.

Vilmar, A. F. C. *Collegium Biblicum. Des Alten Testaments zweiter Teil,* 1882.

Vischer, W. "Das Alte Testament als Gottes Wort," *ZZ* 5(1927), 379–395.

————. "Das Alte Testament und die Verkündigung," *ThBl* 10(1931), 1–12.

————. "Der Gott Abrahams und der Gott Isaaks und der Gott Jakobs," *ZZ* 9(1931), 282–297.

————. "Das Alte Testament und die Geschichte," *ZZ* 10(1932), 22–42.

————. *Das Christuszeugnis des Alten Testaments,* Vol. I: *Das Gesetz,* 1934, 1946[7]; Vol. II: *Die frühen Propheten,* 1942.

Vogel, H. "Kreuz und Hakenkreuz. Thesen des Protestes, der Frage und der Bitte an die 'Glaubensbewegung Deutscher Christen,'" *ZZ* 11(1933), 201–206.

Weber, O. *Die Auslegung der Heiligen Schrift als theologische Frage,* 1934.

————. *Grundlagen der Dogmatik,* Vol. I, 1959[2].

Westermann, C., editor. *Probleme alttestamentlicher Hermeneutik. Aufsätze zum Verstehen des Alten Testaments,* 1963².

———. "Das Verhältnis des Jahweglaubens zu den ausserisraelitischen Religionen," *Forschung am Alten Testament,* 1964, 189–218.

Wolff, H. W. "Der grosse Jesreeltag (Hos. 2:1–3)," *Gesammelte Studien zum Alten Testament,* 1951/52, 1964, 151–181.

———. "Hauptprobleme alttestamentlicher Prophetie," *ibid.,* 1955, 206–231.

———. "Das Geschichtsverständnis der alttestamentlichen Prophetie," *ibid.,* 289–307; *PAH,* 1960, 319–340.

———. "Das Kerygma des Jahwisten," *Gesammelte Studien zum Alten Testament,* 1964, 345–373.

Zimmerli, W. "Verheissung und Erfüllung," *PAH,* 1952, 69–101.

———. "Ezechiel, ein Zeuge der Gerechtigkeit Gottes," *Das Alte Testament als Anrede, BEvTh* 24(1956), 37–61.